D1250639

Voices from a Southern Prison

Voices from a Southern Prison

Lloyd C. Anderson

The University of Georgia Press | Athens and London

MW

© 2000 by the University of Georgia Press

Athens, Georgia 30602

All rights reserved

Designed by Kathi Dailey Morgan

Set in 9.75 on 14 Primer by G&S Typesetters

Printed and bound by Maple Vail

The paper in this book meets the guidelines for

permanence and durability of the Committee on

Production Guidelines for Book Longevity of the

Council on Library Resources.

Printed in the United States of America

04 03 02 01 00 C 5 4 3 2 1

Library of Congress Cataloging-in-Publication Data

Anderson, Lloyd C., 1947–

  Voices from a southern prison / Lloyd C. Anderson.

     p.   cm.

  Includes bibliographical references and index.

  ISBN 0-8203-2235-0 (alk. paper)

  1. Kentucky. State Reformatory.   2. Kentucky. State Reformatory—Trials, litigation,

etc. 3. Prisons—Kentucky—La Grange.   4. Prisons—Law and

legislation—Kentucky—La Grange.   5. Prisoners—Kentucky—La Grange.

6. Prisoners—Legal status, laws, etc.—Kentucky—La Grange   7. Prison reformers—

Kentucky—La Grange.

I. Title.

  HV9475.K42 K453 2000

  365'.9769383—dc21   00-020949

British Library Cataloging-in-Publication Data available

To my wife, Wendy, and my children, Lyle, Lloyd, and Jessie.

In memory of my father, John Gerry Anderson.

Contents

Acknowledgments   ix

Introduction   xi

Shorty   1

Judge Johnstone   22

Wilgus   40

Walter   64

Politics and Litigation   91

Judge Johnstone Visits LaGrange   107

Negotiation and Settlement   115

Compliance: Obstacles and Impact   146

Personal Struggles   171

Substantial Compliance and Collateral Litigation   199

Aftermath   221

Epilogue   239

Appendix A: Methodology   245

Appendix B: Direct Observations   247

Appendix C: Court Records and Other Legal Documents   249

Notes   261

Bibliography   269

Index   275

Acknowledgments

Research for this book was supported by a Faculty Improvement Leave of the University of Akron School of Law and by a David L. Brennan Summer Research Fellowship. Richard Aynes of the School of Law offered encouragement throughout the long process of making this book a reality, and Paul Finkelman provided crucial assistance as well.

The Legal Aid Society of Louisville, Kentucky, and its director, Dennis Bricking, made the commitment that permitted me to allocate nearly all of my professional time for three years to the litigation that is the subject of this book. My co-counsel, Joseph Elder, Alan Schmitt, and Leslie Abramson; the plaintiffs' attorneys in the companion litigation, Oliver Barber and Richard Burr; and U.S. Department of Justice attorneys Shawn Moore and Adjoa Burrow made valuable contributions to the litigation and hence to this story.

Inmates, corrections officials, lawyers, a newspaper reporter, and Judge Edward H. Johnstone cooperated in providing the candid interviews that form the oral history portion of this book. Barbara DeAngelo, longtime secretary to Judge Johnstone, provided many of the archival records. Student research assistant Carrie Bayliss reviewed much of the related literature on prison-reform litigation and pinpointed those portions of the literature most relevant to this book.

The tedious task of transcribing the interviews and typing the early versions of the manuscript fell to Kathee Evans, Mary Strukel, and Debbie Brown, who performed the task cheerfully and skillfully. Lori Morris performed the vital role of typing the final manuscript. Dr. Susette Talarico, professor of political science at the University of Georgia, made the major intellectual contribution: her broad perspective and detailed critiques brought this book into focus.

Finally, this book would not have been possible without the compassion and integrity of Judge Edward H. Johnstone, and to him I extend my heartfelt gratitude.

Introduction

America has conducted a "war on crime" for more than three decades.
This war has consisted largely of legislation creating new crimes and mandating longer prison sentences for violent and drug offenses. For example,
some states have passed "three strikes and out" laws, under which a person convicted of three felonies automatically spends the rest of his or her
life in prison. At the federal level, Congress passed sentencing-guidelines
legislation that deprived federal judges of most of their discretion in imposing sentences for federal crimes and assigned to a special commission
the authority to set strict guidelines for sentences.

Critics have charged that the war on crime has failed because the prospect of longer sentences deters very few people from committing crime.[1]
Defenders of tougher sentencing policy argue that it incapacitates the
most dangerous criminals and that it is, at long last, helping to cause a
reduction in crime.[2] The one indisputable point, however, is that tougher
sentencing policy has resulted in sending more people to prison for longer

periods of time and in turn helped to fuel an explosion in the U.S. prison population.

In 1969, at the start of the war on crime, fewer than one hundred thousand people were locked up in American prisons and jails. By 1986 the number of prisoners had grown to more than half a million, an increase of 500 percent in less than two decades. Prison population topped a million for the first time in 1994 and nearly doubled again by 1999, when more than two million American residents were locked up. The annual average rate of increase was nearly 8 percent from 1987 to 1997. The rate of increase has dropped to under 5 percent, but because the base prison population is so much greater than it was just eight years ago, the annual increase in number of prison inmates today is nearly as great or even greater than the increase in years with higher rates of increase.[3] If the U.S. prison population continues to double in less than ten years, it is conceivable that there could be more Americans in prison than in free society by 2065.

The subject of this book is not the debate over the wisdom of contemporary crime policy but rather prison-reform litigation that has had a profound impact on the conditions in which this vast, ever-expanding population of convicts will live. In 1978 a federal judge appointed this author, then a young lawyer in Kentucky, to represent prison inmates who had filed their own lawsuit claiming that living conditions at the Kentucky State Reformatory (KSR) near LaGrange were unconstitutional. Their two-page complaint charged that overcrowding, cockroaches, filthy food, and intermingling of young inmates with homosexual and hardened criminals violated the Eighth Amendment to the U.S. Constitution's prohibition against cruel and unusual punishment. I spent the next three years meeting with a committee of prisoners organized to express the views of more than two thousand inmates, preparing the case for trial, negotiating a settlement in the form of a consent decree, and working to assure that state correctional authorities complied with the settlement.[4] The nearly twenty years that have passed since my involvement in that lawsuit have afforded an opportunity to reflect on the dynamics and outcome of the case, to observe the process of implementing the reforms envisioned in the settlement, and to learn more about the lives and beliefs of the major participants in the cases, particularly three inmates who were the acknowledged spokesmen for the prisoners. This book is the product of that experience and is primarily a story of the contributions of major participants in the lawsuit: the three most prominent inmates, the judge, the state's top prison official, and a newspaper reporter who covered the case from beginning to end.

This case was not an isolated phenomenon. For more than three decades, extensive litigation has occurred in the federal courts to reform prison and jail conditions in America, and federal judges have intervened extensively in the administration of prisons and jails in an effort to correct unconstitutional living conditions. It was not always so. Prisons in America were not the product of a public thirst for revenge against criminals but instead were initially a result of reforms achieved by a nineteenth-century movement to replace corporal punishment, death, the pillory, and the like with quiet meditation in isolation from society as a more humane method of punishment. These institutions were called *penitentiaries* to reflect the philosophy that the inmates were to engage in penitence for their crimes. A later reform movement, disillusioned by the failure of penitentiaries to achieve their goal of repentant inmates, led to the establishment of reformatories—one of which was KSR—with education, job training, and other treatment programs designed to rehabilitate criminals.[5] Well into the twentieth century, the courts took a hands-off approach to prisons on the rationale that prisoners had no rights, that intervention into prison administration would drown the courts in a flood of lawsuits, that judges lacked the expertise to reform prisons, that attempts to impose reform would cause anarchy inside prisons, and that the judiciary had no authority to interfere with executive-branch functions.[6]

The abandonment of this hands-off approach began in the 1950s and continued into the 1960s when it became increasingly apparent that appalling, brutal living conditions existed in many American prisons, particularly in the South. A new prison-reform movement that sought to alleviate these conditions emerged in the 1960s as part of the broader civil rights movement. The U.S. Supreme Court, which was itself engaged in a process of expanding civil rights, laid the legal foundation for litigation to reform prison conditions in its decision in *Cooper v. Pate*.[7] In *Cooper* the Court ruled that a prisoner had the right to sue state prison officials for violation of his constitutional rights under 42 U.S.C. Section 1983, which provides that any person acting under color of state law who deprives another person of rights guaranteed by federal law shall be liable to that person. Section 1983, as it is generally known, thus became the primary legal remedy for prisoners who claimed that a wide variety of their constitutional rights had been violated, as well as the authority for federal courts to order remedies for constitutional violations. The hands-off era had ended. The most prevalent and most effective type of lawsuit claimed that the totality of living conditions in a prison—overcrowding, crime, inadequate medical treatment, and guard brutality, to name a few—constituted cruel and unusual punishment in violation of the Eighth Amendment. From early decisions in Arkansas, Mississippi, and Alabama in which federal judges ruled that the totality of conditions in those states' prisons were unconstitutional and ordered sweeping reforms, federal judges all over America either found similar violations and ordered sweeping reform or presided over settlements that provided for such reform. Whether by court order or agreement, however, these judges embarked on the lengthy follow-through process of assuring that state prison officials complied with the orders or agreements, so that the prisons would change in the way the reforms contemplated.[8]

There is a rich literature on prison-reform litigation in America. Some of this literature consists of studies of specific prison-conditions cases and provides analysis of the extent to which court-ordered reform was effective and what factors determined the effectiveness of reform. In *Prisons under the Gavel,* for example, Bradley Chilton tells the story of *Guthrie v. Evans,* the litigation over prison conditions in Georgia; examines whether intervention by Judge Anthony Alaimo made the prisons safe and more civilized; and identifies factors that would help judges and other key decision makers become more effective in such an enterprise. He concludes that *Guthrie,* despite constant delays and frustrations, "worked to achieve the desired change" and that the most important factor in this success was that the judge took an active role in encouraging the litigants to agree to reform through negotiation rather than through a coercive court order.[9] In a similar vein, Larry Yackle, in *Reform and Regret,* assesses Judge Frank Johnson's ability to make Alabama's policy makers respond to the need to improve the state's prisons. Unlike Chilton, however, Yackle contends that although significant improvements were made, they fell far short of what had been ordered, and Judge Johnson's "attempts to cooperate with state authorities, his deference to state concerns, his flexibility and boundless patience, often failed to generate the synergy he intended and, indeed, exacerbated resistance to judicial interference in penal affairs."[10]

Litigation to reform the Texas prisons is the subject of at least three books. Ben Crouch and James Marquart, in *An Appeal to Justice,* and Steve J. Martin and Sheldon Ekland-Olson, in *Texas Prisons,* contend that Judge William Wayne Justice's sweeping orders were followed by a wave of violence and disorder in the prisons that resulted from prison officials' failure to respond appropriately to the court's orders rather than from deficiencies in the orders themselves. These authors contend that once state leaders ended their resistance and accepted the authority of Judge Justice's orders, Texas prisons underwent a massive transformation from a system of brutal repression characterized by reliance on an inmate elite to a new and more stable regime run by professional corrections staff.[11] John DiIulio, in *Governing Prisons,* argues that the most important factors in determining whether prisons are orderly and habitable are the prison officials' correctional philosophy and management practices and that officials who enforce a strong code of "civilized conduct" for inmates are more likely to maintain clean and safe prisons than officials who do not. DiIulio acknowledges, however, that judicial intervention such as occurred in Texas fostered the development of "constitutional government" under which prison administrators maintain control over inmates but are themselves answerable to codes of civilized conduct.[12]

Another portion of the literature on prison-reform litigation focuses on the proper role of federal judges. In *Judge Frank Johnson and Human Rights in Alabama,* for example, Tinsley Yarbrough examines the life history of the judge who presided over the Alabama prison lawsuits. Yarbrough notes the fierce debate between those who criticize federal judicial intervention into areas of traditional state authority—such as prisons—as antidemocratic judicial lawmaking and defenders who argue that such intervention is warranted by judges' independence from political pressure and commitment to dispassionate legal analysis. He contends that since few case-law precedents existed to guide the decisions in the Alabama prison cases, Judge Johnson was influenced primarily by a pragmatic approach to constitutional interpretation. Consequently, he viewed the Constitution as a living document whose guaranteed rights should be shaped to meet the current needs of society so that detailed standards for prison conditions could be found "in the shadow of constitutional guarantees."[13]

Judge Johnson responded to his critics by claiming that he was merely interpreting the Constitution, but Malcolm Feeley and Edward Rubin contend in *Judicial Policy Making and the Modern State* that he was in fact making policy rather than providing traditional interpretation, though it was a different sort of policy making than the judge's critics had in mind. Feeley and Rubin assert that "judicial policy-making," properly understood, is a legitimate exercise of authority because it is a natural outgrowth of the role of courts in a modern state dominated by bureaucracy. In their view, judicial policy making occurs when the relevant legal text—such as the Constitution—is cast in broad, general terms without explicit standards for decision, so that the judge treats the text as a source of jurisdiction over the subject matter of the case rather than as a guide to decision. Having used the legal text to assert authority, the judge then relies on various sources, including personal judgment, to reach a decision that is based largely on what the judge perceives as a desirable result.[14] Feeley and Rubin argue that prison-reform orders by federal judges are the clearest example of such judicial policy making because no reasonable interpretation of the Constitution could encompass the elaborate and detailed standards these judges fashioned for administration of prisons. Instead, the phrase "cruel and unusual punishment" contained in the Eighth Amendment formed the basis for exercising jurisdiction over prison conditions, from which exercise of authority the judges established standards for prison governance that, in their best judgment, would foster decent living conditions for all convicts. In so doing, Feeley and Rubin contend, judges such as Johnson violated traditional, eighteenth-century principles of federalism, separation of powers, and rule of law, but such principles should be reformulated for the modern administrative state, in which the judicial branch must play an active role in confining ever-more-powerful bureaucracies to legitimate exercise of authority.[15]

A significant gap in this literature, however, exists because very little of it consists of the perspectives and contributions of the prison inmates whose complaints and pleas for help both initiated and shaped prison-reform litigation. Some of the literature on the effectiveness or legitimacy of judicial intervention into prison conditions is based on research into the roles played by key participants in the litigation. For example, Martin and Ekland-Olson give much attention to the contributions in the Texas litigation of Judge Justice, the attorneys, and state corrections officials. In the Alabama cases, Yarbrough's chief focus is Judge Johnson. DiIulio highlights prison administrators in three states. These participants are undoubtedly key decision makers in prison-reform litigation, so that the literature would be incomplete without telling the stories of their contributions. This story of the Kentucky case also recounts the role played by the judge and state corrections officials. The central focus, however, is three prison inmates who played key roles in the effort to reform KSR, and their story will begin to fill this gap in the literature on prison-reform litigation.

It is important to tell the stories of these inmates because prison-reform litigation typically is brought as a class action on behalf of thousands of prisoners who are represented by a few attorneys. The attorneys spend much of their time with expert witnesses, state's attorneys, and the judge and, as in class-action litigation in general, the clients themselves—the prisoners—tend to recede into the background. The case's focus shifts from the clients to the attorneys, from the clients' needs to the drafting of documents and payment of fees and costs.[16] A frequent complaint about class actions, of which prison-reform litigation is one type, is that the clients benefit very little and the attorneys reap most of the rewards. Whatever the general validity of these criticisms, such was not the case in the Kentucky prison litigation. Inmates, chiefly the three depicted here, made valuable contributions in uncovering the miserable living conditions at KSR, providing direction for the litigation, and negotiating and enforcing the settlement. This is not to say that these three inmates were the most important figures in the case. Unlike ordinary litigation, prison-reform litigation includes numerous key decision makers who interact with each other over an extended period of time, and in this case the judge was probably the most important figure. Nevertheless, it would afford an incomplete picture of the litigation to ignore the contributions of these inmates. As Crouch and Marquart observed in *An Appeal to Justice,* in the current rush to build more prisons to hold more criminals for longer periods of time, "extensive use of incarceration, together with ignorance of what that incarceration entails, is a formula for disaster."[17] Nobody knows better than prisoners what incarceration entails, and it is important to listen to them as they tell their stories.

This book, then, is the story of three inmates in Kentucky—James M. "Shorty" Thompson, Wilgus Haddix, and Walter Harris—who participated actively in the litigation to reform living conditions at KSR. It is also the story of Edward H. Johnstone, the federal judge who took the inmates' complaints seriously; of George Wilson, the reform-minded head of the Kentucky prison system; and of Sheldon Shafer, a newspaper reporter who covered the lawsuit for the state's leading newspaper, the *Louisville Courier-Journal.* I observed and interacted with each of these people during my years of active involvement in the lawsuit, and I also subsequently interviewed them. Except for Judge Johnstone, these interviews were recorded, transcribed, and edited to make the material coherent and readable. The interviews with Judge Johnstone were reconstructed from notes and recollections. Any mistakes in the editing or reconstruction are entirely my responsibility.

I refer to the inmates by their first names throughout the book, although I use surnames for the other participants. I intend no disrespect to the inmates. Rather, I was concerned that use of their surnames might make it difficult to distinguish them from the other participants, thus sinking them into the obscurity that all too often is the fate of plaintiffs in class-action litigation. Thus, the use of the inmates' first names is intended to afford proper respect for their contributions to prison reform.

Although this book offers observations about the effectiveness and legitimacy of the federal judiciary's role in addressing living conditions in American prisons, its main focus is the lives of three ordinary prison inmates who played extraordinary roles in the day-to-day struggle to achieve human dignity in the squalor of a neglected, overcrowded, filthy, lawless prison. Their stories include how they grew up, became involved in criminal activity, and took on the challenge of helping to transform KSR into a better place for all the inmates to live and how they continued to struggle to achieve lives of dignity in the aftermath of the litigation. There is good in the worst of us, just as there is evil in the best of us. Convicts are human beings. Shorty, Wilgus, and Walter all committed serious crimes for which they were sent to prison, yet in their struggle to improve living conditions at KSR, each man discovered a capacity to achieve positive results through lawful means. Through participation in the effort to reform the prison, each achieved a measure of reform within himself. That is not to say they became perfect human beings, for in the years after the lawsuit they made serious mistakes. They did, however, manage to improve their lot. In their stories, there is a message concerning the management of American prisons at the dawn of the twenty-first century: society must continue to listen to the voices of prison inmates. The voices of prisoners, through *pro se* complaints filed with federal courts, sparked prison-reform litigation in the latter half of the twentieth century. Scholars who have studied the results of that litigation have concluded that prisons are now run, or should be run, as a "constitutional government" or "bureaucratic order" in which clearly articulated rules are enforced against both inmates and staff.[18] Prisons will remain grim institutions despite such litigation, for incarceration entails repression, loss of freedom, and minimally adequate living conditions, but prisons will be safer and cleaner and offer prisoners a better chance of rehabilitating themselves. DiIulio, in *Governing Prisons*, hypothesizes that the best model for managing prisons may be a "paramilitary prison bureaucracy."[19] If his vision of a paramilitary prison operation includes ignoring or silencing inmate protests about the way they are treated, it is, in Crouch and Marquart's words, "a formula for disaster."[20] Although prisoners often make frivolous demands, articulate inmates genuinely concerned about the treatment of the average convict can make valuable contributions in bringing to light horrendous living conditions of which the public and even prison officials may be unaware or powerless to change. To ignore inmates' voices will create a grave risk that the wave of new prisons, built in response to the precipitous rise in incarceration, will encounter a crisis of inhumane living conditions that, because of the vast increase in prison population, will far exceed the crisis that led to extensive judicial intervention in the past three decades and create the need for even more extensive intervention in the years to come.

Shorty

Shorty got fed up with the bugs and the rats. They were everywhere. Cockroaches were the worst. When the lights clicked on in the morning at 6:00, the roaches were crawling on his blanket. He knew they had been crawling on him all night long. It made his skin creep. He rose from his bunk, pulled his clothes off the wall hook, and shook them. Bugs came tumbling out. The other guys were getting up and shaking out their clothes. Flap! Flap! Flap! These were the sounds of morning on a cold November day in 1978 at the Kentucky State Reformatory (KSR) outside the little town of LaGrange.

Shorty headed for the washroom. Bugs were crawling on the washbasins. He combed his hair with care and watched in the mirror for lice — they were everywhere, too. There was no point in taking a shower because there was no hot water. It had been a cold November, and a pipe had probably burst, so he simply washed up at the basin. Shorty returned to his bunk, shook more bugs out of his clothes, dressed, and walked to the mess hall. It was a familiar routine: stand in line outside in the snow, get your tray, pick up your food, try to pick out the bugs. He had had enough. It was time to do something.

Shorty did not look like a man who would shake things up, and he did not fit the stereotype of a convict. He was a tiny little man with a trim body, less than five and a half feet tall. His tightly curled sandy hair was cropped short. He was clean shaven except for a neatly trimmed mustache with flecks of gray. He spoke in a matter-of-fact way, in a flat, nasal southern twang, rarely raising or lowering his voice. The eyes gave him away—pale blue, steady gaze, narrow under heavy lids. They were not mean eyes, just eyes that took in everything and kept their focus. His jaw was square and firm, with the mouth set in a straight line, suggesting a stubborn personality. A closer look at Shorty afforded an impression of a man who saw things clearly, made up his mind, and stuck with his decisions.

The main reason I filed the suit was because of the dirty living conditions down 'ere at LaGrange—well, dirty and overcrowded. . . . Place was nasty, and I figured there should be some way to do something about it. I can't remember any one thing or event that prompted me to file suit back in 1978. I just looked around me and decided that people were not s'posed to live like that. There were roaches and rats. The buildings leaked when it rained, and you nearly froze to death in cold weather. We were stacked like cordwood, with no room to move. Half the toilets didn't work, and there weren't enough of them to begin with. I wasn't raised under these conditions, and it made me mad when I realized what the state was subjecting me to. People treat their livestock better than we were treated. The whole place was really a mess. The way I felt, for them to have killed me would have been an act of mercy.

Shorty Files a Lawsuit

On that cold November day, Shorty walked over to the prison law library to do some research. He found Section 1983.

At the time I didn't know anything about research, research and law. I went to the law library and got checking around. And I found Title 42, Section 1983. I got to looking at that and I figured the federal courts had jurisdiction on the thing. That's when I decided to file it in federal court.

I knew that we couldn't do anything about it in state court because it was a state institution. I didn't believe we coulda got anything done in state court. I just found the civil rights thing, and I filed under that. It deals with human rights. I figured even though we was convicts, we're still human.

After Shorty did his research, he handwrote a petition to the federal court in Louisville:

This is a petition signed by only six prisoners. We hope that it will be treated as a class action petition.

If we were permitted to do so, we could get several hundred other prisoners to sign. However, it is our understanding that it is against institutional rules to circulate a petition. Also, most prisoners feel that the administration would take reprisal action against them if they signed.

We hope that the Court will overlook any misspelling, bad grammar and punctuation.

We sincerely hope that the Court will investigate our complaint and that we can get some relief soon. Especially now that winter is comeing on and our living quarters will be even more crowded because of bad weather and people will be staying inside more.

Shorty was not very impressed with his work.

I don't think I done a very good job of [drawing up the suit]. I hadn't fooled with the law very much at that time. I know I didn't word the suit properly. I've never had any training or studied law. I just wrote down the way things were and hoped the magistrate or judge would do something.

Shorty and the five other prisoners who signed the petition knew it was risky business for a prisoner to bring a lawsuit against the wardens and guards.

At that time at LaGrange you couldn't sign a petition. The Corrections Bureau had a rule against circulating a petition. If you was even caught with a petition, you was placed in segregation. I talked to my brother and several other guys about signing the complaint if I drew it up. Five agreed to sign it. Them was the only ones that had enough nerve to sign it. Guys were afraid of being th'own in the hole. You could get placed in the hole for signing a petition or circulating a petition or possession of a petition.

I told the guys, "I don't believe that rule is right, and if we could get the judge to accept this case, I don't think he'd allow you to be punished for trying to assert your rights, to get this case in court. I don't believe a judge would allow that." I was going into federal court. I don't have any faith in state judges, but I don't believe a man will be appointed a federal judge unless he was fair and impartial and unless he would do what he was s'posed to do.

After the other five men signed the petition, Shorty put it in an envelope, addressed it to the U.S. District Court in Louisville, walked over to the prison mail room, and put it in the morning mail.

This simple act triggered a chain of events that Shorty never imagined. The head of the prison system fell from office, the state's leading newspaper carried front-page stories and wrote editorials about the lawsuit, the federal court monitored the prison system for seven years, and the governor fired a high-level cabinet officer. Part of the case reached the U.S. Supreme Court, and the Kentucky Supreme Court levied a $4 million fine against the prison system. The state spent more than $200 million to reform the prisons. The prisons were changed forever, and the lives of every person connected with the lawsuit changed. For Shorty, starting up this long-shot lawsuit turned out to be a major step in restoring meaning and worth in his life.

Getting Up at 3:30 Every Morning

Shorty's life began in 1935 on a farm in Bath County, Kentucky, on the periphery of the Appalachian Plateau. Life is a struggle for most of the people who live in Appalachia, a land of beautiful mountains and some of the most wretched poverty in the United States. Like most Appalachian people, Shorty's ancestors were a mixture of Scottish, English, and Irish blood, carrying names such as Spence, Holton, and, like Shorty, Thompson. These emigrants left the British Isles for the New World many generations ago. Shorty's grandparents were natives of Kentucky, farmers and loggers who made railroad ties and lumber. James McClellan "Shorty" Thompson was the first child born to Ed and Anna Mae Thompson, but he was not Ed's first child. Ed Thompson had already had thirteen children by an earlier marriage, and he fathered nine more children by his second wife, Anna Mae.

It took a great deal of work to support this Thompson family. Ed was a hardworking tenant farmer, raising corn, hay, tobacco, and cattle and cutting firewood. Shorty grew up knowing how to work hard, for the Thompson family lived on what it could produce from the land. Ed had no money for hired labor. Children provided the labor, led by first-born Shorty.

I started work when I was about five years old, doing what I could. Carrying firewood, water; feeding the hogs; gathering eggs. We had an old fireplace. . . . Most of the heat went up the chimney, so you had to keep a big fire in it. And we had the cookstove in the kitchen. We certainly didn't have a furnace. Later on, I think we got a coal-burning stove. We never had central heat or electric, telephone, water, or anything like that. So I cut the firewood and carried it in after school. Didn't have water in the house either. We had to carry water from the spring. We had a spring about a hundred yards behind the house over a hill. I carried a million gallons of water up that hill.

When I got to be seven years old I started milking—get up when the old man did, 3:30 in the morning. . . . As soon as he eat breakfast he'd go out and hitch up the mules, getting ready to go to work. It was still dark, and we used a lantern, a kerosene lantern. We had cows. We had anywhere from five to seven cows. . . . The cows run loose on that farm. I had to hunt 'em up every morning, get 'em to the milking gauge. . . . I milked anywheres from five to seven cows. Go back to the house, take the milk in, go feed the hogs. Took care of six to eight hogs. If I wasn't going to school, by daylight I'd go out to where the old man was working at and either chop tobacco or corn or whatever needed to be done. I did field work.

Quit work at 7:00. Be down to catch the school bus at 8:00. School would get out about 3:00, 3:30, or something like that. Then ride the bus to where we got on, to the gate, walk up to the house, take your clothes off, change clothes, and go to work. That's when I chopped the firewood. . . . When I was seven years old, my sister—my next oldest sister—was old enough to help carry the water and do other stuff. Of course I had to milk the cows again. Milked the cows twice a day. Chop the firewood and kindling, feed the hogs.

When I got big enough to handle the mules, I started working in the field. I was around ten. We'd get up about 3:30 and take a lantern, go to the barn—kerosene lamp—and harness up the mules. Feed them and feed the cows and then come back and eat breakfast while the horses and mules and cows was eating. After I eat breakfast I'd go back and milk the cows, and the old man would take off to the field with the mules. Soon as it got daylight, we was in the field. Old man was plowing with mules. I couldn't handle the plows. I wasn't tall enough to reach the plow handles. I cultivated with mules and a cultivator. It's got wheels on it, and it's just got little plows, and the little plows fit between the rows and plows up weeds and breaks up the ground in between the rows of corn or tobacco or whatever you're cultivating. I wasn't breaking ground, I was cultivating it after the crops had grown.

Nineteen-forty-seven was the first tractor I'd seen. A couple years before that my old man hired a guy that owned a tractor to come in and do some plowing for him. The first tractor we ever owned, the first tractor that I was ever on, was in 1947. My old man bought a tractor, and he didn't know how to operate it. The guy he bought it off of drove it over there and showed me and my father how to operate the tractor. The old man couldn't catch on, couldn't get used to the clutch—put it in gear, and he'd forget to take it out of gear and run into the fence. So I wound up operating the tractor.

We worked from daylight to dark. After the sun was down, we'd stop working. Put the mules in the barn, fed 'em. Seven days a week.

Like many tenant farm families in the Great Depression, the Thompsons lived at a subsistence level, producing nearly all their own food. Anna Mae Thompson was pregnant for much of Shorty's youth, giving birth to nine babies in fifteen years. She managed a primitive, remote farmhouse and spent nearly all her time feeding her family and cleaning up.

The house was about a mile and a half from the nearest road, and the only way to get to it was with a horse, or a mule and wagon, or a horse and wagon, or walk. The house had downstairs four rooms and two rooms upstairs, the fireplace was in the living room, and of course the cookstove was in the kitchen. The upstairs was sorta semiloft. The walls were about four foot high and then ran up to the corner of the roof, peak of the roof. Me and my brothers slept upstairs. My sisters all slept downstairs in the back bedroom. And my mother and father's bed was in the living room. They had to take care of the fire.

We didn't have electric in the house, didn't have water in the house either. We used kerosene lamps and carried water from the spring. We had to have an outside toilet.

I remember when my mother was young and pretty. I was born when she was about eighteen. . . . She worked awful hard, my father and her did, both worked awful hard, and she had nine children. She was always canning. Mostly I remember she was always canning or doing laundry—vegetables outa the garden, corn, beans, tomatoes, cooking sausage, canning sausage. My old man, every year he'd kill six hogs and two beeves. My mother raised a big garden. The only thing we ever went to the store for was coffee and flour, stuff like that. We had butter. We had milk. We had eggs, meat, vegetables. She baked bread. Breakfast would be ham, eggs, sausage, gravy, bacon, preserves, all kinds of stuff. That's all I can remember is her working and taking care of us. She's a little short woman, probably about five foot. She don't have much education. She's got a lot of common sense. She treated us all right.

The family met most of its needs on the farm, so trips to town were rare. Going to town was a major project, because the Thompsons had no car: they would use mules or a horse and wagon for their monthly trips.

Shorty spent his small amount of spare time at the farm, primarily helping to provide food for the family.

I hunted and fished and explored the woods. Back in them days they didn't have television. We had a radio—I think it was a battery-operated radio. People visited a lot on Sundays. We would go to somebody's house for dinner, or they would come to our house for dinner. But I spent most of my time out in the woods hunting and fishing—mostly catfish, some bluegill. Caught turtles, frogs. I never did see a bass. We had fish traps, and we'd catch these fish called red eye. I don't know what kind of fish it was, haven't seen one for years. They're a bass-type fish, a panfish, but it wasn't bass.

I hunted rabbits, squirrel 'n quail 'n grouse—whatever was in season. There wasn't any deer back in this country then. Two old dogs and a rifle—mostly alone. When I first started hunting, I was awful young, I was nine or ten years old. They wouldn't let younger kids have a rifle or gun, especially if you was with somebody. So I didn't even take my brothers and sisters with me 'til they got older. The neighbors wouldn't trust their kid with a gun or wouldn't trust me with their kid if I had a gun, 'cause of accidents. You know children—they're not aware of the dangers of firearms. I always was. My old man taught me how to shoot when I was about seven or eight years old. I always learned never to point a gun at something you didn't aim to shoot. I always keep in mind that a gun can be loaded, whether or not it is. I'll always handle it like it's loaded. So I didn't have all this time, but I hunted and fished. All food for the family.

School was Shorty's major break from producing food for the family. Shorty had already been up and working for more than four hours by the time he caught the school bus. His education was cut short, however, by the need to support the family.

We walked a mile and a half out to the gravel road to catch the school bus. We lived on the back of the farm, so it was a mile and half out to the gravel road. 'Course that was rough walking in the wintertime, especially when it was muddy, and cold. The school was in Owingsville, county seat of Bath County. They had a brick school. It was a big school.

I quit in the seventh grade, to work on the farm. I guess I'm the only one that quit school to work on the farm. All my sisters went to high school, and two of my brothers. I liked school, [but they] needed me on the farm.

Shorty worked full time on the farm for the next six years. He worked side by side with his father, day after day, year after year. They started the day together at 3:30 in the morning and worked until it was too dark to work any more. Ed Thompson remains the strongest influence in Shorty's life.

He was the best friend I ever had. He worked hard. He tried to raise a family and did raise a family. Well, he raised two families. I don't think he ever committed a crime in his life or even thought about it. His criminal record I guess would be maybe a fistfight and maybe in jail for a fistfight or drinking. He was the kind of person, if you had a problem you'd go to him and talk to him about it. If you needed something and he could give it to you, he'd give it to you or loan it to you. That's the kind of person I consider a friend.

The thing that stands out the most in my mind about him was when I joined the Army. I was about eighteen years old, and I came home on a leave—I had gone overseas. And this little ol' hick place he lived at didn't have a train stop. You had to flag a train down to get on it. I stayed with him the last night 'fore I caught the train, about 12:00 or 12:05. The last thing I remember—what stands out most in my mind—just before the train arrived he reached in his pocket and give me his pistol. He said,

"Now take that with you and take care of yourself." That's what I remember. I don't know what his reason was.

I admired him because of the way he was, I guess. He was honest, and he was a nice person. He tried to live right. He was always willing to help somebody. He worked hard.

When Shorty left the Thompson farm at age eighteen, it was 1953, and the Korean War was winding down.

I got in on the last of Korea. I went over there to Korea in April '53, and the war was over with officially in July '53. I was in the infantry. I wouldn't call it combat. They'd shoot at us, and we'd shoot back at them. They had a DMZ up 'ere, with sniping and stuff. There was no battles. They had had a truce going—'course neither side stuck with the truce.

I did a tour of duty in Iceland, . . . at the air base. I was in the army, we was on guard protection. I did four years.

Shorty received an honorable discharge in 1957.

Ten Years on the Run

There was no family farm waiting for the young veteran, but it mattered little. The eldest son of the tenant farmer knew the hardships of subsistence farming in and near Appalachia.

By that time my old man had left the farm and went to work for the state highway department. Farming definitely just didn't pay, 'specially if ye didn't own it. I liked it, but I seen my old man scuffle all his life, and he never did get ahead. I don't mind working on a farm. I wouldn't try and make a living at it. We could never get ahead on the farm, as far as ever having anything. My old man, he struggled all his life on the farm. He made a living, he made a good living, but we didn't have anything extra. He never owned his own home 'til after he went to work for the state highway department. Didn't own any property—no TV, no electric.

The young veteran chose instead to learn a trade in a town one county over from the old farm. He found a job at the Chevrolet dealer, where he did bodywork on cars. He got married, and the couple had a baby girl they named Teresa. Shorty appeared ready to settle down into normal family life in a quiet town in rural Kentucky.

It was not to be. There is no simple explanation for why he turned to a life of crime. His early life did not fit the profile of someone who was likely to become a criminal. His upbringing seemed wholesome enough, the kind that produces hardworking, law-abiding citizens. Shorty got along with everyone in his big family. He had responsibility early in life, he worked hard, and he had plenty of wholesome food. Shorty looked up to his father for working hard and taking care of his family and was an army war veteran with an honorable discharge. None of Shorty's brothers and sisters became career criminals.

There were some danger signs, however. Shorty was poorly educated. Family life was not perfect, for Ed and Anna Mae were divorced just before Shorty joined the army. His prospects on coming out of the army were bleak: sixth-grade education, no farm to which to return. The trouble began at the Chevrolet dealership where the young husband and father was learning auto bodywork.

When I first went to work down 'ere—1959, January or February—I was making thirty dollars a week. The man that hired me told me, said, "You work six weeks down here, and if everything works out, you can get a raise"—which I needed. Thirty dollars a week, and they was holding Social Security out and income tax on that, too. I don't think I ever made over twenty-eight dollars take-home. So anyhow, six weeks goes by, and I don't get the raise, and I go talk to the man that promised me the raise of two dollars and a half. Now, when I started down there, I didn't know anything about the job. All the experience I had was army and military and farming. Of course, I had a little mechanic experience on the farm, but I worked down 'ere, I worked hard. We worked 8½ or 9 hours a day and 5½ days a week. I didn't feel like he was paying me enough.

So I kept after this man for a raise. And instead of giving me a raise, he give me more work. There was a service station next door, Sinclair service station. They bought that so they could have the parking space and their own gasoline and everything and put me over there. I run that for 'em. I worked there a year, no raise. So finally I quit because I didn't get any pay raises. . . .

So I quit, and I'm broke. Like I say, I needed the money. I got a family to support, and I don't have any money, and I don't have any job. We didn't have everything we needed, but we didn't lose any weight, I want you to know. We wasn't starving to death. There was food on the table, but it was a hassle. I was working when I could on farms. It wasn't steady. I trimmed trees, stripped tobacco for maybe a week, maybe help put out a fence or set a fence line. Take a mechanic job when I could get it. I tuned up cars. I overhauled two engines, three maybe. But they was few and far between. It wasn't every day, maybe once or twice a month or something like that.

So I just said, "Well, I know where his money's at and I think they owe me." So I went down and got it—at the service station. They had a little safe in there, and I opened it. I still knew the combination, and I think I got—I don't remember—I believe it was $280.

I was arrested on two charges—felonies—of storehouse breaking. I had some misdemeanors—fighting, drinking, raising hell—when I was a kid. This was the first felony. I was twenty-six years old. I was indicted on both felonies at the same grand jury, two separate indictments but at the same grand jury. I stood trial by jury, and the jury give me, on one charge they give me a year in LaGrange—judge didn't believe in probation. I don't remember any probation back in them days. Since I was a first offender, the commonwealth agreed to file away the other charge, put it on the shelf, on the condition that when I got out of prison, I didn't get into more trouble for a year.

OK, so I go down to LaGrange and do nine months, . . . and I get out and I go to Florida. The reason I went to Florida was because my wife, Teresa's mother, had divorced me while I was at LaGrange. I was still crazy about the woman, and I moved to Florida to get over her. I realized that if I was around and saw her with another man, I would be in trouble again. I worked at Hialeah, Florida, went to work for Van Horne's stables at the racetrack down there. And I stayed down 'ere for about six months. My mother-in-law wrote me that Teresa was sick. I quit the job down 'ere and came back to Kentucky.

I hadn't been in any trouble. My brother was in jail on a misdemeanor—he was doing thirty days—and I went up to jail to see him. Hadn't seen him for six, seven months. While I was in the jail the sheriff came in to take some prisoners over to be sentenced that'd already been tried or pled guilty. He was taking 'em over to court to be final-sentenced. And he told me, he said, "I've got a warrant for you." Of course, I didn't think he did, and I told him, I said, "I ain't done nothing." So he had a bunch of old warrants in his shirt pocket, he went through 'em and couldn't find one on me. So he said, "Let's go over to the courthouse. You just come over to the courthouse with me." So I go over to the courthouse with 'im.

The judge calls these other two guys up 'ere, sentenced one of 'em to two years in the penitentiary for car theft and one of 'em three years in the penitentiary for car theft. And the sheriff goes up and talks to the judge. The judge looks around on his desk, and he finds the old indictment that had been filed away. He called me up 'ere—without an attorney or anything like that, he called me up 'ere. Read the indictment to me. Asked me how I plead to it. And I pled not guilty. So the court appointed me an attorney. They set a trial date. They put me in jail on I believe it was a five hundred dollar bond—it mighta been a thousand, but anyhow it was a small bond.

Shorty's encounters with the criminal-justice system left him feeling that the state had double-crossed him. He had taken money that did not belong to him, and the state had both the right and the responsibility to punish him. After his trial on the first charge, however, the prosecutor had agreed to file away the second charge if he stayed out of trouble. He had served his sentence at LaGrange, moved to Florida, and stayed out of trouble. Now, from his perspective, the state reneged on its promise by jailing him and bringing him to trial on the second charge. Shorty decided to start running from the law.

I was mad, 'cause this charge s'posed to been filed away and everything, so I broke out—1961, I believe in February. The first time I escaped from Montgomery County Jail. It's a old rotten jail built right after the Civil War out of sandstone rock. The jail was heated with natural gas and had a little natural-gas heater in there with a long pipe onto it coming from the outside into the cell block. So I disconnected this steel gas line from the heater and crooked it around into the cell against the wall and turned the gas on and lit it and heated the rock. We heated the rock about two days. It got red-hot, and we throwed cold water on it, a gallon butt can of water on it. The wall just exploded—hot rock, cold water. The wall fell out. So that's the first time I broke outa jail.

I went to Dayton, Ohio, and stayed 'ere until May. I was picked up in Ohio by the Dayton police on a fugitive warrant. I was brought back to

Kentucky and placed in the Clark County Jail for security reasons. Later on that year, October '61, I went to court, and they had a jury trial on this charge that had been filed away in 1960—storehouse breaking. Jury give me two years, so I go to LaGrange and I served eighteen months.

After serving his second prison term for the single act of stealing $280, Shorty quickly got into trouble again, and this time he was on the run for almost ten years. His trail led through Missouri, Oklahoma, California, Oregon, Washington, Texas, Mexico, and Florida before finally bringing him back to Kentucky.

In 1964 I got an assault charge in Montgomery County, and they put me in jail—fourth-degree assault, a misdemeanor. I escaped again. The second time I escaped from Montgomery County Jail, I used the gas the same way, except I went through the ceiling—rock ceiling.

Two of us went to Missouri, me and a guy by the name of Paul Linger. I have a brother who lives out in the western part of Missouri, a little town called Weston, in Platt County. Me and Paul there, we go out there and we go to work. I went to work in a body shop, and he went to work on a farm. We worked out there about four or five months, and of course Kentucky authorities found out where we was. Missouri officials arrested us on a fugitive warrant and took us to the Platt County Jail. We stayed in the Platt County Jail about three weeks, and we broke out. It was three of us broke out that time, me and Paul Linger, the guy that broke out with me in Kentucky, and some kid out of Kansas City, Missouri. I think he was seventeen years old. He was a parole violator. The three of us broke out. The next day Paul gets caught. This kid and myself, we lived out in the woods up 'ere for about two weeks in Missouri. Finally, I got a friend of mine to drive us to Oklahoma City. From Oklahoma City we caught a train to California—Los Angeles.

We didn't have much money. We was on skid row down there in them flophouses, twenty-five cents a night. I got a job in a body and fender shop out there. This kid, he didn't have a trade or nothing, so it was hard for him to find a job. I'm making good money, so I give this kid money ever' day to catch a bus. He's reading these ads in the paper that's got jobs. I give him bus fare, lunch money, and everything, while he was trying to find work. It's a flophouse and there's a wino running it. I guess I'm paranoid about, you know, the law's right on my track, right on my heels. So the guy that's running the flophouse, I told 'im, I said, "I'm wanted by the law. If any policeman come down here asking any questions about me, here's a phone number you can call me and let me know." And I give 'im a five-dollar bill. And every evening when I come in from work, I'd bring him a fifth o' wine.

This goes on for about three weeks while I'm working. This kid still hadn't gotten a job. So I come in from work one afternoon, and this guy that runs the flophouse, he meets me at the door. He says the police arrested the kid at his flophouse. I was supposed to be his uncle. The kid didn't have any identification, and the only reason he could stay there was because I'm supposed to be his uncle. I had ID—phony ID, but I had ID. This kid had got picked up for hitchhiking out in Hollywood. He didn't have any ID on him. When they take him to the headquarters, he calls this flophouse where we're staying and talks to this old man on the phone, tells him when I come in that evening from work for me to come down and identify him, so the police could turn him loose in my custody, supposedly. So when I come in from work that afternoon, the old man met me at the door and told me what happened. So I go to my room and pack my clothes and I'm gone to Oregon, 'cause I don't know what they got the kid for. They may have done fingerprinted him and found out he's wanted. If I go down there I may get caught. So anyway, I caught a freight train to Oregon—Salem, Oregon.

I got to Oregon and I went to work in a labor camp, migrant labor camp, picking. I believe strawberries was in season at that time. Anyhow, I go to work for this contractor, labor contractor. . . . I was only making $1.10 a hour when we worked for these farmers. So this guy tells me that he'll start me out at minimum wage if I'll stay on and cook, take care of the place, and he'll git me one of these winos to help do the dishes. I believe it was seventy-two men at the camp. I'd cooked in the army and at home. The boss lived about twelve miles away. I started cooking at that place. It's just like a little community. I guess I was sort of the mayor or policeman or whatever. I kept order in the place. If winos get in fights, I go separate 'em. Put 'em to bed when they pass out in the yard, raining and snowing on 'em, I'd take 'em in and put 'em to bed. So anyhow, I took care of that place for about six months.

I left there and . . . moved to California. I went to Indio [and] stayed . . . about fourteen months. I worked for Floyd Cooper Body and Fender Shop in Indio. I was arrested once in Indio. They arrested me for drunk driving and threw me in the drunk tank. I wouldn't exactly call this an escape, but while I was in there it changed shifts. Matter of fact, I come in jail as the shift was changing. After I was there about twenty minutes this new jailer called out a guy's name, told him his bond had been posted. This guy was sleeping. I tried to wake him up and couldn't. Me and him was the only ones in the cell, and I tried to wake him up and couldn't so I decided to leave in his place. Actually I wouldn't call that an escape, but I did leave there. In other words, they turned me loose that time.

I quit the job at that body and fender shop and went to Fresno and went to work in a body shop on Ventura Avenue or Boulevard, whatever it is. I worked there about seven or eight months. One night I meet this guy in a bar. He's a ironworker, a disabled ironworker. He's got the money, but he's wanting to get into a business. He can't do ironwork any more. We got to talking about body and fender work. He agreed to rent a shop and furnish the tools if I would run it and show him how, teach him the body and fender trade. [I] moved to Vancouver, Washington, and we set up a body and fender shop. I worked at that about thirteen or fourteen months. He and I had a disagreement over a woman, so I just left everything and took off.

I went to Port Isabel, Texas, and went to work on the shrimp boats. I worked down 'ere at Port Isabel for about six months on a fifty-two-foot wood-hull shrimp boat. The name of it was the Four Leaf Clover. We'd go out and stay anywhere from seven days to twenty-one days, maybe thirty days. We would come in and we would weigh up the shrimp. I got paid on a percentage. We come in one time with a big load of shrimp, and I got a pretty good paycheck. I decided to go to Mexico.

I went to Matamoros, across the river from Brownsville. I had eight hundred dollars on me. I still had a bunch o' body and fender tools, and I had about five hundred dollars' worth o' clothes in the trunk o' my car. . . . I had a guy with me, another shrimper. We go down to a couple o' whorehouses and get our business took care of. We drank in the bars and got half drunk. Started back to the United States. Before I got to the bridges to Texas, there's a four-way stop. There's no stoplight. There's stop signs, four-way stop. So I pulled up to this intersection, and this taxi is on my right at the stop sign. He stops, so I waited. The man on the right has the right-of-way here in the United States. So I waited, and he motioned *me on, so I start through the intersection and here he comes. So I stop and motioned him on. Well, he motioned me on. So hey, I took off again, and he runs in front of me, and I stop, but I don't stop in time, and when he runs in front of me, it scrapes the side of his cab. . . . Didn't dent it, but it scraped the paint off. He jumps out, raising hell in Spanish. I didn't half understand it. He's wanting money, and we're arguing, 'bout to get into a fight. Two Mexican police officers pull up in a '47 Dodge panel truck. They th'ow us, me and the guy I'm with, and the taxi driver in the back of this panel truck to go into jail. . . . We get about two or three blocks down the street, and they pulled down an alley. This panel truck has got a padlock and a hasp on the back door, a screen between the back and the drivers. They unlock the back door and get us all out in the alley. Took my billfold and the guy that was with me's billfold away from us and took the money out of 'em and threw the billfolds down the alley. This taxi driver, he's jab-bering, and they didn't rob him, but they kicked his hind end and sent him up the alley and took us on to jail. Me and this other guy stayed in jail three or four days. When I finally went to court, the judge fined me $125 American and give me twenty days in jail. It was in early '66. . . .*

I stayed in jail twenty days—actually 19½ days. The jail was just like a corral. No building in it. It was just brick walls twenty or twenty-five foot high with electrified barb wire on top. They penned you up just like a cow—no ceiling, no nothing, just a pen. It come two or three West Texas rains while I was there. We had to sleep standing up, leaning against the wall, or you slept on the ground. It didn't have a bathroom or toilet. The only water had been a faucet coming up outa the ground, and somebody had broke the faucet off even with the ground—it's just a stream of water squirting up outa the ground. These Mexicans used the bathroom right around the drinking water—just squat down and take a crap. It gagged you just to bend over and drink water. That's all the water we had. Twice a day they fed us a bowl of beans and three tortillas a little bit bigger than a silver dollar, had gravel in 'em. I guess it was stone-ground. The beans was just cooked long enough to crack the hull. It was harder than peanuts. I stayed in 'ere 19½ days. This guard come in on the nineteenth day. He said, "If you clean the crap up around that water spigot there, we'll turn you loose a half a day early." I was glad to do it. Just for four or five hours, I was glad to do it. I lost about twenty pounds in twenty days—hadn't took a bath, hadn't shaved, had mud in my hair, all nasty where I'd been laying on the ground.

I'm flat broke. No identification. The two bridges outa Matamoros go-
ing back into Brownsville at that time, one of 'em it cost you a penny to
cross it. The other one cost you five cents. I'm on my way to the river to the
bridges. I meet this Mexican guy and his girlfriend or his wife, whatever.
I bummed a penny off of him to cross the cheap bridge. . . .

I went on down to Brownsville to American customs. I talked to a man
about trying to get my car back. He told me it was hopeless. The Mexi-
cans had confiscated my car and whatever's in it. That left me on foot,
so I hitchhiked a ride down to Port Isabel to get on the shrimp boat again.
My boat was out, and 'course I didn't have any money, so I couldn't hang
around. I hitchhiked back to Brownsville and caught a freight train and
headed north.

I finally wound up back in Oregon—Salem, Oregon. I went to work in
a body and fender shop up 'ere. I worked about three years [and then I]
went to Orlando, Florida. I got a job out there, . . . working for a body
and fender shop, Cadillac agency dealer. . . . I worked there about a year,
[came] back to Kentucky, and [then] went out to see my brother in Mis-
souri. He was building a new house. I started to helping him work on the
house. I wound up staying there. We went into business out there—garage
and body and fender shop service station.

Off to Prison

By 1973 Shorty had been drifting for nearly ten years. Shorty's daughter, Teresa, was now thirteen years old, growing up without her father.
Shorty came back home to visit, but he was a wanted man, a fugitive from
justice, so the visits were few. His years on the run ended during one of
these visits.

Late part of 1973 I got into a shooting scrap in Bath County, Kentucky.
My brother Henry D. was going with this girl. She made a play for me,
trying to make him jealous. It worked, and he got mad at me. She told him
I had made a play for her. I went to see her to get things straightened out.
That made things worse. I talked to him and explained what was going
on. He understood. One day I was driving down the road past her house.
She and another boyfriend were out in the yard planting flowers or some-
thing. I was driving my brother's station wagon. As I passed the house
they opened fire on me with a shotgun and an automatic .22 caliber rifle.

I was unarmed. I turned around and went back up to my dad's, where my car was parked, got my gun out of the glove box. I went back down and did a little shooting myself. The station wagon I was driving had eleven bullet holes in it, plus the back glass was shot out with the shotgun.

Nobody was injured in this gunplay, but the police located Shorty and arrested him, placing him in the Bath County Jail on a charge of shooting without wounding with intent to kill.

While I was in the Bath County Jail on that shooting charge, I got a hacksaw blade. I sawed out a bar in the upstairs window and escaped. I went to Clark County and went to work on the tobacco farms down there— housing tobacco, seasonal temporary work. And of course I didn't go far enough. They found out where I was. The Clark County officials arrested me on a fugitive warrant. And I had a gun on me, .22 revolver, so the police also charged me with carrying a concealed weapon.

Shorty defended himself on the weapons charge, acting as his own attorney. It turned out to be the start of a successful career as a jailhouse lawyer.

When the officer arrested me, the gun was laying in the seat beside me. So we have an examining trial before a judge, city police court, on the ·carrying-a-concealed-weapon charge. I questioned the officer that was examining at this hearing and asked him where the gun was when he first seen it. He said it was laying in the seat beside me. I asked him, I said, "Did you ever see the gun in my pocket?" He said, "No." I told the judge, "Well, your honor, I move that this charge be dismissed because the weapon wasn't concealed." So the judge dismissed the charge.

This successful defense did not free Shorty. The long criminal record, laced with gunplay, attracted the attention of federal authorities, and the state transferred him to the custody of federal officials because the gun was in his possession.

The federals picked up the gun charge. Charged me with being a ex-felon in possession of a firearm in interstate commerce. They had me cold. They kept me in the Clark County Jail for security reasons, because I'd never escaped from there, I guess. When they put me in the Clark County Jail it was about 10:00 in the morning. There was four other guys in 'ere sawing their way out. At about 10:30 that night we left, me and four other guys.

*Like a fool I went back to Bath County. My brother-in-law bought a
place that was all grown up with weeds and bushes. I was helping him
clear that. Of course, the sheriff found out where I was, and they arrested
me again, took me back to Clark County Jail. I stayed there about three
months in a solitary cell. I tore the bedspring loose from the bunk and
made a key to the door—actually, I guess you call it a pick. One night
when the jailer come down to serve coffee and donuts about 9:00 at night,
I picked the lock. The jailer and the trusty come in to serve me donuts. Of
course, the jailer is thinking the door is locked. I happened to have it already unlocked. When he reaches to put his key in it, I slammed the door
in his face—took him by surprise—and I run over top of him and the
trusty. I didn't get very far on this escape, only got about a block. I'd been
laying there for three months, smoking two cartons of cigarettes a week,
so I got winded [in] about a block. They was right on my heels, so they
caught me.*

*They had me cold. I pled guilty to the federal charge in Lexington in
Federal District Court. Got two years. I served 'em at Texarkana, Texas;
Springfield, Missouri; and Terre Haute, Indiana—served seventeen
months and five days on it.*

After six successful escapes, Shorty had broken out of jail for the last
time. Now he was a prisoner of the U.S. government. Shorty learned another way, the legal way, to get out of prison while he was at the federal
prison in Springfield, and it was the beginning of Shorty's education in the
law. Learning about law was also a way to stay busy. Shorty had grown up
working and had worked throughout his years on the run, but it was always
work by hand. The study of law was a new kind of work, in which Shorty
had to learn to use his mind to achieve results.

*I first started when I was at Springfield, at the federal prison hospital.
There was a lawyer there. He was a prisoner. It was something to do with
credit cards, embezzlement or something, Texaco Company. He was doing
legal work for inmates. I got acquainted with 'im. He was from Pikeville,
Kentucky. I started helping him do research. I just got interested in it from
helping him.*

Serving hard time in federal prison learning about law did not stop
Shorty's criminal activity. After his release he returned to Kentucky and
found a girlfriend and a job, but he was soon in trouble again.

In the latter part of '77 I was arrested for killing cattle, trying to do a guy a favor. I got an unlawful taking charge on that. We shot 'em and skinned 'em, what it was. This was a young guy, and he'd been married about a year, and his wife had had a new baby. He was broke. He knew some people in Cincinnati that would buy beef—meat. I had money in my pocket. I didn't have to do that. I was just doing him a favor. But anyhow, he come up to my house and asked me if I would go help him kill two beef. So we go out on this man's farm and shoot two beef and skin 'em out, load 'em in his car and he takes 'em to Cincinnati.

This girl I'm shacking with, she hears the next day that two beef had been killed. She goes [to] talk to her mother: "Well, I bet he done it. He come in this morning at 2:00 and had blood all over him." Word gets around, and the law gets wind of it. They charge me with theft over one hundred dollars. I pled guilty, got five years. That's what I was in La-Grange on when I filed the suit.

So it was that the farm boy from Bath County on the periphery of Appalachian Kentucky spent twenty years of his life committing crime and running from the law. The record of convictions is long but not gruesome: one theft of $280, one assault, one instance of drunk driving, one gunfight, one instance of gun possession, and one theft of two cattle. Nobody was injured. Shorty was a small-time criminal and an escape artist.

What drove him to petition a federal court to investigate living conditions in a prison? During his years on the run, Shorty lived in flophouses, migrant labor camps, a Mexican jail, and similar other places. He had experienced squalor and filth firsthand as a free man, so what was different about KSR?

I'll tell you about the Mexican jail. It was dirty and nasty, but we didn't have cockroaches and rats. The way I feel about it, I believe that people down there were ignorant, so they can be excused for them kind of conditions. But here in the United States, here in America, I believe a prisoner ought to at least have a clean place to sleep—no roaches and rats. And a warm place—no cracks in the walls and the roof leaking and the windows all out.

Shorty believed there was no excuse for the conditions at KSR. Shorty had broken society's rules, and society punished him. He understood that situation and felt no resentment, but he also believed that if he had to live by the rules, society had to do so as well. Shorty decided that he would try to use the same legal system that had sent him to prison to improve the living conditions at KSR.

Shorty and the other inmates who joined him believed that they were exposing themselves to significant risk by filing the petition with the court. Prison officials had a history of retaliating against prisoners who sued prisons. Some guards at KSR soon struck back.

> We knew that if the officials got wind of the complaint, we would be in deep shit, so we kept it a secret among the six of us. When we first filed the suit, we got a guy in the so-called legal office to shoot copies of the complaint. Each one of us kept a copy. I mailed it out that morning. About 10:00 later on that morning, here come guards down.
>
> There were six of us, and there's two guards each man, which makes twelve guards. They shook us down. I had told these guys, I said, "Don't let the guards get ahold of this. Don't let nobody see it." Other inmates had seen us together, and the guards had seen us together, and I figured they might shake us down and find this. So we all hid ours except my brother. I gave mine to another inmate [who] wasn't involved, wasn't even in the dormitory that I lived in. The rest of the guys did, too. The only copy they found belonged to my brother. They took 'im to the captain's office. Let 'im sit in the captain's office. It was in a sealed envelope. Took the envelope someplace and brought it back to him and turned him loose. I know what they did, they shot a copy of it. And give it back to him. It was a dangerous incident.

The danger passed for the moment, and the envelope containing Shorty's petition wound its way through the mails to the federal courthouse in Louisville.

Judge Johnstone

Shorty's handwritten petition was assigned to Judge Edward H. Johnstone of the U.S. District Court for the Western District of Kentucky in a roundabout way. The petition arrived in the clerk's office at the federal courthouse in Louisville on November 30, 1978. A clerk opened the envelope and read it. There was a time when that clerk might have shaken his head, stuck Shorty's complaint into a dead file, or maybe even pitched it into a wastebasket, never to be seen again. In those days, people who filed civil rights lawsuits sometimes got a hostile reception in the clerk's office in the federal court. There was an incident in the early 1970s, before Judge Johnstone assumed office, when a clerk saw a couple of lawyers filing a civil rights lawsuit. The clerk remarked, "What happened? Someone step on some poor nigger's toes?" The remark was reported to the judges, who fired the clerk. Their action sent a message that civil rights lawsuits were to receive the same treatment and respect as any other lawsuit. The clerk who read Shorty's petition referred it to U.S. Magistrate George

Long, who on December 15, 1978, ordered "James M. Thompson, et al., Plaintiffs" to file a complaint "on forms prescribed by the Court which will be supplied to the plaintiffs by the Clerk of Court."

Shorty received the forms and, on his bunk bed, using a battered typewriter purchased for a carton of cigarettes, typed out a two-page complaint. The complaint alleged that the dormitories were overcrowded, dirty, and bug infested; the food was filthy; and young inmates were intermingled with and attacked by homosexual and hardened criminals and that these conditions were "in violation of their rights against cruel and unusual punishment." He mailed the complaint to the federal court, and on January 2, 1979, a clerk wrote on it case number "C79-0001L," the first new case of 1979.

It was now an official case. Shorty did not have a lawyer, and engaging in litigation without a lawyer usually is a major disadvantage, but Shorty had the right to do so, and he had no choice. From his prison dormitory there was little chance of contacting a lawyer familiar with such a case, and even if he had managed to do so, it would have been difficult to find a lawyer willing to take the case. What lawyer had the resources to take on the commonwealth of Kentucky? How would he or she get paid?

The clerk's next step was to draw the judge to hear the case. Several federal judges handled the caseload in the Western District. The clerks kept a pile of cards with each judge's name on a card. Whichever judge was next in the pile was assigned the next case, so it was luck of the draw. Shorty's luck was bad at first. Judge Tom Ballantine's name came up. Despite the traditional view of the law as a set of neutral principles applied by dispassionate judges, the assignment of a judge can make an enormous difference. A fierce debate has raged for many years over the extent to which social, political, and other extralegal factors influence judicial decision making. Adherents of a behavioral model of judging contend that judges' personal values and life experiences are a major determinant, perhaps the dominant one, of their decisions.[1] Critics of the behavioral model assert that the impact of such variables has been greatly exaggerated and that the traditional legal model of judicial behavior—characterized by strict neutrality, dispassionate analysis, and reliance on legal text and case-law precedent—remains the best predictor of judges' decisions.[2] A recent study by Gregory Sisk, Michael Heise, and Andrew Morriss examined decisions by hundreds of federal district court judges on the single issue of whether the federal sentencing guidelines are unconstitutional. The study found that many extralegal factors, such as gender, race, age, geographical location, schools attended, and political ideology, had little influence on outcomes, but a few social factors—prior employment and prospects for appointment to an appellate court—played significant roles. The authors also found, however, that case-law precedent, an icon of the legal model, powerfully influenced decision making. Thus, Sisk, Heise, and Morriss concluded that judicial behavior was too complex to be fully explained by any one model and that decisions are the product of a complicated interaction among personal values, life experiences, and the law itself.[3]

Judge Ballantine was known and respected as a fine former state court judge with a particularly good reputation as a trial judge. It was unlikely, however, that Judge Ballantine would have much interest in prisoners' complaints about their living conditions in a state prison. Sisk, Heise, and Morris, for example, found that prior employment is a significant extralegal influence on judicial action and, in particular, that prior service as a state court judge was an influence in favor of upholding the sentencing guidelines. Why this phenomenon would exist is unclear, but one possibility is that a former state court judge, especially one with long service, is likely to be highly deferential to legislative and executive authority.[4] If such is the case, Judge Ballantine, a former state judge, was unlikely to have much interest in intervening in the administration of Kentucky's prisons and probably would have dismissed the complaint early on.

As it turned out, Shorty received a lucky break. Judge Ballantine may not have been interested in Shorty's case, but he thought one of his fellow federal judges in the Western District of Kentucky knew more about prisons and had more experience with prison problems than he did. That judge was Edward H. Johnstone, who already had been assigned a lawsuit involving similar conditions at the Kentucky State Penitentiary in Eddyville. Ballantine and Johnstone met and they agreed that Johnstone should assume control of Shorty's case, so Ballantine transferred case C79-0001L to Johnstone.

Judge Johnstone was and is an unusual man. Although Sisk, Heise, and Morriss conclude that judicial motivation is too complex to be explained by any one set of variables or model, they also found that personal values and life experiences have a greater impact than expected. One extralegal factor about Judge Johnstone was very clear: he was interested in prison conditions and cared about how prisoners were treated. Johnstone had been inside Kentucky's maximum-security penitentiary at Eddyville and seen firsthand some of the monstrous conditions in which prisoners lived. He had seen that years of neglect had led to deterioration in the buildings and mistreatment of the inmates. Shorty's case was transferred to a judge who understood that allegations of filth and overcrowding in prison might be true. Over the next several months, early in 1979, Judge Johnstone made a series of procedural decisions that transformed Shorty's case from a nearly hopeless gamble into a major consolidated lawsuit to reform the state's maximum- and medium-security prisons. Over the next seven years Judge Johnstone would mediate a settlement of the case and oversee the transformation of the state's major prisons from filthy, dangerous hell-holes into modern institutions staffed by people trained to treat prisoners in a humane manner.

There is no easy answer, however, to the question of what motivated Johnstone to take an interest in prisoners, for several factors in his background suggest, at least superficially, that he would have little sympathy for convicted criminals. He was a decorated World War II veteran. He was a successful country lawyer who had practiced for nearly thirty years in Princeton, Kentucky, a small town of fifteen thousand in the remote western end of the state. Princeton, and western Kentucky in general, appear distinctly southern and conservative in social matters. Johnstone and his wife, a schoolteacher, raised four children and belonged to the local Episcopal church. He was active in politics, mostly behind the scenes, and once ran a successful campaign for governor for a former law-school classmate, Edward T. "Ned" Breathitt. When a new state circuit judge post was created, another Democratic governor appointed Johnstone to fill it. Less than two years later, he was appointed to the federal bench. Judge Johnstone thus rose from small-town lawyer to federal judge in less than two years, a spectacular leap by any reckoning and owed in large measure to rich and powerful people in the Kentucky Democratic establishment. A background so rooted in conservative culture and politics would appear, at first glance, likely to produce a person for whom improving the lot of prisoners would be a low priority at best.

There Is Good in Everyone

Judge Johnstone's family background suggests some reasons for his interest in prisoners. His father and mother were the strongest influences on his life. His father, William Johnstone, grew up on a farm in Jessamine County, Kentucky, and graduated from the University of Kentucky in 1916 with a bachelor of science degree in agriculture. His profession led him to Brazil, where, as agricultural adviser to the Brazilian government, he brought knowledge of modern farming methods to the state of Minas Gerais. Bill Johnstone soon met and married Katherine Huggins, a young American woman whose father had been a civil engineer in Brazil. She gave birth a few years later to Edward Huggins Johnstone in a São Paulo hospital.

In 1922 Bill Johnstone accepted a job in western Kentucky as county agricultural agent in Taylor and McCracken Counties, disseminating information about modern farming methods to the local farmers. The farm agent's office was in the courthouse in Paducah, a small town where the Ohio and Tennessee Rivers come together and where Ed Johnstone grew up. His father had a distinguished career in Taylor and McCracken Counties from 1922 to 1937. Forty years after he left the area, Bill Johnstone was still so well remembered that a local newspaper ran an editorial about him after his death in 1978.

When Mr. Johnstone came to McCracken County as the agent of the new university extension service, his task was to help farmers raise more and better crops and livestock and to organize them to sell it profitably.

He succeeded in a remarkable way. He was a new kind of pioneer, leading farmers in the transition from what was an essentially subsistence type farming to the modern type which is the wonder of the world.

Under his leadership our county became a leading producer of strawberries and peaches, marketing them all across the country through organizations which he formed. He pioneered the milk producers organization.

Many farmers had little idea how to maintain their land so it would continue to be productive. Mr. Johnstone initiated the soil conservation movement in our county.

Most farmers still lived by the kerosene lantern and animal muscle. When the rural electrification movement started in the 1930s, Mr. Johnstone helped organize the movement which gave birth to the Jackson Purchase electric cooperative.

His life was dominated by a fascination with things that grow in the soil and the ways in which they could promote human life. He promoted Kentucky 31 fescue grass as a way to stabilize roadsides and farm slopes, to the point that it became a major state issue.[5]

These pioneering accomplishments strongly impressed young Ed Johnstone.

My life to a great extent was molded by growing up in a close-knit, strong family, influenced by the example set by my father. He was a scholar. He insisted upon high academic integrity. He devoted his professional life to the farmers of Kentucky. One of his major accomplishments involved the development and promotion of a grass called Kentucky 31 fescue. . . . Today, Kentucky 31 fescue is known throughout the world. Production of the seed was extremely profitable, but Bill Johnstone never sold a single pound. He was fanatically opposed to using a public position for personal gain!

In 1937, Bill Johnstone accepted a job as extension agronomist at the University of Kentucky. His friends in western Kentucky decided to give him a big send-off in Paducah. It turned out to be quite a night:

They had a testimonial dinner for my father in Paducah on the night of the 1937 flood. I was fourteen years old then, and the whole family was there. The dean of the College of Agriculture at the University of Kentucky was the chief speaker. The water kept rising, and everyone told my father, "You'd better go now while you can still get out of here." He said, "No, I'm going to stay here with my people." And he did stay. He helped with rescue efforts. Meanwhile, his home and furniture and car were destroyed by the backwater.

As extension agronomist, Bill Johnstone continued his distinguished career. A new hybrid grass was developed and named Johnstone Tall Fescue after him. His prominent status as extension agronomist did not rob him of concern for his students, an attitude that impressed Ed Johnstone, as did his mother's optimism about people.

I like to see people of modest circumstances get a chance and achieve. My father and mother invited youngsters from rural Kentucky to stay at their house when they entered the university. The girls occupied the first floor, and the boys slept in a big attic on the second floor. When the school year started, the house was packed with students! My father would make use of his influence to get jobs for them and places for them to stay. These young people have been high achievers since then.

My mother is a devoted parent. She sees a lot of good in every individual. It was from her that I learned to look for the best in people. She believed, as I do, that there is a lot of good and a lot of evil in every human being. We are all about equal in this regard. Our destinies are usually fixed by family surroundings and opportunities others make available for us. Even in the worst of people, there is a good side. If we treat them with dignity and respect, it brings out the good and suppresses the bad.

It is likely that Ed Johnstone came to see prisoners in light of the values his parents gave him. Many years later, as a judge, his actions were consistent with a belief that prisoners had good in them and that it was his duty as a public servant to assure that they were treated with respect for their human dignity.

Country Lawyer

Young Ed Johnstone went to public schools and then enrolled at the University of Kentucky, where he majored in political science. After World War II erupted, he dropped out of school in 1942 to enlist in the army, along with his dog, who did distinguished service in the Canine Corps. Johnstone was assigned to the infantry and fought on the ground in Europe. He was an infantry sergeant in 1944 when Hitler launched his final desperate effort for victory in the Battle of the Bulge. Johnstone was awarded the Bronze Star for heroism in ground combat and the Silver Star for gallantry in action while in combat, but he received more than decorations from the battle:

The Battle of the Bulge . . . made a lasting impression on me. I was an infantry sergeant. The people at the front were not highly educated. Some had ways not acceptable in polite society. But the ones I served with had the courage and guts to fight. These guys were patriots. They did the job without benefit of academic niceties or social polish. I saw too many of them give up their lives or blood so those back home could enjoy individual freedom. The battlefield was a great equalizer. Soldiers had to rely on one another. Our company was one of the first to be racially integrated. In crisis we are just one society.

When the war ended, Johnstone came home to finish his education. He earned a law degree at the University of Kentucky and started his own law practice in little Princeton, Kentucky, out in the western end of the state, not far from Paducah. For the next quarter century Johnstone was a country lawyer in a small town. He liked people, and he saw law as a way to help them.

I began a solo law practice because I didn't want to work for someone else. People came in for divorces. I counseled some of them not to get a divorce, and often they stayed together. I see them today, and they have grandchildren. They come up and thank me for keeping them together. I represented defendants in criminal cases. Sometimes I won their cases, and most of them never got in trouble again. I closed a lot of home mortgages under the GI Bill. I worked for ordinary people. They were very good to me. Maybe that's why I stay in Princeton. We understand each other. They're my friends.

When I was practicing law, it was considered a duty to represent the poor without a fee. I represented many poor people and never got a dime.

One of Johnstone's most celebrated cases involved Dorothy Scott, a young woman whose life was ruined when her car collided with a truck. Her mother and father were killed. She suffered numerous injuries, including brain damage, paralysis, and loss of the ability to speak. Her husband came to Johnstone for help, and he sued the owner of the truck.

The case went to trial on December 17, 1964. During the trial, Johnstone put a doctor on the witness stand to describe Scott's injuries. The doors to the courtroom suddenly swung open, and the woman was carried in on a stretcher and laid, mute and still, in full view of the jury. She remained in the courtroom for a half hour while the doctor pointed out her injuries. The doctor finished his testimony, Scott was carried out, and the trial came to an end. The jurors retired to consider their verdict, and when they returned to the courtroom, the foreman handed the verdict to the court clerk. The clerk began to read the verdict in open court, but suddenly an astonished look spread over his face, and he stopped reading. He handed the note, which was in the foreman's own handwriting, to the judge. The note said that Scott was entitled to recover $400 million in damages and her husband was to receive $250 million in damages plus $75 million for medical bills. The judge talked with the jury and discovered that the foreman had written down three too many zeros. The final judgment was reduced to $725,000. At the time, it was still the biggest jury verdict ever given in Kentucky.

It was a bittersweet victory, however, because the defendants only had $152,600 in insurance. There was no more money available to pay the judgment, so that is all Scott received. Furthermore, she never knew about her victory because her brain was dead. She remained in a rest home until she died. No amount of money can restore a ruined life. The Scott case, however, earned Johnstone a reputation as a skilled courtroom lawyer.

Johnstone's Princeton law office was across the street from Herby's Barber Shop. Johnstone continued to have his hair cut there even after he became a federal judge in Louisville. Herby's Barber Shop is just a little place, a couple of barber chairs and a row of seats for people waiting. One wall is covered with miniature billboards, set in frames built into the wall, advertising more than forty local businesses and churches. Some people came in for haircuts, and some people just dropped in to sit and talk and listen. Johnstone dropped in every Saturday morning, whether or not he needed a haircut. Sometimes he swept up the floor for Herby. Herby's Barber Shop was more than a place to get a four-dollar haircut. It was a political listening post. Western Kentucky is Democratic country, but Herby, although a son of poor tenant farmers, was a staunch Republican. He needed to stay informed about what people were thinking, so he welcomed and encouraged people to come in and talk politics. A cross-section of citizens came to Herby's—farmers, shopkeepers, mechanics, lawyers. Area politicians came to Herby's to find out what was happening, what was bothering people, what people's opinions were. Johnstone learned more about politics at Herby's Barber Shop than anywhere else. He made many friends stopping by Herby's, practicing law and just helping people out.

Johnstone also made friends in politics. Not long after he helped Breathitt get elected governor, Breathitt asked Johnstone to represent the state in a lawsuit to acquire land for Lake Barkley State Park. In 1968 he sued more than fifty landowners to acquire their property for the park and pay them fair market value for the land. The lawsuit made headlines all over the state and made Johnstone well known outside his local area.

A riot erupted in the early 1970s at the Kentucky State Penitentiary in Eddyville, just west of Princeton. Governor Breathitt appointed an advisory committee to study the penitentiary and make recommendations to prevent future riots, and he appointed Johnstone to the committee. Another member of the committee was Robert Stephens, who years later would be elected Kentucky attorney general and then chief justice of the Supreme Court of Kentucky. Both Stephens and Johnstone eventually would play major roles in reforming the state's prisons. Johnstone already knew something about the maximum-security penitentiary by the time he joined the advisory committee because he had defended inmates who were locked up at Eddyville. Now he took a hard look at what the penitentiary was really like.

> We all thought the prison was fine, until we actually looked at it. It was wrong, what we saw—bugs, human refuse, overcrowding.

The committee submitted a report, but it had little effect, and prison conditions remained the same. Johnstone, however, remembered what he had learned about the Eddyville penitentiary.

Johnstone began his rise in official public life when another Democratic governor, Julian Carroll, appointed him as the first judge of the newly created Fifty-sixth Judicial District for the commonwealth of Kentucky. This multicounty court included Caldwell County, where Johnstone lived. Johnstone was a highly respected, competent attorney, but he also had powerful political friends. He was unopposed for election the following year. The position of state circuit judge gave Johnstone the chance to do something about the conditions at the Eddyville penitentiary, because the Fifty-sixth Judicial District also included Lyon County, home of the penitentiary. He took the unprecedented step of holding court right at the prison.

> We established a courtroom in the penitentiary at Eddyville. They used to bring the prisoners over from the penitentiary to the courtroom in Lyon County in a van and leave them in the van outside until their case was called. They kept them in shackles. They brought them into the courtroom,

still in shackles, in the view of the jury. I told the county they couldn't do that anymore. Oh, they were upset! I ordered them to build a courtroom within the penitentiary at Eddyville. Well, I didn't actually order it— I suggested it. I used my authority as a judge very little. I try to persuade people first. So I talked to the warden at Eddyville about building the courtroom. He was glad to do it. He liked it. It was less trouble for him that way. The prisoners liked it, too.

Less than two years after Johnstone's appointment to the state circuit court, a vacancy opened up on the U.S. District Court for the Western District of Kentucky. Kentucky had created a citizens' commission to screen candidates and make recommendations to the ranking senator to ensure that candidates for federal judgeships were qualified for the position. Senator Wendell Ford had already announced that he would support whomever the citizens' commission recommended for the new vacancy.

The commission recommended Johnstone. One important factor in his selection, aside from his reputation and political connections, is that he made a commitment to hear cases anywhere in the Western District of Kentucky the chief judge assigned. The Western District sprawls from just east of Louisville to the Mississippi River and down to Tennessee. There are federal courthouses in Paducah, Owensboro, Louisville, and Bowling Green. Despite the fact that more than half the cases in the Western District arose outside the Louisville area, its federal judges historically had preferred to reside and hold court in Louisville, in the northeast corner of the district. This practice left the western and southern areas feeling neglected and caused litigants, witnesses, and their attorneys a great deal of inconvenience. The citizens' commission was concerned about this problem. Johnstone made it clear to the commission that he was willing to hold court in Paducah, Owensboro, and Bowling Green as well as Louisville and to do whatever traveling was necessary.

Senator Ford kept his promise and recommended Johnstone to President Jimmy Carter, who nominated Johnstone for the judgeship. The American Bar Association ranked Johnstone as well qualified for the position, a strong endorsement for a nominee with less than two years of judicial experience. Johnstone breezed through his hearing before the Senate Judiciary Committee and was confirmed by the full Senate. The one specific act in his career as lawyer and judge mentioned in the confirmation hearing was his creation of the courtroom for prisoners in the penitentiary at Eddyville.[6] Johnstone had arrived at his federal judgeship through a combination of powerful political connections and an outstanding professional reputation. It also helped that people generally liked him. He helped people out, laughed a lot, put on no airs or pretensions, and made friends wherever he went.

Johnstone took office in 1977. His background offers a vivid contrast to that of the prisoner whose case would soon be assigned to him. Shorty's parents were the sort of primitive farmers whose production methods Johnstone's father sought to elevate to twentieth-century standards. Both men were veterans of military service; Shorty, however, returned to civilian life with little education or training, while Johnstone resumed his college education and obtained a law degree. Shorty's life of crime began with an employer's broken promise, and Johnstone in law practice defended many people like him. The two men, however, eventually shared common ground: a belief that the U.S. Constitution is a living document.

A Visit with Judge Frank Johnson

Cases about prison conditions were waiting for the new federal judge. For years, prisoners at Eddyville had been filing lawsuits complaining about conditions. One suit in particular, filed by an inmate named Jerald Kendrick, drew Judge Johnstone's interest because Kendrick's complaint was a broad-based constitutional challenge to the totality of living conditions at the penitentiary. Johnstone decided to learn more about such cases, and so, shortly after he took office but at his own expense, he drove down to Montgomery, Alabama, to talk with Frank Johnson.

Johnson was a federal district court judge in Alabama, but he was no ordinary judge. A lifelong Republican, nominated to the federal bench by President Dwight D. Eisenhower in 1955, Johnson had presided over the dismantling of officially sanctioned racial segregation in Alabama. In a series of decisions over nearly a quarter century, he ruled that racial segregation in Alabama's public schools and a host of other public services was unconstitutional and ordered sweeping changes in all aspects of Alabama public life. Alabama Governor George Wallace seized on these decisions as examples of judicial tyranny, defied the orders, and personally vilified Johnson. As a result of their lifetime appointments, however, federal judges are largely immune from political pressure, and Judge Johnson had the personal courage to withstand the campaign of vilification, eventually achieving official compliance with his desegregation orders.[7]

Supreme Court decisions such as *Brown v. Board of Education*[8] provided ample legal support for the desegregation decisions, but there was relatively little precedent for claims filed in Judge Johnson's court that conditions in Alabama prisons were unconstitutional. Beginning in the late 1960s, prisoners all over America, sometimes on their own and sometimes represented by lawyers, began to file lawsuits complaining about horrible living conditions. These lawsuits brought to public attention what prisoners and many corrections professionals had known for a long time: conditions in numerous American prisons were unspeakably brutal and degrading. These lawsuits claimed that overall living conditions in these prisons—with overcrowding, filth, danger, idle inmates, unhealthy surroundings—were so bad as to constitute "cruel and unusual punishment" in violation of the Eighth Amendment to the U.S. Constitution. The original intent of this provision was to prohibit the various forms of physical torture that were still in use in colonial times, and some scholars and judges have argued that the Constitution should be limited to the original intent of its framers. In this view, the Eighth Amendment should prohibit only the medieval forms of physical torture practiced in colonial times and has no application whatsoever to prison conditions. Others maintain that the Constitution is a living document meant to endure for the ages whose meaning must be derived in part from history but also from the need to address current social needs. According to this theory, the Eighth Amendment was not written in exact language limited to torture but instead contains broad, general language whose underlying purpose is to protect human dignity. Some support for this flexible interpretation was provided by the decision in *Trop v. Dulles,* where the Supreme Court stated that the Eighth Amendment must draw its meaning from "the evolving standards of decency that mark the progress of a maturing society."[9] Thus, when prisoners began to seek relief from the federal courts, they had a relatively slim body of case-law precedent to support their claims.

Nevertheless, federal district court judges, relying on a flexible interpretation of the Eighth Amendment, began to rule in the prisoners' favor. Perhaps the most famous of these early cases, *Holt v. Sarver,* involved the Arkansas prison system. Inmates brought a class action claiming, among other things, that conditions in the Arkansas prisons amounted to cruel and unusual punishment. After a long and arduous trial that revealed unspeakable horrors in these prisons, Chief Judge Smith Henley of the U.S. District Court wrote a 1969 opinion in which he explained the law of cruel and unusual punishment as applied to living conditions in prison: "It appears to the Court, however, that the concept of 'cruel and unusual punishment' is not limited to instances in which a particular inmate is subjected to a punishment directed at him as an individual. In the Court's estimation confinement itself within a given institution may amount to a cruel and unusual punishment prohibited by the Constitution where the confinement is characterized by conditions and practices so bad as to be shocking to the conscience of reasonably civilized people even though a particular inmate may never personally be subject to any disciplinary action." Judge Henley described the conditions in Arkansas prisons: prisoners in control of the prison; overcrowded housing; weapons and intoxicants widely available; no rehabilitation programs; filth everywhere. Based on this evidence, Henley concluded,

> For the ordinary convict a sentence to the Arkansas Penitentiary today amounts to a banishment from civilized society to a dark and evil world completely alien to the free world, a world that is administered by criminals under unwritten rules and customs completely foreign to free world culture.
>
> After long and careful consideration the Court has come to the conclusion that the Fourteenth Amendment prohibits confinement under the conditions that have been described and that the Arkansas Penitentiary System as it exists today, particularly at Cummins, is unconstitutional.

Henley then ordered the state to undertake massive prison reform.[10] The Court of Appeals affirmed his decision, and the state appealed only one part of Henley's decision to the U.S. Supreme Court: his order that a prisoner could not be placed in isolation for more than thirty days. In 1978 the Supreme Court handed down its decision in the case (now called *Hutto v. Finney* as a result of changes in the leading parties to the lawsuit). The Court upheld Judge Henley's statement of the law: "The Eighth Amendment's ban on inflicting cruel and unusual punishments, made applicable to the States by the Fourteenth Amendment, 'proscribe[s] more than physically barbarous punishments.' It prohibits penalties that are grossly disproportionate to the offense, as well as those that transgress today's 'broad and idealistic concepts of dignity, civilized standards, humanity and decency.' Confinement in a prison or in an isolation cell is a form of punishment subject to scrutiny under Eighth Amendment standards." The Court agreed with Henley that under the law, conditions in the Arkansas prisons, including the isolation cells, constituted cruel and unusual punishment; therefore, he had the authority to place a thirty-day limit on isolation as part of the overall effort to remedy the constitutional violations.[11]

Building on precedents such as *Holt,* Judge Johnson found that Alabama's prisons were horrendously overcrowded, the buildings were dilapidated and filthy, violent and mentally ill inmates intermingled with the other inmates, there were too few guards, and inmates lacked any meaningful opportunity for education, work, or recreation. Johnson concluded,

> The conditions in which Alabama prisoners must live, as established by the evidence in these cases, bear no reasonable relationship to legitimate institutional goals. As a whole they create an atmosphere in which inmates are compelled to live in constant fear of violence, in imminent danger to their physical well-being, and without opportunity to seek a more promising future.
>
> The living conditions in Alabama prisons constitute cruel and unusual punishment. Specifically, lack of sanitation throughout the institutions— in living areas, infirmaries, and food service—presents an imminent danger to the health of each and every inmate. Prisoners suffer from further physical deterioration because there are no opportunities for exercise and recreation. Treatment for prisoners with physical or emotional problems is totally inadequate.

In a passage that remains as relevant today as it was in 1976, Judge Johnson responded to political charges that prisoners should not be coddled: "The Court now acts in these cases with a recognition that prisoners are not to be coddled, and prisons are not to be operated as hotels or country clubs. However, this does not mean that responsible state officials, including the Alabama Legislature, can be allowed to operate prison facilities that are barbaric and inhumane. Let the defendant state officials now be placed on notice that failure to comply with the minimum standards set forth in the order of this Court filed with this opinion will necessitate the closing of those several prison facilities herein found to be unfit for human confinement." Johnson ordered wide-ranging improvements in the prisons. Most important, he forbade the admission of new prisoners, except escapees and parole violators, until the population was reduced to the level for which the prisons were designed.[12] Governor Wallace, Johnson's old nemesis from the desegregation cases, immediately refused to comply with these orders, and thus began years of state intransigence and resistance to change during which Johnson continually prodded the state to obey his orders.[13]

Ed Johnstone thought he might learn something from Johnson, and so he did. The single most important step Johnstone could take, according to Frank Johnson, was to invite the U.S. Department of Justice, Civil Rights Division, to participate in the case as amicus curiae, or friend of the court. The Justice Department employed lawyers with experience in these cases, had ample resources to help conduct the litigation, and assumed a position of formal neutrality on which the judge could rely for an informed and objective viewpoint. Armed with this advice, Ed Johnstone returned to Kentucky.

Procedural Maneuvers

At first, Johnstone paid his attention to Kendrick's lawsuit. The Eddyville prisoners were represented by able lawyers, but as a first step, following Frank Johnson's advice, Johnstone invited the U.S. Department of Justice to intervene in the case as an amicus curiae and granted the department's subsequent motion to intervene. Formally, this move brought federal government lawyers into the case to counsel the judge. In practical terms, these lawyers had resources and experience that could be used to hire experts, gather evidence, and prosecute the case. The move also had great symbolic value, for intervention meant that the U.S. government was interested in Kentucky's prisons.

Soon after this maneuver, Shorty's case was transferred from Judge Ballantine to Judge Johnstone. Within a few months, Johnstone made a series of decisions that transformed Shorty's original one-page, handwritten petition into one of the major prison lawsuits in the United States. These decisions did not concern the great constitutional issues of the day but were rulings on procedure, on how the lawsuit was to be conducted. Legal procedure is a mysterious subject little understood by people outside the legal system and poorly understood by many lawyers. At first glance, procedural rules are merely neutral principles governing the conduct of lawsuits and appear to have nothing to do with the decision on the merits of the case. In fact, however, the procedures employed in a case can have a tremendous impact on the final result. In Shorty's case, Johnstone's procedural rulings would assure a full and fair hearing of the prisoners' complaints, for he was determined to air the issues in public. His next step was to appoint lawyers to represent Shorty and his group. With the lawyers in place, Judge Johnstone then consolidated Shorty's lawsuit over conditions at KSR with the Kendrick lawsuit over conditions at the penitentiary in Eddyville. Combining the two cases meant that conditions in the state's two major prisons would be investigated and prosecuted both by lawyers for the prisoners and by Justice Department lawyers counseling the judge.

Once Shorty's lawyers were appointed, they met with Shorty and the other five inmates who had signed the complaint. The lawyers also researched the law, toured the prison, and, as a result of this investigation, moved the court for permission to file an amended, twenty-three-page complaint. Judge Johnstone granted permission to file the new, amended complaint and greatly expanded the case's scope. Shorty's lawsuit was now about more than bugs, dirt, bad food, and overcrowding, although they remained central concerns. It was also about crumbling dormitories, inadequate security, fire safety, jobs, recreation, education, classification, medical care, libraries, religion, visiting, and virtually every other aspect of prison operation. The suit had become as much about how prisoners were treated as about bricks and mortar.

By mid-1979, the lawsuits were combined, nearly every condition in the two prisons was at issue, and the lawyers were in place, but thus far the KSR case only concerned six prisoners. The interests of more than 2,300 other prisoners at KSR were also at stake, so the next step was to employ the class-action procedure, in which a few named plaintiffs represent the interests of many people in the same situation. All these prisoners were living in the same conditions at KSR, so Judge Johnstone ruled that Shorty's case would proceed as a class action. That ruling gave the judge the power to decide about the living conditions of every prisoner at KSR. Johnstone ended this flurry of activity by ruling that the case would go to trial in less than a year, on April 7, 1980. He set aside twenty-five days for the trial, an unusual amount of time for a civil trial, indicating that this lawsuit was a top priority for the court.

Very little in the rules of procedure required Judge Johnstone to take these early steps in the litigation. He was not, in this case, following the traditional role of a judge who passively waits for litigants to bring issues to the court and then rules on those issues. It is difficult to say whether he was motivated by respect for the dignity of all human beings and a belief that there is good in everyone, by professional experience in defending people accused of crime, by personal knowledge of the appalling conditions at the penitentiary, by a philosophy that the Constitution should serve the nation's evolving needs, or by a complex interaction of these and other factors. It is nevertheless quite clear that, like Frank Johnson before him, Johnstone took an affirmative, proactive approach to the Kentucky prison-conditions litigation. Johnstone's rulings, however, would never generate the sort of controversy and resistance Frank Johnson encountered.

Wilgus

Wilgus Haddix arrived at KSR soon after Judge Johnstone made the procedural rulings that transformed Shorty's petition into a major class-action lawsuit. Wilgus was eager to do something about conditions in the prison by joining the lawsuit, all because of a blanket. He was doing hard time at the penitentiary in Eddyville when he met Jerald Kendrick, the inmate who had brought the penitentiary lawsuit.

I was in cell 4D21. I was next to Jerald Kendrick. . . . He was a little comical, ordinary, plain, everyday-looking person.

So it got on up into the wintertime. It was twelve below zero, and I had ice in the commode. Pigeons was flying in and out of my cell. I had an old broom handle and one o' these little mops —you know these little toy mops you buy for kids, for little girls to play in their dollhouse? . . . That's the kind of mops they give us, and the little toy brooms to sweep our cells out with. Cockroaches were ever'where. Guys was stabbing one 'nother.

Ever'thing in the world going on. I thought, "What in the world am I amongst here?" I thought, by God, I'd been a little bit of ever'where and seen a little bit of ever'thing. The first day I went out on the yard, I went down to take a good hot shower on the yard where everybody took a shower together. . . . By God, I seen some few things that I don't know in that shower! Never seen nothing like it in my life!

Well, 'bout three days after I'd been there this tour came through—four or five guys. They had on suits and neckties. One of 'em had a briefcase, and this one was giving all the directions and he was talking tough.

One guy near me said, "Hey man, what are y'all gonna do about—?"

"Ain't doing a goddamn thing about it. Beat your goddamn brains out if you don't lay down, punk," says the tough guy.

I thought, "Well, who in the hell is this guy? He must be the boss of this place." Well, I had an old half a blanket. So I said, "Sir, do you got something to do with this joint?"

"Have I got something to do with this joint? Why, you happen to be looking into the eyes and talking to none other than Donald Lee Bordenkircher. You're goddamn right I got something to do with this place. I'm the warden here."

"Well, I'm glad that you're the main man. I'd like to know, could I get a bigger blanket?"

"Whatsa matter with that one?"

"Well, it's too short, and I'm about to freeze to death."

"By God, file a goddamn writ on me. If you want a different blanket or a bigger blanket, you oughta stayed where you was at. File a writ."

And he went on. Hell, I didn't know what a writ was. Shoot, never heard tell of a writ. Jerald Kendrick said, "That's the same thing the son of a bitch told me. That's why I've got him sued now."

"What's he talking about, a writ?"

"I'll explain it to ye tomorrow. Come up to the Legal Aid Office and I'll show you what's happening."

So I went up and I looked over what all he said and done. He had filed a lawsuit maintaining that the conditions at the Kentucky State Penitentiary were inhumane. He said, "But nothing will ever come of this 'cause I'm getting ready to leave and there's nobody to take it to."

I said, "Well, I wish there's something I could do to help after you leave."

He said, "Well, there is." And he explained to me what could happen if I'd be a main plaintiff.

I told him, I said, "I tell you what, I'm not up to date on this stuff. But somehow or 'nother I can get hooked up with this and get my name on it. I would certainly like to become a part of the team." He was gonna add me as a plaintiff.

Kendrick did not have enough time to add Wilgus to the lawsuit over conditions at Eddyville, because prisoners who sued the warden were marked men in those days. Soon after Kendrick filed his lawsuit, prison guards came to his cell in the middle of the night carrying shotguns. One guard held his shotgun to Kendrick's head while the other guards told him they wanted the lawsuit dropped. Kendrick refused, and the guards left. Cooler minds found a quieter way to try to kill the lawsuit, which was to get him out of Eddyville and transfer him to another prison as far out of the way as possible. If Kendrick was gone from Eddyville, he could not carry on the lawsuit. It was a bit tricky to find a place for him. He had a long criminal record, which is why he was in Eddyville, Kentucky's maximum-security prison. The medium-security prison, KSR, was a risky transfer in Kendrick's case because the filth and overcrowding there were just as bad as at Eddyville, so Kendrick might file another lawsuit at KSR.

That left the minimum-security prisons, known to prisoners as camps, where prisoners often work outdoors without fences around them. Prisoners who present a low risk to society usually go to camp, so Kendrick might not qualify for minimum security. It was a strange move, but the authorities sent Kendrick to Harlan County Forestry Camp, deep in the backwoods of the Appalachian Mountains. When prison officials learned that Wilgus and Kendrick were allies, Wilgus was transferred to several different prisons, ending up at KSR in LaGrange in July 1979, shortly after Judge Johnstone's series of procedural rulings. Wilgus remembered the blanket at Eddyville, however, and embraced the opportunity to try to change the way Kentucky prisoners were treated.

It was what Bordenkircher said to me about the blanket. I thought, "Well, I shouldn't be here to start with. And what kind of person, what kind of country, would put its people in this situation and put him in 12 below zero weather and not give him something to keep warm with?"

I got mad first. But then after I got to thinking about what I'd seen in the shower house and the amount of money that they paid people to work and the conditions we were living under, then I changed my opinion and said, "Well, I don't need to be doing what I'm doing to hurt people or to make the taxpayers pay a big lot of money." Then I became genuinely interested in the plight of my fellow man around me. . . .

There was a guy come to me, that was of Eddyville, that knew that Jerald Kendrick and I were buddies, and he said, "You might oughta get involved in it now." So I said to myself, "Well, if I'm gonna do what I promised him, now's the chance to do it." Well, once I looked at the list of people that were involved in the lawsuit, I didn't like it. I didn't like the character of 'em. There was some on there that would tell everything that was going on, there was some on there who was weak. Some was on there just to be on there. Some of 'em didn't even know what was going on. I knew we had to have some intelligent people on there. And we had to have a few, not a lot.

So I went to Shorty Thompson. I talked to Shorty and I explained to Shorty where I was at with Jerald Kendrick and how it was and I explained to him how I felt about some things. And [Shorty] said, "OK, I'll tell you what let's do. Let's do this. We'll take you up to the next meeting and get yer name added to the list." So the next meeting it was had, I came up. Shorty brought me up. And it was something said about it amongst some of the other inmates on the yard and Shorty said, "It's my lawsuit. I say Haddix goes on."

Shorty was the leader, so the lawyers added Wilgus Haddix as a named plaintiff in the lawsuit, representing every other prisoner at KSR. His name would now appear on legal documents in the case, he had the right to meet with the lawyers appointed by Johnstone, and he had the duty to voice the complaints of all the other prisoners.

Wilgus was now a member of an influential group within the prison called the Plaintiffs' Committee. All the prisoners who added their names to the lawsuit, about a dozen men, were members of the committee, which met every week with the lawyers. In those meetings the committee members provided information about conditions at LaGrange and told the lawyers what the prisoners wanted to achieve in the lawsuit. The lawyers in turn provided information about legal maneuverings. Committee members then relayed the legal information back to other prisoners. In the eyes of the other prisoners, members of the Plaintiffs' Committee were powerful, not because they had guns and knives, not because they were a prison gang imposing its will by violence and threats, but because they were in control of information about the lawsuit and had direct access to the lawyers. The committee members were in a position to change conditions in the prison through the law and in the federal court.

Hillbillies

Working within the legal system was a new experience for Wilgus. His adult life until 1979 had been full of violence and bloodshed. To say Wilgus was committed to peaceful change through law would have astonished every person who knew anything about him. He was a hillbilly, a native of Appalachian Kentucky. Understanding Wilgus requires a brief look at one version of Appalachian history. According to Harry Caudill in *Night Comes to the Cumberlands,* in the early seventeenth century in the coastal British colonies of Virginia, North Carolina, and South Carolina, the plantation economy required large amounts of human labor. There were not enough African slaves to go around, so plantation owners looked to the British Isles to fill their labor needs. Under acts of Parliament, some workers came legally—orphans, debtors fleeing life in prison, thieves, and men avoiding military conscription. Other workers were imported illegally, kidnapped by thieves who were in the business of stealing children and adults for sale to the plantations in America. These kidnapped workers were, in effect, white slaves, and from them, according to family oral history, came Wilgus's maternal ancestors.[1]

Some of these white plantation laborers escaped and fled into the interior, then a nearly trackless wilderness. Throughout the latter half of the seventeenth century and into the eighteenth century, they trekked to the Piedmont, into the foothills of the Blue Ridge Mountains, and on to the Cumberland Plateau, the heart of Appalachia. The ancestors of the Appalachian people thus were established in the mountains between 1750 and 1775. The descendants of these pioneers continued to move deeper into the mountains. They had inherited their forefathers' deep anger and bitterness toward established society and fierce desire for freedom from social control of any sort. They sought to find good land for growing crops and herds of game to hunt and to escape their neighbors. As soon as new neighbors settled land a few miles away, many of these mountain families simply packed up and moved on.

This migration into the mountains began to decline after 1812 and largely ended by 1830. Few new settlers arrived after 1830, and the mountaineers of Appalachia were finally left alone. Most of them were poor and illiterate, had little organized religion, and functioned with almost no formal government or law. Throughout the nineteenth century and well into the twentieth, many Appalachian people resolved their own disputes, often with guns. Thus arose the feuds in which entire clans would simply shoot it out. The feuds or "troubles" in Breathitt County, Kentucky, home of the Haddix clan and Wilgus's birthplace, were so violent that the county became known as Bloody Breathitt. Men were often gunned down on the premises of county courthouses to settle scores, and one of these victims was Wilgus's great-grandfather.

Wilgus's life offers a miniature history of the Appalachian people, at least as recounted by Caudill. Wilgus was born to John and Pauline Combs Haddix, and the Haddix and Combs families were among the earliest settlers of Appalachia. These settlers, both Combs and Haddix, came out of Virginia into the Appalachian Mountains and established families that have remained in the vicinity of Breathitt County for more than two centuries.

Gingerbread

Wilgus came from a broken home, but he did not grow up in a loveless environment. John and Pauline Haddix were divorced in 1946, shortly after Wilgus was born. He was sent to live with his mother's parents, Rollin and Idie Combs, who owned a farm up a hollow in the hills of Breathitt County, near a little place called Peg Fork. The farm was remote and primitive, like the farm on which Shorty grew up. The farm is also full of fond memories for Wilgus, for he had the benefit of great affection from his grandparents.

My grandfather was probably the most influential person in my early life. I used to go into the woods with him to watch him work. He would go to the barn and gear up the mule, and we'd put wire on the sled and go on top of the hill. We'd build a fence, and I'd watch him cut trees, and he would explain things as he was going along.

The most outstanding thing that I remember about him was one day he didn't eat his gingerbread. Every day he would want gingerbread. He'd always ask Granny to bake him some gingerbread, and she'd bake gingerbread for him. . . . He carried the gingerbread [to work] in his bib overhauls. . . . He would unzip, and he'd reach in and get me a piece and him a piece, and we'd eat the gingerbread. . . . He'd tell me a big tale about when he was a young boy. . . . But one day he did not eat his gingerbread, and his feelings were obviously hurt. His feelings were hurt so bad that it distracted me and him both the rest of the day. Our little dog that was with us—which was his dog, called Trixie—Trixie realized that something was wrong. Even the mule acted different. . . . I thought he was sick.

We got back home, and he called my grandmother into the kitchen. He said, "Idie, I didn't eat this bread today. And I don't want any more bread like this as long as I live." And she says, "Why, Rollin, what in the world is wrong with that?" He just pulled his brogans off and went straight to bed. . . . My grandmother said, "Rollin, are you sick?" And he said, "Yes." And she kep' on 'im and kep' on 'im. . . . That next morning when they got up I heard 'em talking in the kitchen. This was the first experience I ever had of love between man and woman. She said "Rollin, you never hugged me last night and you always hug my back." That started the conversation. She knew something was wrong. . . .

So he said, "Idie, one of the most enjoyable times during the day in my life is the time that I spend with you. The time away from you is misery for me, even though I'm just on the hill, and I can come to you any time I want to. The gingerbread, Idie, that you sent with me yesterday did not have your handprints in it." . . . When she put the gingerbread in the pan, she'd always mash all of it. . . . When they baked, her fingerprints would be right up on top of the gingerbread.

[But] she didn't have her fingerprints baked in it that day. That's why he wouldn't eat it. 'Cause they pulled what was left out of the warmer. And she said, "Well, Rollin, here's my fingerprints all over this bread."

He said, "But there's none on this." And he pulled it out. He still had it. She just missed [one piece in the corner]. . . . He felt so neglected that she didn't send part of her with him that his feelings was hurt. . . . That was his thing. That's the way he expressed his love to her. . . . She said, "Rollin, it'll never happen again." And I watched. Every time that she'd bake bread

*I'd try to make it my business to be in the kitchen. She'd put her hand-
prints on every biscuit or piece of gingerbread in that pan. And boy, before
she'd put it in that stove she done it again.*

*That little incident right there explained to me how people operate who
love one 'nother. . . . They smoothed that out without ever mentioning it
again.*

Grandfather Combs gave Wilgus some early lessons in politics. Buying
votes on election day was an old tradition in Appalachia, and Rollin Combs
followed his father into local politics, handing out patronage jobs and buying votes.

*People in the community who wanted a job would have to see my grandpa.
He was the man that you would see to get things done. He was the precinct
ward heeler. He would gitcha job with the state highway department. He'd
gitcha job with the school system. He was the man you had to see. And
they couldn't circumvent him. . . . Even jails, people getting out on bond.
I've seen my grandfather send a note to the jail with a deputy sheriff who
couldn't read. And the jailer would read it and bring the guy right back. . . .*

*They would put me in the loft at the polling place and give me a ballot,
and I'd mark down how ever'body voted. I was a kid, 'bout eight or nine.
They was outside buying votes, twenty dollars at a wap. They was running in to vote, just lay the ballot down, and they had a little stamp, a
little wooden thing [that] looked like a cigar [and] had a X on the end of it.
Stick it in an ink pad. Stick it over on the ballot. Fold it up, put it in the
box. While they was doing that I was looking down through the crack.*

*Well, at dinnertime they come 'round there and slipped me a R. C. Cola
and a moon pie and some tater salad up in the loft and said, "Send me
down the ballot you got." Well, I sent it down. Oh man, hell broke loose
when they seen that. They said, "Hell, you marked these down on the
wrong side!"*

I said, "No, I marked it down on the side ever'body voted on."

"Well," they said, "the goddamned son of a bitches double-crossed us!"

*So they went on horseback. They was 'til 12 o'clock midnight gitting
ever'body back out and made 'em vote again. They got ever'body, they
moved ever'body, they brought 'em all back out. Shot the ballot box all
to hell. Made 'em vote right on the table, where they could see 'em.*

Old Rollin also taught Wilgus some lessons about making his way in the world. The Combs farm near Peg Fork was in steep hill country and used mules to work the land. It was difficult work that required Rollin to teach his grandson special skills.

Nowadays, kids, I don't know how they begin to feel about their developing manhood, but back in those days, when your father or grandfather trusted you to do something that he had always done, he gave you the sense that you had gained respectability and that you were a man and that he recognized that. That was the most important thing that he could do.

Now, when we would go into the barn and milk the cows, he'd sorta show me how to do that. But that wasn't too big a thing because it never was the big manly thing. But when they had a mule that was mean, that would kick you, you'd have to handle him in such a way that he knew you were the boss. You'd go into the stall and speak with a commanding voice that that mule knew that you was there for no stuff. That you were there to put the gears on him and take him out in the field and work him. And he obeyed.

My grandfather had a way of gitting things to obey him, either by carrot or by stick. Well, my grandmother would always caution him, "Rollin, don't you let that young 'un around that ol' dangerous mule! Now you heerd what I'm telling you! You're up 'ere and you're not paying no attention now what you're doing, and that young 'un'll run in behind that thing, it'll kick his brains out! Don't you bring him back to this house hurt!"

"OK, Idie, I know what I'm doing. I'll watch. Don't worry. You cook the bread, I'll gear the mule."

Well, see, I was always, "Stand back," or "Stand over there," or "Now I'm gonna move him around and you stay over 'ere." But one day Granny said, "Rollin, I've got to have some cake flavor and I've got to have some flour and I've got to have it today."

And he said, "Well, I'll go to the store. I've got to have some cow feed anyway. . . . But I've got to go down here and get these chickens back in. If I don't, they'll every one be in the woods and the foxes'll catch 'em and we'll not have a hen. But it's getting late and I've got to have some help here."

Then he said, "Gray, come here." (They called me by my middle name, Gray.) . . . He said, "Let me tell you something. Now I want you to go to

the barn and I want you to gear the mule up." Well, that was my first deal-
ings with him on the basis of man to man. He was handing me the responsibility of a father handing a boy the keys for the first time to the car and
saying, "Now listen. I'm gonna let you go on this date, but now here's how
you're gonna drive the car. Stop at stop signs." See? He pulled me off to
the side. And the very last thing he said, "Now you've seen me do this a
thousand times. Can you do this?" I said, "Yes, Grampaw, I can do this."
I hightailed it to the barn—excited, heart beating in my chest. I went in
and I did it just exactly like he did it. Step by step. No one was in the barn
with me. That gave a chance and an opportunity to really throw out my
force—to be dominant. To go in and take charge of this mule that was
mean. She would kick your brains out if she caught you in the wrong way.

So I went in and got this bridle off of the hook and I opened the door
and I spoke to her just like he did. And she acted like she didn't want to
give me her head. I done just exactly what he did. And she obeyed. I got the
bit in the mouth and got the bridle on her, and I let her out of the stall and
tied her up to the pole. I put the collar on her. Picked up the harnesses and
threw the harnesses over her. Tied 'em around the collar and backed 'em
off. Done everything just perfect. I spoke in a commanding voice several
times, even when I didn't have to. I was letting her know that I was on the
scene.

The more I went, the farther I got along in this process and nothing going wrong, the more confident I became. Then I led her out and I backed
her up to the sled. Grampaw did his chore and he was coming and Granny
was standing on the back porch. She had seen what had happened, that
I had did the job well. And I felt great.

That was my very first delegation of authority. I was delegated a man's
job there, a man's work. Where I come from, men's work and women's work
is separated. And a boy is sorta in the middle. He does a lot of women's
work until he becomes a man, and then he does men's work. Boy, that
thrilled me to death.

Well, I backed the mule up and had the swingletree laid out and laid
the trace chains out to hook to the swingletree. But I got so excited at going
around checking everything. Grampaw'd come and he had so much confidence in me that he just set down on the sled and he said, "Are we ready?"
And I said, "Yeah, we're ready." And I set down on the sled with him. . . .
Well, I didn't hook the trace chains to the swingletree, in all this excite-

ment. When [the mule] took off, she took Grampaw right off the sled and right down over into the gully, over into the holler where we went and right down through the bottom. Me and the sled was setting back. He went with the mule 'cause he had to drive. I didn't have the mule hooked to the sled. Down through the bottom he went, tore him all to pieces! He couldn't turn loose of the mule. If he did, she'd hit the woods and be gone for a week. . . .

When he got her stopped, he was hot. He was mad. Had high blood pressure and, boy, he'd chew his tongue, he'd bite his tongue. He run up into the woods, tied the mule up to a tree and grabbed him a switch.

And here come Granny. She was watching the whole time. Now she said, "Rollin, what are you gonna do with that switch?"

"I'm a-cutting it."

"No, you're not. You're not gonna touch that young'un 'cause you know that's a dangerous mule and you know he ain't nothing but a baby and you had no business having him fool with that ol' dangerous mule! He's lucky he got done what he did do. You ain't hitting him nair lick! And now you hear what I told you! . . . You will not touch him! If you do, you and that mule both will sleep together tonight in the barn! You listen! You're not touching that young 'un!"

Well, he didn't, but I was sorta injured, my stature in the family. If there had been another brother that he could have delegated some authority to and he could have carried it out successfully, I would have been killed.

A little later on he taught me a lesson about being overconfident. He and I sat down and talked about this. He knew that I had gained too much confidence, wasn't paying enough attention to what I was doing. I didn't follow out the process step by step. When you back the mule to the wagon, you hook it up. That's the next thing you do.

So I was taught a very valuable lesson. And that stayed with me. When you have a process, you go one, two, three, four, five, six. You never go one, three, five. You never shortcut. . . .

Years later I realized what he was doing. The tradition that he was passing on, that he had learned and been taught by his father, and it was coming down as a tradition. And it affected how I looked at the world. He was developing my worldview according to his worldview. And though my place in life has changed many times, that worldview is basically stayed the same. He made a survivor out of me.

The happy childhood years came to an end in 1958, when Grampaw Combs died. Wilgus was eleven years old, still a boy. Grampaw was the protector, the teacher, the dominant person in the boy's life. His death left Wilgus without a mentor and left Granny with a terrible sadness.

One time after he was dead—he died in 1958, January the 18th in 1958— Granny and I were setting out on the porch. It was in the spring of the year, around May, and we'd been out in the garden planting beans. The graveyard was out on the hill right in front of the house. She had that long, faraway stare in her eye and was looking way, way off. She had that old big wedding band on that they had bought in 1901. They got married in 1901, and he died in 1958, so they was married fifty-seven years. I said to her, "Granny, do you see anything up on that hill?"

"No, I don't, child, but I wished I could see your grampaw coming off that hill."

"What're you talking about, Granny?"

"Now Gray, I'll tell ye. I may live many years, and I may die tomorrow. But if your grampaw could get up outa that grave and I could just see 'im coming off that hill with his arms open, I could walk right into 'em. I'd go back to the grave with him tonight."

And big tears ran down her cheek.

Smoking Guns

Disaster struck within a year. While visiting at his mother and step-father's house, Wilgus accidentally shot his sister. The shot did not kill her, but she was very badly injured. Wilgus was beaten viciously, which might have been the end of the incident, but Wilgus's mother had him sent to a children's home. Wilgus was convicted of a juvenile criminal offense called being an unruly child. At the age of eleven, he was taken from the farm near Peg Fork and sent to faraway Lexington to live in a children's home. He ran away from the children's home and was captured, but he escaped again. He found his way back to the Peg Fork area and, according to his own account, lived in the woods like an animal for three years. His home was a cave. His food consisted of berries, roots, and any other edible thing he could find in the woods. An old man finally found Wilgus, sick and very weak. The old man took Wilgus to the nearest hospital, where he was di-agnosed with hepatitis. After treatment, he was discharged and sent to the Kentucky Reception Center in Lyndon.

These four crucial years changed his life forever. The boy had done a terrible thing when he shot his little sister, but in his eyes it was an accident brought on by his own carelessness. He had not intended to hurt her, and the adults bore some responsibility for leaving children alone with loaded guns. The criminal-justice system, however, intervened heavy-handedly and sent him to a children's prison. The system sent Wilgus a message that he was a criminal, an evil person. People usually behave in accordance with the way they are treated, and this treatment, wholly out of proportion to his carelessness, taught him to go on the offensive, to attack before someone else attacked first and hurt him. This formula meant lasting trouble, because now the teenager saw the world as having two kinds of people: aggressors and victims. Wilgus had already been a victim once. Now he would not trust the government to resolve any of his disputes. He would try to leave others alone, but, if there was trouble again, he would take care of himself and attack.

I grew up in a place, where if you and I had a falling out, that's exactly what it was, it was a falling out. And if you threatened me, then we settled it. We didn't let it go any further. If I felt like my life was in danger, I would take your life. You didn't call the police. Hell, there was no police. You'd have to ride a horse to get there. . . . It's just part of that old tradition. I guess it goes back to, hell, the 1700s, into the feud days. If I had something against somebody or somebody stole something from me, I didn't go to town and get a warrant for 'im. Hell, I just laywaid 'im or went to him and said, "Give it back."

Where I come from, you can't go and draw a pistol on a man and intimidate him or embarrass him and get your property back that he stole and go home and live comfortably. You've either got to go git it without the pistol and take a chance on being killed, or you got to get it with the pistol. When you get it with the pistol and you pull it, you got to use it. You can't bullshit. He's not gonna back down. You gonna have to use it. If you don't, you're a dead man. And when you're killed and laying in your coffin, people will say, "Well now, he's pulled a gun on that feller and goddamn poked him 'round and didn't use it." Boy, it was the worst thing you ever done in your life is pull a gun and never use it. You don't do that kind of stuff. Just like in the penitentiary, you don't threaten a man, tell him, "I'm gonna go get a knife and come back and cut you," and then come back around at lockup and not have a knife. Don't make the threat unless you're gonna carry it out right on the spot.

The police and courts represented the government and were not to be trusted, as far as Wilgus was concerned.

If you go to the police it makes ye less a person, makes you less a man. That's why the women from eastern Kentucky is one of the most closed-mouth segments of society on earth. They see, hear, tell nothing. They was raised up to never tell anything on anybody.

You don't run to the cops 'cause the deputy sheriffs is everybody's enemy. He's got that badge on for one purpose and it don't make any difference who y'are. He's out to do something for no reason other than having that badge on his chest.

That's what we never could understand. I could never understand why he even had one. It's just like somebody in the community. Let's take a community of fifty people. They grow corn and they raise their gardens and they try to live and try to feed their families. Now all of a sudden somebody in that community puts on a badge and a gun. Well, why? Is he gonna protect you from somebody else?

We protect our own self. We don't need any certain person to put on a badge to protect us. What he is, he's a rat amongst the rest of us. He's turned sour. He's looking for something that we're doing. 'Course if I git into it with my neighbor and have a harsh word with him, he's gonna come up and try to arrest us both. After he pulls that badge off he could never get back into the community. He's never accepted. If you got a community where there's nobody having any problems, or they're solving their problems themselves, why need him? Now, if he was there just to arrest people who kills one 'nother after the feuds, fine. But here's a guy who's gonna arrest ye for anything ye do—for taking a drink o' liquor. For whatever you do he's gonna be meddling in it, trying to put ye in jail.

These people don't want government interfering in their business. The government's got too much now. Hell, they've got Social Security numbers tacked on to ye, and a number for this and a number for that, taxes, and all that crazy stuff.

The lineage of people that I come from came into eastern Kentucky to get away from all that stuff. They don't want government inspectors and government people saying this and that. If the people in my part of the country had anything to do with it, there would be no roads. All the inter-states, that stuff was forced on 'em, man. They didn't want that. They had their own whiskey, their own women, their own way of life.

Good education sometimes salvages children headed for trouble, but the schools in the Appalachian Plateau rarely were up to that task. The schools were run as a system of political patronage. Many teachers received jobs as a reward for helping to secure votes, not for showing ability to teach. In Wilgus's view, hillbillies left home for four years, got degrees, came back home, and taught other hillbillies. Wilgus finished twelfth grade without a usable academic or vocational skill.

He did, however, know how to use a gun. Shortly after he left school, he became involved in an argument with another man and, in the Breathitt County tradition reinforced by the criminal-justice system, shot him without killing him. Wilgus was arrested, but no charges were filed against him. Local authorities instead told him to leave the state. Wilgus enlisted in the army a year later, served three years with the Second Infantry Division in Korea, and received an honorable discharge. Like Shorty, however, he returned to civilian life with little in the way of marketable skills.

Cy Bend

The next decade of his life was filled with drugs, gunplay, and killing. A few weeks after he returned to Kentucky, Wilgus became involved in an argument with another man. They exchanged gunfire, but both missed. A charge of malicious shooting against Wilgus was dismissed, and he left Kentucky for Indianapolis to live with his father. They soon argued, and Wilgus left, this time for Cincinnati. He eventually returned to bloody Breathitt County and renewed an old feud with a former deputy sheriff, Jeff Turner. As was the tradition in Appalachia, the two old enemies soon confronted each other again.

It was him and me out in the woods, and I got him first.

Wilgus and Turner exchanged gunfire. Turner was hit seven times and killed. Authorities charged Haddix with first-degree murder, but he claimed that he acted in self-defense. At his 1969 trial, the jury acquitted Wilgus.

Wilgus married the same year, and the young couple soon had two daughters, Shannon and Thadda-Rhea. But as in Shorty's case, family life did not last. Wilgus was charged in 1971 with the crime of receiving stolen property, a battery and alternator. This time Wilgus was convicted and served one year at KSR. After returning home to his young family at Peg Fork, Wilgus argued with a neighbor. Both men pulled their shotguns and fired away, and both were wounded with buckshot. Authorities charged Wilgus with shooting and wounding. Instead of facing the charges, he hit the road for Florida. He was now a fugitive from justice, like Shorty. Wilgus spent four years wandering among Florida, Michigan, and Kentucky. In 1975, Kentucky authorities picked him up on an old charge, which was then dropped. He returned to Florida.

During these years Wilgus was taking a wide variety of drugs, and to pay for his habit, he was buying and reselling every kind of illegal drug on which he could lay his hands. There was one interlude when Wilgus tried to get straightened out, and it was in the tradition of his Appalachian forebears.

Those were my dark years. I came back from Florida, and I knew that I had to do something. I had to go somewhere and get someplace away from society. I had to seek some solitude. I had gotten to the point where life was nothing.

So I got straight, and me and a friend of mine, Ishmael, built a fishing cabin on the North Fork of the Kentucky River. We started on it in '76. It's in the Cy Bend section of Breathitt County, where the North Fork comes down and goes in. . . . It was six and a half miles in if you walked—no road. . . . We went down in that part of the country, and we built the cabin. We got the boards out of an old house. . . . We couldn't get the lumber down to where we needed to git it. So what we did was, we got the lumber on a truck and drove to the closest point upstream and got it off of the truck and onto the river bank and put a cable around it. Then we went down to where we was gonna build the cabin and stretched a cable across the river from one tree to another tree. . . . There was [a shoal] between the point of the lumber and where we was going to build the cabin. We couldn't use a boat, 'cause we couldn't get a boat through the shoal. We had to wait till the water got up so we could float the lumber down the river over the shoal to the cable. The first tide came up when it rained, and the water raised.

We got the lumber in the water and we got on top of the lumber with two nylon ropes and lock hasps, and we went down the river. And when we come to that cable we just snapped the lock hasps on that cable and locked up. Then when the water went down we shimmied across the cable over to the bank. We had a rope tied to the lumber, and we just pulled it across to the bank. . . . Then we went down and laid the foundation—laid the floor and set the corners and then built it up. After we got it up, we took the logs and instead of putting the whole log against it we sawed the log in half [and] used straw and mortar to stick it together. . . . And then we put in white paneling that we took outa the ceiling [of an] old house. . . . We even put a fireplace in it—just picked up rock all over the hillside and washed 'em off and used straw and mortar to stick it together. Put in sliding windows.

I took furniture down on a boat. I took an old iron bedstead with me and what my granny called a davenport, which is a couch. And we had an old hutch which was solid cherry and an old buffet which matched it. And took a table down and a little heating stove. I got my coal where the coal had washed into the river. I'd pull a boat along the banks of the river and git my coal to burn, right out of the river.

I had running water. From where the cabin was built, about three hundred feet up the hollow was a ten-foot drop in a creek. I went to the hardware store and bought 340 feet of black plastic pipe hose. I plugged the lower end up and I went up to the other end at the drop and put a funnel in it, and I filled the hose full. Then I pulled out the funnel, put a screen wire over that end, and put the hose back in the water and laid a rock on top of the hose. I went down to the plug in the other end and pulled the plug and I had a force—gravity.

I dug a hole for a firebox and made me a firebox with mud and rock and I put a barrel in there. I put a spout in the bottom of the barrel. I took me a piece of the plywood, cut a hole in it where it would drain, and laid it down. When I wanted to take a shower, I would run that barrel half full of water, build a fire under it, and then I'd run it full of cold water and heat the water in the barrel. I had hot water for a shower. I put a spray nozzle on my garden hose. I'd hook the garden hose up to the spout with a water clamp and just hang it over a limb of a tree and I had a shower. I could take a shower right out in the middle of the woods. . . .

I built me an outside toilet and set it right astraddle of [a] stream so that when the water come down it would go right into the creek and into the river. And I had me a vegetable garden, and a hemp garden, too.

*So I started fishing. I had a barrel that I used for my fish barrel and
I kept running water on it all the time. And I stayed down there. . . .*

*People knew I was in there, sure. And the community was watching.
They was hoping that people would leave me alone and let me get straight.
They knew I was in bad shape. . . . It got me almost to the point where
I could reenter society. That winter I trapped five red fox and I sold them
for eighty-eight dollars apiece. I dug some ginseng and I sold quite a bit o'
catfish. I'd even began to put some stuff on paper about my thoughts, because I could be out in the woods alone.*

Wilgus was now trying to do what his forefathers had done: escape from
society and start all over again. He sought solitude to break free of the drug
culture and stay out of more trouble. Wilgus just wanted to be left alone,
do something constructive, and get his life straightened out.

It lasted less than a year. On June 23, 1977, Wilgus went to visit his
father, now living in the little town of Campton in Wolfe County, just
across the line from Breathitt County. When he arrived in Campton a fight
was breaking out. As Wilgus tells the story, a gang had come into town
looking for action and was beating up people. Having learned to settle
problems on his own, Wilgus intervened to break up the fight. The gang
members started drifting away but only to fetch their guns. They returned
and cornered the intruder who had broken up their fun. They discovered
his identity, held rifles to his head, and told him to get down on his knees
and say his last words. Wilgus figured that the gang members really wanted
to show that they were the toughest men in Breathitt County, and he
talked them into taking him on with their bare fists, one at a time. As they
were walking down the road, Wilgus suddenly broke free, raced over to his
truck, whipped open the glove compartment, pulled out his pistol, and
started shooting. The gang members were no match for Wilgus in a gun-
fight. He shot and killed two men, and the rest of the gang fled.

The police arrived, arrested Wilgus, and charged him with two counts
of manslaughter. At trial, the jury found Wilgus guilty on both counts. The
judge sentenced him to ten years in prison for one killing and twenty years
for the other killing. The two sentences were to run concurrently rather
than consecutively, so Wilgus effectively had a twenty-year sentence. He
was headed for prison, although he would be eligible for parole in four
years.

Wilgus arrived at the Kentucky State Penitentiary near Eddyville, a grim fortress at the end of a lonely two-lane road in the remote western backwoods of Kentucky, towering over the bank of Lake Barkley, an artificial lake created by a dam on the Cumberland River. The huge, gray stone building is topped with turrets and battlements. The cell blocks are high, narrow rectangles of dirty stone, like giant matchbooks placed parallel to each other. Wilgus met his neighbor, Jerry Kendrick, and learned of Kendrick's lawsuit about conditions in the penitentiary. Less than a year later, Wilgus was transferred to KSR, where he talked Shorty into letting him join the lawsuit and become a member of the Plaintiffs' Committee.

The Plaintiffs' Committee

Wilgus entered a new world when he joined the Plaintiffs' Committee, a world in which people could not solve their problems with force. People in this new world had to think, discuss, evaluate, and create ideas for solving problems. Wilgus had to lay aside ingrained habits of reacting to problems on impulse and with violence. He had to learn to employ reason, think through problems, and arrive at rational solutions. Joining the lawsuit meant that Wilgus would participate in the effort to change the prison. It also meant that he would have to change as a person.

One of the first things Wilgus had to learn was how to deal with the lawyers appointed by Judge Johnstone. Wilgus was still angry about his numerous transfers around the Kentucky prison system. He wanted to get even with prison officials, but the lawyers were not interested in his personal feud. In this early phase of the lawsuit, they needed, above all else, reliable information from the inmates.

> *After I got to thinking about what I'd seen and the conditions we were living under, I forgot about the bones 'cause that's the first thing that the lawyers said, they said, "Well now, wait a minute. Do you have a bone to clean with these people at Harlan County because they transferred you? Or do you have a genuine interest in this thing here?" And I said, "I have a genuine interest in this lawsuit." That's when I forgot about how they screwed me over in Harlan County and moved on with it.*
>
> *Now, we knew that if we could ever get anybody from the outside to look at what the lawyers were telling and we were telling the lawyers, it was a winner all the way. That's why before ever' meeting we screened each other.*

"What have you learned this week?"

"Well, there was a guard down there and he said—"

"Well now, wait a minute. Where is the proof at? Let's don't go to the lawyers with anything that we don't know for a fact and anything that we can't prove, 'cause when they take it to the wardens and the state's lawyers, those people will come back with it and say, 'Oh no. This is not true. Your boys were lying to ye.' We don't wanna do that. We wanna be straight with what we're doing."

Members of the Plaintiffs' Committee played a vital role in providing the lawyers with information about prison conditions. This information had to be accurate, because the attorneys intended to prepare an amended complaint that, while retaining Shorty's original complaints about overcrowding and filth as the core of the litigation, would greatly expand the scope of the case to include medical care, recreation, job training, education, and virtually every other facet of the conditions at KSR. Information is usually no better than the people who provide it, and Wilgus did not like the character of most of the people on the committee when he first arrived. He wanted to eliminate those inmates from the committee and recruit new plaintiffs. He started organizing, using some of the political skills passed on by Grampaw Combs.

Once I got on the committee, then we started making our moves. We started getting rid of the guys that we didn't want and the guys that we knew that didn't have a good working knowledge of the prison, didn't know how to manipulate. What we needed was people who could play specific roles, 'cause we knew this was gonna get down to the nitty-gritty and we had to have someone who could deal with certain regions of the prison.

We had to have a man who could deal with prison industries. We had to have a man who had communication skills who could deal with academic people. We knew that we had to have people who had skills that could deal with the mess-hall people. We knew that we had to go into these areas and git information not from the inmates but from the staff. We knew that we had to have people that the staff trusted.

Like I went to the library and said to the librarian, "Look Joyce, how much money would you need, if you go home tonight and daydream about making this library a library like you'd want it? Bring me back the dollar amount tomorrow." So she did. She brought me back a list. So when the

*lawyers said, "Well, how much money would they have to have to bring
this library up to where it would be serviceable to all the men on the
yard?" that's where the fifty-thousand-dollar figure come in at.*

Shorty was the leader of the Plaintiffs' Committee because he had filed
the lawsuit. Wilgus too came to feel that he was playing an important role
in doing something constructive.

*We got together and made out what we's gonna do, and Shorty presented
it. Shorty had a good sense of what needed to be done. Shorty's strongest
point is that he's a compromiser. And he had a very keen sense and a very
good knowledge of what the law is and should be. And you could sit down
with Shorty, and Shorty could see it and have a good, good view of it. But
he would have some strings a' hanging that wasn't just exactly right and
it would be killing his whole program.*

*My job was to snip those strings off. But I'm telling you, I got what
I wanted. 'Cause when we sat down we would horse-trade, but I could get
the most information from the yard. I had the most spies in the most different places, and the staff members would talk to me. They would tell me
the most. Anytime some men is sitting down and talking about what's happened during the events of the week, I was the man who knew the most.*

The Plaintiffs' Committee knew that the judge assigned to the case
would be making important decisions. Shorty's case had already been
transferred to Judge Johnstone, but Johnstone had a reputation among
some prisoners as a law-and-order fanatic who was tough on criminals,
not a judge who would take seriously prisoners' complaints about living
conditions. Some of the committee members wanted to make an issue
of the judge and maybe have him removed from the case. Wilgus asked
around the general population, and he heard some interesting stories
about the judge.

*We were talking about it in the dormitory, and a guy said, "Johnstone's
not a bad fellow."*

*"The hell he's not! He's out of that Fifty-sixth Judicial District down
there. He was the circuit judge in Lyon and Trigg County. Hell, he's
burned every convict up that ever come over there from Eddyville!" . . .*

And the [first] guy said, "Yeah, but Johnstone was beholding then. He's not beholding now. He's a federal judge. The only boss he's got's God. So his view might be a little different."

"Well, how you know 'bout this?"

"My father worked for Johnstone all of his life. My daddy's done lots of work for him."

"Well, tell me something about him."

"What do you want to know?"

So we compiled this list of questions that we wanted to know about him. Did he like to hunt? Did he ever hunt? Was he into animal husbandry? And we just did a full-scale evaluation of him.

This guy put us in contact with a guy at Eddyville who gave us some information. And he told us that they called Johnstone "Big Foot." He said he wore about a thirteen or fourteen, maybe a fifteen size shoe, but his feet was actually much bigger 'n that. While they were hunting, nobody liked to hunt with him because he was clumsy and fell over things and made too much noise. But he was always wanting to go. Ever' time they was getting ready to go duck hunting, he was right there and they'd say "Oh God, here comes Big Foot!" So they never did like to hunt with him.

I said, "Well, can you give me something that sort of has something to do with the law? A decision he's made, can let me see some human characteristics in him?"

"Well, I kinda wrote some bad checks one time on him. I wrote some bad checks, and Johnstone told me, said, 'Well hell, you don't need to go to the penitentiary. We need to find you something to do!' And he got his money back that way." . . .

From those rumors and tales and stories we decided that that's the man we ought to go with. We seen humaneness, we seen a character of a man who had a heart, who cared about people enough to not send a man to the penitentiary for writing cold checks. He'd realize that [a man] needed a job and not send him to the penitentiary.

And we seen a man who had flaws, a man who caused trouble on hunting trips by falling down and making noise. We seen a man who knew that he was hunting with guys that probably didn't want to hunt with him. We seen a man that was Kentucky. We seen a man that was country.

We seen a man that had dealt with prisoners before. One of our big goals was to get him inside the prison. We knew if we could ever get him there that we had the case locked up. This is a guy with heart. And it turned out we were right.

Despite the committee members' position as power brokers, it was difficult to serve on the committee. Their position was well known within KSR, and they believed they were being harassed by some of the guards and by other prisoners acting on orders from those guards. It was a learning experience for the young hillbilly from Bloody Breathitt.

I'll tell you, when you're doing these kind of things, it's hard on you just to keep a straight direction. There's a couple of times when Captain Sharp and them sent Tom Payne and those guys out on the yard and tried to get us piped. Me and Steve Brannun went in the law library. Ol' Tom Payne made him climb the goddamn wall with knives, 'cause Sharp brought the word out that the guys on the lawsuit ought to be piped 'cause they was gonna mess the penitentiary up.

And they closed the legal aid office off to us and wouldn't let us use the copying machine. The inmates over there did. They wouldn't even let us pay 'em to run stuff off. We was finding stuff in the mailroom—all them old court orders and things that was two or three months old. We's trying to get copies of that stuff. They'd layway me on the way to the mailbox and cut my letters open and plant marijuana on me during the day. Inmates was doing it.

It was kind of hard for me to not to get to do a lot of things for spite. It's difficult to keep from becoming vindictive. There have been times when we were negotiating and I would say, "Yeah, I'll bust their nuts here." And then I'd think, "Well, no, I need to get a different direction on this stuff." I wasn't interested in gitting anybody fired. I wanted to get something for the convict.

It made a whole different person out of me. I was taught patience. I was taught to just keep knocking on the door. Regardless of what . . . people [are] trying to do to ye that's gonna make you mad and make you want to get even, now that you got a fine chance to get even, don't do it. Forget about [it]. Just keep your direction. Keep your head on straight and keep going. Git something good for the institution and for ever'body that's gonna be here later on.

Considerable tension among the guards and prisoners exists in prison, and prison-reform litigation can intensify that tension, as Wilgus and other members of the Plaintiffs' Committee learned. Wilgus asked the lawyers to take legal action against the harassment, with the support of the Plaintiffs' Committee. The lawyers conferred with their counterparts in the consolidated Eddyville case and filed a joint motion to prohibit harassment of the plaintiffs for their participation in the case.

Judge Johnstone believed that any person, including a prisoner, who brought a lawsuit in federal court had the right not to be punished for doing so. On September 24, 1979, he issued an order that prison guards were forbidden to harass inmates for being involved in the lawsuit. The harassment order did not solve all problems, because some harassment continued. Wilgus was on his way to a meeting of the Plaintiffs' Committee one day when a squad of guards surrounded him and took him into a windowless room. They ordered him to pull down his pants, bend over, and spread his buttocks. Wilgus obeyed, but nothing happened, and eventually the guards let him go. The guards were violating the harassment order, but it was difficult to prove. Wilgus had no physical injury, no witnesses. If the lawyers filed a motion to hold the guards in contempt, it would be one inmate's word against a squad of guards. Wilgus had to swallow his anger and keep on with the lawsuit.

The harassment order remained a significant victory. Perhaps for the first time in Kentucky history, a judge had come to realize that a prison guard was capable of punishing a prisoner simply because the prisoner had complained about inhumane living conditions. The judge was following legal precedents set by judges in other states, but his order signified more than that to the inmates. The harassment order was a sign that Johnstone cared about people, that prisoners were still human beings, and that the problems of prisoners deserved the attention of the court. The harassment eventually dropped off. KSR was starting to change.

Walter

Walter Harris joined the Plaintiffs' Committee about the same time Wilgus Haddix did. Walter had already served nearly six years at KSR as part of a life sentence for murder and armed robbery. He had stayed out of trouble all six years in prison, and he wanted to keep it that way. Walter's rule was to stay out of sight and blend into the woodwork. He wanted no part of any lawsuit against the prison because he did not want to be transferred back to the Eddyville penitentiary. Walter had, however, received a job at the KSR inmate legal office, helping other inmates with their individual legal problems.

The inmates on the Plaintiffs' Committee had a related problem: given prison officials' propensity to transfer named plaintiffs in prison-reform litigation to other prisons, Shorty and his committee had agreed on a plan to arrange for a replacement in case any one of them was transferred. Larry Alexander, one of the committee members, was black, and about one-third of the prisoners at KSR were black. Larry decided that proper representation for black inmates required that he seek a black for his re-placement, and he approached Walter Harris. Walter was a tall, well-built, good-looking man from a big-city black ghetto. He was a quiet man who spoke in a deep voice and used slow, carefully constructed sentences. It took some convincing to bring Walter on board.

It was a question of representation of blacks on the committee. There were blacks on the committee, but none as bold as [Larry] was. There was a problem on the committee. It was predominantly white. Outside of Larry Alexander there was only one other black guy that was doing any talking, and he wasn't too articulate. Larry couldn't reason with him. The guy wasn't really thinking on the issues before he spouted off at the mouth. It was more like he was trying to impress the fellas.

LaGrange was segregated at that point, and there was a lot of racial tension. All blacks were housed primarily in dormitory 6 and dormitory 5. There were no white folks in those dormitories. The only integrated dormi-tories were dormitory 8 and dormitory 2, which was more or less [run] by people of the persuasion of the Aryan Brotherhood. They fancied them-selves to be Ku Klux Klan members. That was their territory and they [didn't want] to have any of us in there.

People were just paranoid. You always walked with your back to the wall. All blacks went through one line at chow hall, and all whites went through another line. If any white person approached the black line, every-body got uptight, wanting to know what was getting ready to jump off. And vice versa when blacks approached the white line. You didn't do that. Blacks [were] eating on one side of the cafeteria and whites [were] eating on the other side of the cafeteria.

Even on business, you didn't speak to each other. I mean, just passing somebody that you worked with, you didn't say "Hi" to them or their people.

Unfortunately, very few of the black inmates were in a position to voice their gripes in an effective fashion because of the hostility. Larry wanted a replacement, but he wanted somebody who wasn't going to do what he thought all the other blacks on the committee were doing at that point. I don't really know what made him choose me. Of all the guys he knew, I was kind of surprised that he came and got me.

You see, there were points of view to be expressed. The general view

*of an inmate at that point in time was that he had a sixth-grade educa-
tion—functionally illiterate, incapable of any serious discussion of legal
issues. I was a self-taught jailhouse lawyer. I thought I was marginally
proficient. Guys considered me kinda good at it.*

*Larry knew that I was working for the legal office. He was aware of the
work that I had done for some other guys. And I had coordinated a criminal-justice seminar for the Jaycees [with] Larry Alexander and a few
others. . . .*

*So having been acquainted with me in the past, Larry sought me out.
I was working in the legal office. I was on my way to lunch. He stopped me
on the yard, he said, "Walt, you know about this Plaintiffs' Committee?"
I said I had heard about it, but I haven't taken an active interest in it or
for that matter an active interest in finding out what was going on. I was
just listening to what the guys were saying around the yard, but that was
going in one ear and out the other. Larry ran the situation down to me.
There was a serious racial problem at the institution at that time. He felt
that it was the obligation of the blacks who were on the committee to ade-
quately represent the interests of the entire black population, and that
wasn't happening. He felt that blacks on the committee were knuckling
under because they were intimidated by the process of just having a discussion of that magnitude with attorneys as well as with the guys on the
committee who were white, who were better educated than they were, more
verbal, and more persuasive. To his way of thinking, he was doing all the
talking for blacks. Everybody was looking up to him when it came to what
blacks had to say about this, that, and the other. He didn't like that. He
wanted to voice his opinion but not to have all the weight on his shoulders.*

*I was kind of reluctant. I didn't think I was ready for that sort of a chal-
lenge at that particular point in time. After we got finished talking, I told
him he had gotten the wrong guy. I didn't have the education or the legal
training in this.*

*He wasn't put off by that. He said, "The worst you can do is what these
other guys are doing now, and I know you're not gonna do that, so you're
going to make some type of contribution. What it amounts to in the long
run [is that] neither one of us will probably be around to find out. Give
it a try."*

*So I did. He convinced me to give it a try. The reason he brought me on
was 'cause he knew I was an opinionated SOB. I kind of stuck to my guns*

once I made up my mind about something, unless I saw it was a hopeless cause. Then I just let what was gonna be, be. That's how I initially got in.

Walter joined Shorty and Wilgus on the Plaintiffs' Committee. He was a loner, and speaking out for causes and groups was not his way. Walter quickly realized that he would have to learn a great deal about how the prison operated before he could speak out for anyone, black or white. The men on the Plaintiffs' Committee were engaged in an effort to change the prison to make it a better place for the average inmate to live. KSR was a huge prison housing more than two thousand inmates, and running it was a complicated enterprise. Walter soon grasped that prison-reform litigation was a complex process that would require much research, extensive interaction with lawyers, and a great deal of thought. Walter saw in this process a tremendous challenge to his ability, not a racial cause.

Ghetto Child

Meeting this challenge would require some personal development on Walter's part. He grew up in an urban black ghetto. There was extreme poverty in his neighborhood and, as socioeconomic status is closely related to crime, the condition of poverty gave rise to high levels of crime. Walter McKinley Harris is a son of Mary Betty Harris and Sylvester Gee. Mary Harris grew up on a farm in rural Virginia and came to the big city as a young woman.

It was the first time she had been in a big city. Shortly after she got here she met my brother's father, Junious Venable Sr. She thought they would get married because she was light-skinned. At that time there was a thing about light-skinned women amongst dark-skinned black men. He led her on for a while, and she got pregnant with my brother. My brother went to live with his father.

Sometime after that she met my father. My brother and I were born a year apart. She was in love with him, as she says, but he was a real rascal. All he wanted was a place to lay up and somebody to sleep with from time to time. He was into using people for what he could get from 'em. He had gotten what he wanted from her. She was no further use to him. Took a little pleasure on the side. She finally got the message that their relationship wasn't going anywhere and she let him go.

She came into some money. She started getting welfare checks. He thought he was going to get that, because my mother was kinda stuck on him. But she didn't give it to him. So he just went on his merry way.

Walter's parents never married, so he was an illegitimate child carrying his single mother's name.

It was pretty much a typical black family—poor, living in the city. My mother had four children. There was me, my brother, and two of my sisters. We weren't on the bottom of the scale. We weren't too far above it for a while. Mom was on welfare when we were coming up. She kinda kept things together. She did the best she could.

Walter's father, Sylvester Gee, mostly ignored his family. He worked a little, chased women, and fathered thirteen children in all. Walter has bad memories of his irresponsible father.

I don't know how the hell to describe my father, outside of being a general asshole. He liked money. He just couldn't be trusted.

He was living off of his father, my grandfather, Russell Gee. My grandfather had been into mechanics all of his life. He was good at it—owned several garages. He was living very well. My father would work about six months out of the year, for-hire things like painting houses. Then he'd run home to Daddy and work a little while, get a little money, but earn it. My grandfather wouldn't give him any money straight out unless it was an emergency. Then [my father would] be gone. And primarily he just worked on women and laid up on 'em.

Every time my father had an opportunity to work with my grandfather, he would do something stupid. Like when my grandfather was repairing vehicles, it was cash in advance, half up front. So the people who worked for him got the money. They had to be trusted to bring the money to him. When he wasn't there, he'd leave my father in charge. Well, my father would stick around long enough to collect a sizable sum and then he would just disappear with it. He knew my grandfather wasn't going to prosecute him. If he needed money and couldn't find a job, my grandfather would always let him work in the garage, but my grandfather never let him work for him after that in the sense of being in charge of anything.

My father didn't care about nobody but himself. The only thing he did for me in thirty-five years, before he died, was bought me two suits when

I was a youngster somewhere between the ages of seven and nine. That's
about the time I threatened to kill him if he put his hands on my mama
again. And two weeks after he bought 'em and gave 'em to me, he came
back and got 'em and gave 'em to my brothers. After that, he never bought
anything or even pretended to give it to me. And every time I ever asked
him for something, I never got it. I got a long song and dance about it.
I mean, I couldn't even borrow five dollars from him.

Walter was on his own much of the time as a little boy, and, with poverty
and crime all around him, he started breaking the law about the same time
his father took back the two suits.

I grew up in the streets. I started stealing when I was about nine. My
mama wasn't into taking care of me. I guess she was going through her
thing of getting back at my daddy.

   I got put out of school, too. The first time I got put out, I was going to a
small kids' disciplinary school. I got put out because I hit a teacher with a
chair for beating my cousin. We had kind of a close relationship, we kids.
We were going to the same school. We were laughing and joking in class,
as kids do. The teacher smacked my hands with a ruler. I was one of those
stubborn kids—didn't wanta cry. So she didn't get any satisfaction out of
that. She went to my cousin. She was whaling away on her hands. Her
hands turned red. My cousin was dropping. Teacher just kept on going,
so I told her not to hit my cousin again. She hit her again, and I hit the
teacher with a chair. They sent me to a school where they send troubled
children. I stayed there till I was about thirteen.

Walter graduated from elementary school and junior high. He got into
some trouble, but at first his offenses were minor, at least compared to
much of the violent crime in the ghetto. After a day in school he usually
headed onto the street with his friends. Walter eventually joined a teenage
gang. Gang life led to trouble with the police. Walter was arrested on a
burglary charge when he was in the tenth grade, and he realized it was
time to leave the gang behind.

[I] just wasn't into the gang anymore because it wasn't leading any-
where. . . . The guys we knew who were going to school with us at the time,
they were graduating. They weren't going anywhere—just hanging out on
the corner. They didn't want to go in the service. There were plenty of jobs

working in restaurants as dishwashers, busboys, factory positions, and that sort of thing, but they didn't have any skills to get a meaningful job.

We started trying to make a break from the subculture. To some extent, we were successful. We were still in school. We got jobs. Stopped being on the street and stealing. We were employed for a while.

Pagoda Valley

In November 1969, when Walter was in twelfth grade, he was eighteen years old and still facing the burglary charge. There was a large demand for new recruits to send to Vietnam, so Walter dropped out of high school, and he and his friend, Eddie Edwards, enlisted in the Marine Corps as a way to break out of the gang subculture.

I went in the Marine Corps to get out of the ghetto. I didn't need any more living on the street. What got me in the Marine Corps, outside of being in a little bit of trouble at the time, was that Eddie had enlisted, but he had gotten such a poor score. He only got a five on the test. That put him in a position where they would take you, but only when they got good and ready to.

He got to telling me about it. I went down and talked to the recruiter. I told him what my situation was. I had a juvenile record. I was facing a burglary charge. He said that wouldn't matter, that if I got a good enough score on the test, they'd have my record sealed.

Sounds like a winner to me! So I took the test. I got a thirty-one, which was higher than he expected. And when they resolved everything they were willing to take Eddie in with me on the buddy plan. And off we went to boot camp.

After basic training, Walter was sent directly into combat in Vietnam, like many disadvantaged young men who bore the brunt of jungle warfare in Vietnam. Walter was a tough street kid, a survivor, when he shipped out to Vietnam. When he came home nine months later, he was also cynical.

I actually arrived in the country of Vietnam July 10 of '70. It was an experience. I don't talk about it too much, except when I get gabby. It wasn't traumatic or anything like that, just not much to brag about.

I was in combat the whole time. Just outside Da Nang. I was at Khe

Sanh, the Pagoda Valley. The war was kind of petering out. There were still engagements, some close calls. I was one of the lucky ones. There were firefights. Gotta keep your head and ass down if you don't want it shot off. There was a definite danger, but constant exposure to it minimizes your anxiety. You just gotta take it and survive.

I probably killed some enemy, moving with the machine gun like I was and doing all the shooting that I was doing. Being as good as I thought I was—and was—I probably hit somebody. Never saw 'em.

I don't bother reading the books or watching the movies about Vietnam, or even the shows that they have on TV. They don't even come close to what it was really like. I mean, it's not romantic.

It was every day. The lesson that I learned was that there are no heroes. There are just ordinary people who do the unexpected and that winds up being declared as "going beyond the call of duty." Perhaps they did no more than was imperative to save their lives or a buddy's life at the time. And they got a medal for it. I used to listen to some of the citations being read at award ceremonies, and it was a bunch of the damnedest garbage you're ever gonna hear. Some of the stuff never happened! But listen to 'em write it up and, good God!

A friend of mine got a Purple Heart. We were on the edge of Pagoda Valley one night—where they have cemeteries. We were right on the edge of the cemetery, in the rice paddies we'd dug into. We were in the cemetery during the day. We had to move to a different spot at night so that we wouldn't be detected. That didn't keep 'em away. We started taking 'em incoming. I was bucking away on the machine gun. My old buddy Dawson goes, "Oaah, I'm hit, I'm hit!" I looked at him. I said, "Where? I don't see no blood." He just kept on screaming, so I called the corpsman. Corpsman came over, tore his pants open, looked at his knee. Dawson had this wee incision there. Corpsman dug in there and pulled out a little ol' piece of scrap metal. He got hit by a piece of scrap metal in front of the knee. The scrap metal wasn't even as big as a pinhead! It wasn't as bad as a scratch you'd get from a piece of elephant grass.

That got him the Purple Heart! They read this damnedest citation off. We died laughing right there in formation as he was getting the award. Oh, my God! They threatened to write us up for it.

Guys get it and deserve it. There's no question of that. But sometimes there's ordinary things that they just blow out of proportion. Guys that *are there don't attach that much significance to it. We kinda play it down. There are some awards that are given to people that shouldn't get them. Some asshole officers endanger people's lives unnecessarily to get written up in the paper and get promotions. There ain't a whole lot you can do about that. That's the system. You buck it and you wind up going down. There are no heroes.*

Vietnam replicated Walter's ghetto experience. Whereas Judge Johnstone saw combat in World War II, was cited for heroism in the Battle of the Bulge, and came home a war hero, Walter fell into the quagmire of Vietnam and came home with no recognition of his effort. There were no victories, no heroes, and no parades. He wound up simply trying to stay alive, relying on his marine comrades to help him stay alive, and waiting for the day he was sent home. The danger and the disillusionment of service in Vietnam and ready availability of drugs led Walter, like many of his fellow soldiers, to become a heavy drug user.

I came back March 31, '71. I left 'Nam with the First Battalion, Fifth Marines. This was the third unit I had been assigned to. We landed in San Francisco. When we reported back, we were reassigned to another unit at Camp Pendleton.

Shoot, just about everybody that I came back from 'Nam with—overall 1,099, something like that—was into drugs. I was using it, and I was using it regularly in California. Marijuana and cocaine and whatnot, doing all of that, especially mixing it all up together. I was a naive little fella.

They had this drug program. One day the first sergeant came out and read a little proclamation off to everybody about general discharges. It was supposed to be drug related. If you had a drug problem and you wanted to take a general discharge—no questions asked—they would give you this general discharge.

Pshew! Out of the battalion, there were less than ten people who didn't take it. All our illusions had been shattered by the Marine Corps by then. Just about everybody was disenchanted and looking for a way to get out or to ride out our tours, and that'd be it.

I shoulda took it, but I didn't. I didn't have a drug problem anymore than most of the guys did that took it. It was just a way out, and they wanted it.

Life in the Fast Lane

Walter received bad news about this time: his grandfather, Russell Gee, had died while the young marine was in Vietnam. Walter had expected to inherit part of the garage business, but the court administering the estate awarded the business to his father, Sylvester Gee. Sylvester had promptly ruined the business, so that, like Shorty and Wilgus, Walter had little means of making a living when he left the military.

When my grandfather died, the garages were supposed to go to me and his two youngest children—my uncles. He told me this. He had indicated prior to his death that he was going to leave the garages to me and his two other sons. . . . At that time they were about thirteen and fourteen.

He said he didn't want his two youngest sons to go through what I went through. At that point I was several years older than them, and they couldn't take the property and manage it. He said that he was going to give each of us a one-third interest in the garages. That I would have controlling interest of the property until they reached the age of majority, at which point they would take their inheritance, and we would share equally. . . . He was going to bypass all of his children outside of the two sons he was living with.

What happened was, my grandfather didn't have a will. That was the problem. Well, my father found out about it. And I was overseas. Because my grandfather hadn't written a will, my father took it to court with his sister and they managed to get just about everything. . . .

He was running the business. They kept it going for a while. Then he lost it. He got it and he lost it.

Walter's father was not someone on whom he could rely for a positive role model, but his grandfather transmitted some positive values to Walter.

I've never considered my father my father. He was just a father in name only. I considered Russell, his father, to be my father also. He did some of the things that my father should have done. When I got in trouble, he was the one come down to the police station to see about getting me out. My mother couldn't get bail. She needed help. Or he was the one that arranged for transportation for her to get to the station. If somebody was needed, he was the one.

My grandfather was one of those people who believed that if you have friends, you take care of your friends. You have family, you take care of your family. If you don't look after your family, then when you're in a pinch you can't expect anybody to do anything for you.

Walter drifted into the California drug culture while stationed at Camp Pendleton.

At first it was like work. They'd sound reveille regularly at four o'clock. It was too much like being overseas, back in the boondocks. You'd look up, there's a mountain. They've got you playing these war games that didn't really mean a damn thing anymore.

The frustration just built up. It got to a point where I just didn't give a damn anymore. So I took off and stayed AWOL, running around.

I was into drugs. I was moving in the fast lane, or what I thought was the fast lane at the time—just doing a lot of partying, hanging out with the fellows that were working and spending nice money, or what seemed like nice money in that day. Nice cars, nice apartments.

Liberty from the base was supposed to start Saturday at 4:00. If the first sergeant didn't sign me out, at 4:00 I was gone anyway. I just got in the damn car and left. Then I'd come back in the morning about five minutes before formation. I had my uniform on and walked out there and played the game during the day. At 4:00 I was ready to go again. I might have to use a little ingenuity from time to time to make my exit, but I managed to.

Then it got to the point where that wasn't enough any more. I kinda got fed up so I just said, "The hell with it." I tried to get court-martialed one time just to get out. I came on base and walked around. I knew everybody on that damn base. They had to know I was higher than a kite. The only person that said something was the gunnery sergeant. He asked me what I was trying to do. It was his job to write me up. But he didn't do it. He just let it go. And I took off for about a week. I reported back in AWOL and turned right around and signed myself back out on liberty.

That made 'em madder than hell! They wanted to know where I got the gall to report in from being AWOL and turn around and go back out on liberty five minutes later! At that point I didn't really care. I knew sooner or later it'd be over.

Walter was court-martialed and confined to the stockade at Camp Pendleton. He was released after serving his sentence, placed on leave, and finally discharged for bad conduct. He immediately joined the fast lane of civilian life and was soon in trouble and on the run, like Shorty and Wilgus after their military service.

I was running from that ever-haunting fear of having to return to the ghetto with virtually nothing, no meaningful skills and no money, to keep from falling back into the old routine, the ghetto being in a sour prospect at that time.

I started to hustle — robbing. That didn't work out. I got a possession-of-stolen-property charge that they were going to break down into several other charges. They were getting ready to send me to the penitentiary, but I decided I didn't want to go.

I had a way out. At the time this was going on a friend of mine was working for the Veterans' Administration. He was somebody I met in San Diego while I was on leave pending my discharge. He wanted to leave and go to Kentucky for a promotion. I asked for the money I had saved while I was in the Marine Corps, plus money I had hustled up, and I was still a fair hustler at the time. So I tagged along behind him. So off I went to Kentucky.

Walter arrived in Lexington, Kentucky, with a long string of failures behind him. He was on drugs and he had no job skills, but he knew how to use a gun. Disaster struck within a year.

We stayed in the Holiday Inn in Lexington for a week. Between his room and mine and the food we ate, that got kind of expensive 'cause we took three meals a day there, plus eating out on the street. Each room was $119 at the end of the week. The $3,000 we had wouldn't have gone very far. So I rented an apartment for us, and we stayed there.

It was kinda all right. I thought I was making some headway. I still wasn't where I needed to be because I needed to get back in school. I was trying to get into the University of Kentucky.

I was still hustling — robbing. I was trying to break away but not quite succeeding. I just picked up a pistol and knew how to use it — pretty good shot. At least I thought I was — 'til that night of June 18 of '73.

That's when I robbed a liquor store and killed a man, killed the operator, in what I thought was self-defense, but of course nobody agreed. He provoked it because he came after me with a bottle. The guy died a couple weeks after the robbery of blood poisoning.

The police did their little tampering with the evidence to ensure that it appeared to be an unprovoked murder. The police had done it when they were examining the scene and taking the photographs giving them the best possible view of everything. There were pictures that they never produced at the first trial that showed the counter had been moved all the way up against the wall so it appeared that the operator had been shot in front of the counter rather than behind. And they testified that there was no glass. The pictures showed that there was, in fact, a glass bottle.

Armed robbery was just one of the charges. In the course of a robbery, you are guilty of anything that transpires in the course of a robbery. Despite my intent of not meaning to kill him, they also charged me with willful murder under the theory that no one forced me to pull the trigger.

Walter was convicted on January 4, 1974, of armed robbery and murder. The judge gave him two concurrent life sentences, one for each charge, which made him eligible for parole in five and a half years.

Inmate Advocate

Walter arrived at the Kentucky State Reformatory in LaGrange three days after he was convicted. Now twenty-three years old, Walter decided to spend his time in prison staying out of trouble, going to school, and holding a prison job. He also started to work on overturning his murder conviction on the grounds that the police had tampered with the evidence. This effort led to the beginning of a legal career, though not as an attorney.

They initially wanted to send me to Eddyville, but I was just twenty-three at the time. I was too young in those days. So they sent me to LaGrange. I kinda stayed in the woodwork for eight years, being Mr. Loner.

I started off working as a clerk in the academic school. Then I got my general education degree, and then the senior clerk left, and I became chief clerk for the academic school. I basically coordinated the clerical work for the principal, Dave Vislisel, while I was there. In his absence the teachers thought of me as the versatile one in school, administratively.

During that time I was interested in my case. I just couldn't afford to pay anybody to do what I wanted done. I was trying to get some sort of training so that I could look in the books myself and do it seriously.

I had no idea where to start or how to start until I met Don Ault. He had just come down from Eddyville. He was living in Dorm 8 with me. He gave me a couple of Nutshells, what we call Nutshells. They were on jurisprudence and legal research. Just told me to read 'em. I read 'em.

Just about the time I finished 'em they decided to have this pilot paralegal training program, which they called the paralegal training project. I enrolled in that, which was for two weeks, eight hours a day. Completed it and went to work in the legal office.

Walter achieved the position of prison legal aide, which was part of an official program at KSR to provide legal help for prisoners. The purpose of this program was to give prisoners useful skills and to discourage prisoners from using unofficial jailhouse lawyers, inmates who do legal work for other inmates without permission from prison administrators. In this job, Walter assisted men who sought to have their convictions overturned or who had complaints about how they were being treated inside the prison. As Walter looked into the complaints of mistreatment, he took them seriously and voiced them to responsible officials. His assertive attitude soon led to his being transferred out of the legal office.

I wasn't arrogant or argumentative, but if a guy had a legitimate complaint I would stand my ground on any position that I took on his behalf.

There were problems with caseworkers being available. Claude Turpin, the chief caseworker, didn't care for that. He had a policy whereby if an inmate called a caseworker, he didn't want to hear anything about the caseworker not wanting to talk to the inmate until the caseworker came back to the inmate's dormitory. I called Claude Turpin and told him that this one caseworker had refused to talk to an inmate until he returned to the dormitory. Turpin went and talked to the caseworker about it.

I had contacted a number of officials about various problems, nonlegal problems, that inmates were having. Our job description was kind of broad at that point. Whatever came up, you had to deal with it one way or another. If it wasn't a legal issue you had to refer it to someone at the institution who's responsible for dealing with that particular type of problem. Other employees didn't particularly appreciate that. The warden, Steve Smith, had made it known that if any employee got a call from a legal aide about a matter, he wanted that matter addressed. He didn't want it just set aside.

So they went to Steve Smith with their complaints about what I was doing on behalf of other inmates. One day they called me up to Steve Smith's office. When I went in I didn't see anybody else. He asked me to have a seat. I sat on the couch in front of his desk. He said, "Walter, they tell me you're too much of an inmate advocate."

I laughed. "How so?"

He wouldn't elaborate, 'cause then he said, "I think we're gonna need to assign you somewhere else."

I said, "Well, as long as you don't put me out in prison industries I'll be all right. In fact, I was thinking about going into drafting class. If you can give me some assistance in that regard, I'll be more than happy to change assignments."

He said, "We'll look into it."

I was too much of an inmate advocate. That's what Steve Smith told me. And I had to leave the legal office. So for about two months I was roaming around without a job.

The news that Walter Harris had been fired for being "too much of an inmate advocate" traveled quickly among the general prison population and established his reputation as an aggressive spokesman for inmates' rights. This reputation prompted Larry Alexander to goad Walter into joining the Plaintiffs' Committee.

Heavy Stuff

Larry brought Walter to his first meeting of the Plaintiffs' Committee, where he met Shorty, Wilgus, and the other plaintiffs as well as the lawyers appointed by Judge Johnstone. As discussion about the lawsuit proceeded from one topic to another, Walter listened quietly and experienced mixed emotions.

My initial impression was that this is some heavy stuff. Get outa here before you get lost.

I didn't understand all of the issues. If you didn't have a particular job or weren't privy to certain exchanges between inmates—that subculture which you have in a penal setting, where certain inmates tend to know what's going on amongst inmates and prison personnel, who have a grasp of the hierarchy outside the institution, who you take certain complaints to—you really can't speak out on anything. Because of the nature of my

charge I was restricted to assignments within the compound. The only
things I knew of were what went on in academic school and vocational
school and out on the yard.

At that first meeting they were talking about prison industries, OSHA,
the electrical wiring. What was OSHA? I ain't never heard of OSHA at
that time. I knew about the living conditions. I knew they were deplorable,
and we wanted to do something about it, but from a technical perspective
I had absolutely nothing to say.

Then I thought, "Well, what else am I doing?" The things I was doing
and the legal issues I was handling at that time, it was no real challenge.
Intellectually, I wanted to take my thinking along a different route, but
I didn't have the stimulation I needed to go in another direction. I think
that made me stay.

Once they got me started, I kinda liked it. It just began to make me look
at things differently.

Although Walter had grappled with legal issues and prison problems as
an inmate legal aide, his concerns had focused on individual inmates.
Shorty's lawsuit encompassed the common problems of more than two
thousand convicts—safety conditions in prison industries, nutrition guidelines in the chow hall, medical treatment at sick call, and dozens of other
aspects of prison administration. Walter had little information or knowledge to contribute to the discussion, but he found it interesting. He decided to read all the legal papers that had been filed in the lawsuit and to
educate himself about the constitutional rights of prisoners. A new world
was opening up, a world in which skills learned on ghetto streets were of
little use. He had to learn new skills, one of which was politics.

Early in his involvement with the Plaintiffs' Committee, Walter had to
come to grips with the racial tensions among the inmates. He did not view
his role as limited to representing only the interests of black prisoners.
He intended to speak for all the prisoners, because he had learned from
months of combat in Vietnam that survival requires reliance on people
with common interests, without regard to their race.

The gripes of the black inmates weren't really all that different from the
white inmates. They were basically the same concerns but became focused
on color because either blacks brought the issue up first or whites brought
the issue up first. If it was brought up by whites first, then it's a white con-

*cern. If it was brought up by blacks first, it's a black concern. There tended
to be very little mingling of the two, no common ground that anybody
would acknowledge.*

Getting beyond race and seeing the common concerns was in Walter's
control, but other problems on the committee were not. As Walter listened
to the discussions, he watched the other inmate plaintiffs carefully to determine who was doing most of the talking in the meetings and what the
talkers were trying to achieve. What he saw and heard bothered him, because it seemed that the committee was not a team working for a common
goal of improving the prison. Instead, Walter felt the group was dominated
by a few individuals promoting their own selfish goals.

*In the early days, Shorty basically called the shots. We all just conceded
that he was the principal plaintiff. If the case ever went to court, he was
going to be the one who would speak out for everybody. What he said and
didn't say would be the end of the issue.*

*So at that point there was a lot of sucking up to him. Leslie Brannum
was the most successful at that. He had Shorty's ear. He was able to voice
some of Shorty's thoughts more effectively than Shorty could. They became
thicker than thieves after a while.*

*Brannum was effective. I have to hand it to him. In spite of his selfish
interests or his personal interest, he did pursue the other issues. He had
to give something to get what he wanted. He basically gave Shorty what
Shorty needed. And that was some insight and support at the right time.
He kept things going.*

*Wilgus was Brannum's best friend, if there are friends in prison. Bran-
num and Wilgus had more in common than Brannum and Shorty, so they
pretty much called the shots—Wilgus, Brannum, and Shorty. Haddix and
Shorty and Brannum were the main voices on the committee. They were
going to have their way. All they were after—well, not all they were after—primarily what they were after were things for themselves. Oh yes,
initially! No doubt about it!*

*There was some prison politics going on. Initially, it was nothing more
than the lawsuit being exploited to the advantage of certain individuals—
mostly white inmates.*

Whether or not Walter's perception of the politics of the Plaintiffs'
Committee was accurate, it is clear that he did not trust the other representatives of the class. He also did not fully trust the legal aid lawyers ap-

pointed by Judge Johnstone to represent the prisoners, and race was part of the reason. The lawyers for the plaintiffs were all white. Conversely, the two lawyers for the U.S. Department of Justice, Judge Johnstone's legal advisers, were black, and Walter trusted them. His perception of the two sets of lawyers involved more complex factors, however, than a simplistic racial bias. He also took their roles into account, and perhaps Walter felt that when the Justice Department lawyers spoke, they were reflecting the views of the person they were advising, Judge Johnstone.

I didn't trust anybody who was appointed on our behalf. It wasn't a personal thing. It was a reservation born of my experiences of the public-defender system and with the legal aid societies. It wasn't all that faithful.

I was constantly on the alert for the quick deal, anything that wasn't a real good deal. Like someone saying, "Well, you're not going to get any more of this," before a particular issue had been fully explored—just writing it off and winding up with just another case. The case out of Rhode Island was the worst I saw, where they just repainted the institution and didn't do anything innovative or worth speaking of, where the guys were hotter than hell afterwards. They had signed onto this lawsuit that they thought was going to be very productive. And it wasn't. Years later, they were sitting back in the same conditions, and there's nothing they can do about it.

So I was on guard against something like that happening. The legal aid lawyers were attempting to educate us about realities and prison cases and consent decrees: "There's only so far that you can probably get and no further." But all of us were shooting for the stars.

The Justice Department lawyers being black, there was a natural tendency for me to gravitate towards them. But it was more than that. I sensed early on that they would be straightforward. If I advanced an opinion that was ludicrous, they would tell me that. On the other hand, if I advanced one that had some merit, they would explore it with me.

What I was doing was weighing all of the factors against each other, playing both ends against the middle. With respect to Justice and the Legal Aid Society, I was weighing and playing both ends against the middle. The Justice Department had their own reasons for getting involved in the case, and the Legal Aid Society had its own reason for getting involved in the case. While the legal aid lawyers were telling us some things, Justice was telling us some things in addition to that.

So it wasn't as though I disliked anyone. I was afraid to place absolute trust, blind trust, in anyone at any point where it wasn't absolutely essential that I do so.

Since Walter did not fully trust his own lawyers, he decided to do his own independent investigation. He set out to find out as much as he could about the conditions in the prison. He read law books to discover legal precedents in litigation concerning prisoners' rights to decent living conditions. It was a monumental challenge, and it was just the challenge Walter needed. Up to this time, his great motivating impulse had been to escape the ghetto, but Walter had no interest in trying to escape from KSR. Shorty's lawsuit became for Walter an opportunity to engage in a productive effort to improve prison living conditions.

Putting the Pieces Together

The time Walter joined the Plaintiffs' Committee happened to coincide with an unprecedented opportunity to learn about the conditions prisoners endured at KSR. In the fall of 1979, Shorty's lawsuit entered the phase of discovery, the process of obtaining information about a case prior to trial. The plaintiffs' lawyers began this process by touring KSR themselves, in the company of an expert hired to inspect the prison. Shorty, two assistant wardens, Justice Department attorneys, and lawyers for the state also came along. The exterior entrance into KSR is an impressive and rather attractive tower designed in an Art Deco style, a dramatic contrast to the squalid interior where the prisoners lived. As the lawyers came through the outer door, they encountered bitter and nauseating smells and the harsh, jarring sounds of iron doors opening and closing. On the other side of this huge tower sat a large outdoor area known as the Yard. The Yard was the prisoners' world, a surprisingly quiet space containing nine dormitories. Prisoners were scattered around the grounds, a few walking about, others chatting in small groups, the rest just sitting. As the expert and lawyers entered the Yard, the prisoners stared at them, intently aware that an important investigation was about to begin.

The tour continued into the first dormitory, where more than two hundred convicts lived in space designed to hold eighty men. One unarmed guard watched over the entire dormitory. Prisoners strolled around freely. The dormitory had four wings: two on the ground floor and two on the second story. Bunk beds packed the wings. Men lay on their bunks, some sleeping, a few writing letters or reading books, the rest chatting in small groups. Almost all were idle, and there was no place to be alone.

The floors and walls of the dormitory were cold and hard. Paint was worn and chipped. Trash and dirt were everywhere. Cockroaches skittered along the floor, on the beds, in and out of the men's clothing. One man lifted up his radio, and a nest of cockroaches scrambled for cover. Window frames were rusted. Windows were broken. In the bathroom, one shower out of four was working. Toilets were broken and overflowing. Stench filled the air. The tour moved on. Nearly every dorm was the same. The assistant wardens said that there was nothing they could do about the conditions.

The plaintiffs' lawyers had never seen anything like it. Shorty's original complaint said the prison was overcrowded and filthy. The allegation was true, but words alone could not convey the sense of squalor and inhumanity within the walls. It overwhelmed the attorneys with a feeling of depression. One of the lawyers for the state, a young woman, sat down on an empty bunk and burst into tears. "I can't defend this," she sobbed. She withdrew from the case soon after this tour.

The expert and the lawyers saw the same degrading conditions throughout the other eight dormitories. It seemed clear that the "reformatory," with its impressive Art Deco facade, was in reality a human garbage dump. Accepting the proposition that prisoners remain human beings—people who have made serious mistakes and done bad deeds but who also have the potential for good in them—KSR was a dysfunctional prison destined to bring out the evil and suppress the good in any human being.

The lawyers' impressions were confirmed by the hard facts that poured in during the discovery process. The state's answers to interrogatories revealed that KSR was built in 1937 to house a maximum of 1,200 prisoners, 1,080 in the dorms and 120 in the intake unit and disciplinary cell blocks. By 1979, however, KSR housed about 2,100 men. Whereas the dormitories were designed to house 120 men each, they now held between 200 and 240 men. Those numbers provided empirical evidence that KSR was massively overcrowded.

Physical sensations and numbers alone, however, were insufficient to build a case that conditions at KSR had fallen so far below acceptable norms of civilized existence as to constitute a violation of the constitutional prohibition against cruel and unusual punishment. In addition, the evidence had to be organized in a form that Judge Johnstone, who had never seen KSR, could understand. Part of the answer was provided by professional standards, mainly the standards of the American Correctional Association (ACA), an organization of experts who work in the administration and operation of prisons. The ACA over many years had developed a set of minimum standards that all prisons ought to meet if they are to be run properly. These standards cover how much living space a prisoner needs, common living areas, security, food service, medical care, and every other area of prison operations. To forge the link between the evidence and ACA standards and explain how conditions at KSR fell below acceptable professional standards required the assistance of experts in prison administration.

It was at this juncture that Judge Johnstone's invitation to the U.S. Justice Department to participate in Shorty's lawsuit as amicus curiae first played a critical role. Experts charge fees, and the plaintiffs' legal aid lawyers lacked a budget to pay such fees. The Justice Department, however, had a large budget to pay litigation expenses, and so it performed the crucial role of bringing in most of the experts to inspect KSR and render written opinions on its conditions. Several experts inspected the dormitories and talked with prisoners. One expert in criminal psychology, Dr. Richard Korn, commented on the overcrowding:

> The major and universal symptom [expressed] by inmates is tension brought about by overcrowding in dilapidated, filthy, vermin-infested dormitories. The degree of physical compression fails to provide the minimum amount of privacy and personal space required for maintaining mental health. One inmate expressed the representative feeling: "There is no privacy. No place to be alone. No way to get away from it, unless you go to drugs, and that's only until your high is over. I've been here ten years, and if it weren't for the drugs and some of the home-brew, I'd be down on the nut ward."
>
> Constant over-exposure and over-stimulation leads to bizarre and degrading forms of tension-release. Homosexuality, both consensual and coerced, is endemic, public, and inescapable even to non-participants who are forced to be spectators to noisy, night-long orgies in neighboring bunks. Disturbances of sleep and prevention of sleep are widely reported.[1]

The dormitories themselves were firetraps and breeding grounds for disease. Walls were cracked and filled with mold and fungus. Paint was peeling, lights were broken, and electrical wires were exposed. The roofs and windows leaked so that during storms water dripped on the men and pools formed on the floors. Water pipes leaked and water faucets and toilets were broken. Some inmates attempted to make the plumbing work by poking holes in sewage lines. Odors from human waste escaped through these holes and drifted into the dormitories. Raw sewage sometimes overflowed from the pipes and collected beneath the dormitory floors. Mattresses and blankets were filthy. Some men had no pillows. Fire hoses and fire extinguishers were missing. Five dorms had no fire escapes, and guards did not know how to open the fire escapes that did exist. An expert in environmental health and safety, Theodore Gordon, inspected KSR as well as Eddyville, saw these conditions, and concluded,

> The ventilation systems at both institutions are totally inadequate to remove the obvious accumulations of cigarette smoke, body odor and other odorous impurities. . . . [T]here are five effects resulting from human occupancy of the poorly ventilated living quarters: (1) the oxygen content is reduced, (2) the amount of carbon dioxide present is increased, (3) organic matter and odors are given off from the skin, clothing and mouth of the occupants, (4) the temperature is raised by heat generated in the body processes, and (5) the humidity is increased by the moisture in the breath and evaporation from the skin. . . .
>
> [A] feeling of oppression is experienced in insufficiently ventilated areas and the respiratory organs (lungs) may also be adversely affected. . . . [U]nhygienic air can cause physiological reactions such as nausea, vomiting and depression of breathing. When temperatures and humidity are both high, as often occurs in poorly ventilated cells and dormitories, the inmates may be unable to lose sufficient heat. The body temperature rises, the pulse rate increases and the blood pressure becomes unstable. . . .
>
> [T]he plumbing (handwashing basins, commodes and showers) [was] defective. Countless numbers of leaking plumbing fixtures were observed and it was obvious that the institution had no effective plumbing maintenance program. . . . There were several instances (kitchen, hospital, etc.) in which plumbing connections were such that the drinking water supply could be contaminated with water of unknown or questionable safety. These connections were simply a hose extended down into a sink full of contaminated water. The development of a pressure differential could have moved the contaminants toward the drinking water system and caused a prison-wide water borne disease epidemic, such as dysentery or infectious hepatitis. . . .

Sixty (60) square feet per inmate is considered a minimum space allotment in penal correctional facilities. This allocation of space is not provided under the current average occupancy of the institutions.\. . . . The attack rate of meningococci infection, tuberculosis and other infectious diseases may rise to abnormally high incidence in crowded and confined populations. . . .

There was substantial evidence of a rodent infestation (i.e., rats and mice) especially noticeable in the food service areas, cell blocks, dormitories, and the surrounding exterior premises. The institutions were infested with roaches, as indicated by roachy odors and roaches observed in dormitories, food service, cells and food storage areas. . . .

[I]nsects and rodents can be responsible for the mechanical transmission of bacterial agents that cause infections. Salmonellosis (symptoms: nausea, vomiting, diarrhea and abdominal cramps usually attended with fever) is of particular importance and can be a serious complication for confined persons in crowded facilities. Domestic rodents—rats and mice—are common reservoirs of this organism and it can be transmitted mechanically by filth-breeding insects such as houseflies and cockroaches which seek out food preparation and food storage areas.[2]

Idleness was also a major problem, despite the fact that part of KSR's official mission was to provide opportunities for rehabilitation. There was little for many prisoners to do to pass the time. More than five hundred men at LaGrange had no jobs (an unemployment rate of about 25 percent), meaning that these men did nothing except eat and sleep. Hundreds of men had jobs in places like the kitchen, industrial shops, and the laundry, but all too often more men were put on the jobs than were actually needed. Some jobs officially described as requiring eight hours of work a day could actually be completed in about fifteen minutes. Thus, prisoners often came to regard their jobs as superfluous. It was a poor way to teach a work ethic.

KSR had a vocational school to train prisoners in useful job skills, but the school had only 113 slots. The waiting list had 147 men on it, and prisoners often would be paroled or transferred to another prison before reaching the top of the list. There was an academic school where men could take courses and earn credit toward a degree, but, like the vocational school, there were not enough slots. Men often waited for months to get into school and finally gave up.

The rehabilitation programs did offer caring and skilled instructors to help a relative few men. Dave Vislisel, the academic school principal, was a hero to the men who were admitted into the school. Vislisel was interested in the men as human beings, understood the educational deficits nearly all of them had, and gave the men a good education. But the great majority of prisoners could not get into this gem of a program. At best, KSR was doing very little to prepare the majority of prisoners for life in free society. At worst, the prison was instilling disrespect for work and destroying the men's motivation to improve themselves. In the early 1970s, a few studies were conducted comparing the recidivism rates for prisons with rehabilitation programs with those rates for prisons with no rehabilitation programs. The researchers—particularly Robert Martinson in his article "What Works? Questions and Answers about Prison Reform"—found that the respective recidivism rates were about the same and concluded that prison rehabilitation programs had failed to achieve meaningful results.[3] These studies were exploited by others to justify a "nothing works" doctrine that prison cannot rehabilitate criminals and prisons should be used simply to keep criminals off the streets and punish them.[4] Very little attention was given to whether the rehabilitation programs studied by Martinson and others were adequate or meaningful. It was obvious that the rehabilitation programs at KSR—despite laudable goals and dedicated teachers—were inadequate. At KSR at least, there was no evidence to support the "nothing works" doctrine, because true rehabilitation—such as the school run by Vislisel—never had a chance to serve the majority of prisoners.

Idle men find different ways to pass the time, and at KSR inmates had nearly free rein. Inmates were locked in their wings from 6:00 p.m. to 6:00 A.M., so that for twelve hours fifty to sixty convicts were packed together, largely unsupervised, in space designed for thirty. The guard on duty often was called to the mess hall before 6:00 A.M. to help supervise breakfast. During these early morning hours the entire dormitory would have no guard at all. The result was that stronger prisoners committed massive amounts of crime against weaker prisoners, crimes that can never be detected or recorded: robbery, assault, homosexual rape. If a younger, weaker prisoner was afraid of being raped in his bunk, his solution at KSR was to find a "daddy," an older, stronger homosexual who would protect his charge against rape in return for sex whenever, wherever, and however he wanted it.

Weapons such as knives, pipes, and guns were readily available to inmates who wanted or needed them. A prisoner could buy a sawed-off shotgun on the Yard in about fifteen minutes. It was easy to get drugs and alcohol. If a man wanted moonshine to help pass the time, for example, the only question was whether he wanted apple, strawberry, or some other flavor, for prisoners had stills. Inmates used cash and cigarettes to pay for their contraband and illicit activity. There was a great deal of cash on the Yard, much of it in large denominations, since small rolls of fifty and one hundred dollar bills were easier to hide than large wads of one or five dollar bills.

This idleness and lawlessness threatened the safety and security of the vast majority of average inmates, who wanted only to serve their sentences and go home, in Dr. Korn's opinion:

> The physical safety and security of inmates cannot be protected by custodial staff in the dormitory setting. Inmates are wholly vulnerable to each other and at each other's mercy. The comparatively low number of reported assaults is no index of the degree of intimidation and terror exercised by individuals and groups over others. Effective intimidation does not require overt violence, except on exemplary or unusual occasions. Extortion, exploitation under threat of physical harassment, all forms of oppression are practiced. The only escape possible for the victims is transfer to protective custody—which involves the additional danger and degradation of proclaiming one's helplessness and incurring the reputation of "rat."
>
> Institutional services are so poor and controls so lax that inmates have found it necessary and possible to create their own economic market system, based on cash, exchange of services, contraband and stolen goods. This private economy successfully competes with, and degrades, the system of institutional services, thereby victimizing those who are too poor or too scrupulous to participate in it.
>
> I. Inmates seeking well-laundered and pressed clothing employ a laundry boy, who gives their clothing special attention for a price, while giving minimal attention to the clothes of non-customers.
>
> II. Sandwiches are openly sold in the yard to inmates who cannot tolerate waiting in long lines in the cold for institutional meals.
>
> III. There is widespread belief that green money can buy anything at La-Grange, including:
>
> 1. More desirable jobs or quarters,
> 2. Transfer to a minimum[-security] facility,

3. Drugs, home-brew,

4. "Contracts" on enemies,

5. Knives, pipes, other weapons[5]

An expert in prison operations, Dr. David Fogel, concluded that the people supposedly in control of the prison—the guards—were themselves victims of these conditions:

> The plight of the guards at Kentucky State Reformatory is particularly woeful. The scant coverage exposes them to extraordinary risks resulting in a natural fear to intervene strenuously into unlawful inmate behavior. As a consequence of such timidity (occasioned by staff shortages) inmates are more lawless and potential victims are placed in greater jeopardy of predators. In case of an attack or injury after evening lockdown a guard must be alerted. He in turn has to call Central Administration and request assistance because he is alone. The response time to such an emergency can be as high as thirty minutes. . . .
>
> I also found that KSR is about the most lawless correctional agency I have ever investigated. The money available, smuggling, illicit market, hold-ups and even a kidnapping all combine to make KSR a hazard to the public safety.[6]

Other experts found violations of ACA and other professional standards in other areas of the prison. Working conditions in several industrial shops were dangerous. The classification process was dysfunctional because younger, weaker prisoners were assigned to living units along with older, stronger prisoners, as Shorty's complaint had alleged. There was little treatment of mental illness except to disable sick convicts with drugs.

The lawyers shared this information with the inmates on the Plaintiffs' Committee. Walter listened, and he started to put the many little pieces together. A fuller picture of the prison began to emerge in which the prison could be conceived as a community, with homes, schools, churches, workplaces, a hospital, a kitchen, police, drugs, crime, and unemployment lines. This community was in serious trouble. The wardens and guards knew it, but they were powerless to change it. They were prisoners of their own system.

The challenge Walter set for himself was to understand this community and the forces that had the power to change it and to help formulate some solutions. Walter began to think about the broader issues such as health, safety, and rehabilitation. Conversely, meeting this challenge was beginning a process of personal change in Walter. He was educating himself about the prison so that he could help forge solutions to the problems. Other prisoners started to look to Walter for answers about the lawsuit. Walter had no desire to be a leader, but men were starting to look to him for leadership.

Politics and Litigation

Prison-reform litigation in America is a widespread but extremely complicated process that, unlike ordinary litigation, involves numerous key participants and decision makers. In particular, improvements in inmates' living conditions to even the minimum levels of decency mandated by the constitutional prohibition against cruel and unusual punishment typically require massive new expenditures of public money.[1] Long-accepted principles of federalism, however, prohibit the federal judiciary from directly ordering state and local governments to appropriate funds to remedy constitutional violations unless there is no permissible alternative that would provide the remedy.[2] In the context of prison-reform litigation, these principles severely limit the authority of federal courts to order state legislative and executive officials to fund the cost of improving prison conditions, so it is essential to obtain their agreement to do so. If these officials do not agree or are reluctant to provide the necessary funding, federal litigation can become a form of political leverage, influencing state political and budgetary processes to achieve funding. This phenomenon has been demonstrated in several studies of prison-reform litigation. Bradley Stewart Chilton, for example, notes that Judge Anthony Alaimo, in the Georgia case of *Guthrie v. Evans,* persuaded Governor George Busbee to seek funding for prison reform and that state corrections officials successfully lobbied the legislature to approve such funding, which ultimately totaled nearly $100 million.[3] In the Alabama case, *Pugh v. Locke,* which was marked by far more resistance to prison reform than was *Guthrie,* Larry W. Yackle describes how, despite an apparently willing legislature, executive branch officials led by Governor George Wallace stymied efforts to fund prison improvements, prompting Judge Frank Johnson to engage in a protracted process of achieving funding by patiently prodding the responsible officials.[4]

The Kentucky case provides another example of federal litigation operating as an instrument of political leverage in the world of state politics and budgets. Politics within the Plaintiffs' Committee was mild compared to the political infighting within the Kentucky state government that had been sparked by the litigation attacking conditions at KSR and at Eddyville. The government lawyers defending the commonwealth of Kentucky against Shorty's lawsuit had a dilemma. From both correctional and legal perspectives, they believed that only an idiot could look at Kentucky's two major prisons and not see a need for change. The lawyers knew the prisons were overcrowded, filthy, and out of control and were fully aware of the legal precedents set in other states. In states such as Arkansas, Louisiana, Alabama, and Mississippi, federal judges had found prison conditions beneath human decency, ruled the conditions unconstitutional, and ordered reforms that cost hundreds of millions of dollars. Kentucky's lawyers were convinced that their state faced a similar legal liability if the case went to trial. Moreover, they thought it was bad financial and corrections policy to continue to run the prisons in the traditional manner, pumping public money into institutions that continued to deteriorate at an accelerating rate. The physical infrastructure continued to crumble, and many prisoners came out of these crowded, filthy, dangerous prisons angrier and more lawless than when they entered.

The lawyers believed sweeping change was essential, but their client did not, and therein lay the dilemma. David Bland, the commissioner of corrections and lead defendant in the litigation, favored the status quo. Bland had good intentions, but he was an outsider in the prison system. His academic training and professional experience were in the field of education, so he had very little background in prison administration. His appointment as Kentucky's commissioner of corrections was his first job in prison administration. He had some good ideas and was willing to listen to suggestions. Bland, for example, improved prisoners' academic programs. His weakness was that he had little idea how to address prison-administration problems such as overcrowding, filth, crime, and improper classification that were endemic at KSR and the Eddyville penitentiary. Bland turned to the old guard in the Bureau of Corrections for answers to such problems. He was intimidated by the system's old-timers, who had worked in the prisons for many years and had stock answers to the problems. The old guard had one basic answer: "Ain't no riots, ain't no problems." For the most part, Bland accepted that formula and hewed to the status quo. When the state's lawyers talked to Bland about the need to settle Shorty's lawsuit and avoid a potentially disastrous trial, his instructions were to offer to settle the case only on terms that would maintain the status quo.

The state's lawyers tried to go over Bland's head and talk directly to Governor Julian Carroll. Carroll had less than a year remaining in his term of office, and his final budget had no money designated to pay for major prison reform. Thus, when the lawyers met with Carroll in an attempt to persuade him to order Bland to adopt a more flexible, open-minded policy concerning the litigation, the governor had a short response: "That's for the next governor." Early in the litigation, then, Shorty's lawsuit had no effect on state corrections policy.

A Warehouse Prison

Political attitudes such as Governor Carroll expressed had produced the filthy, overcrowded, and dangerous conditions at KSR. KSR was, in historical perspective, a "warehouse prison," a relic of late-nineteenth-century thinking. According to Charles Stastny and Gabrielle Tyrnauer, the history of American prisons encompasses four models of what a prison ought to be, and each model has emerged as the dominant type of prison at some time in American history. The earliest model was the "enlightenment prison," which had its heyday roughly from 1820 to 1900. In colonial times, criminal offenders were believed to be possessed by evil demons. To exorcise these demons and thus save the offender and protect society, authorities employed as punishment various forms of physical torture, such as whipping. In hopeless cases, the offender was executed. Enlightenment thinkers, however, came to believe that criminals were not possessed by the devil but rather acted of their own free will; hence, punishment should seek to reform criminals rather than exorcise their demons. To achieve the goal of reform, large institutions should be built, with individual cells for each prisoner. Prisoners should be isolated in these cells so that they could contemplate their sins, repent, and return to society as law-abiding citizens. Throughout the nineteenth century, huge, grim, fortresslike prisons with row after row of cells were built in accordance with this thinking and thus came to be known as the "enlightenment prisons."[5] The Kentucky State Penitentiary—*penitentiary* is a term derived from the ideal of a prisoner doing penance—at Eddyville was an example of an enlightenment prison.

The fatal defect of the enlightenment prison, in Stastny's and Tyrnauer's view, was the principle of solitary confinement that was its dominant feature. Isolating prisoners in cells for extended periods of time rarely yielded repentance but instead produced bitter, angry, violent, and often insane people. Nineteenth-century thinkers therefore reduced the emphasis on reforming criminals and instead placed higher priority on protecting society, so that the dominant purpose of a prison was very simple: to incapacitate criminals so they would not threaten society. This thinking produced the warehouse prison, which became the dominant model in the period 1900–1950. Since there was little hope of reforming the prisoners, there was little need for individual cells, except for disciplinary confinement. To confine as many prisoners in as little space as possible, they should be housed in open dormitories and allowed to have contact with each other. In accordance with this thinking, the warehouse prison consisted of a large open space dotted with one- and two-story dormitory buildings, surrounded by fences and guard towers. In reality, guards controlled the periphery, but prisoners themselves largely controlled the interior because they had contact with each other and could form gangs and because stronger inmates could exercise power over weaker inmates.[6] KSR was built in 1937, in the heyday of the warehouse prison. It had open dormitories, the interior was run largely by prisoners, and, despite the title "Reformatory," programs for rehabilitating prisoners were woefully inadequate. For the most part, men spent their days doing little or nothing.

A minority school of thought in the nineteenth century did not abandon the ideal of reform, according to Stastny and Tyrnauer, but rather shifted its focus. It was too much, some believed, to expect a criminal to figure out how to save himself. Rather, outside experts should apply new scientific techniques to criminals to change their behavior. These techniques included industrial training, education, recreation, and psychotherapy. This school of thought remained a minority view throughout the first half of the twentieth century, however, and warehouse prisons like KSR remained the dominant model.[7]

Violent riots in the early 1950s in some of the warehouse prisons, however, prompted a fresh look at American prison policy. Experts determined that the causes of the riots lay in the very nature of the warehouse prison. Inmates were packed into overcrowded dormitories, which resulted in inhumane and degrading living conditions; prison interiors were lawless because they were in the hands of the most aggressive and sophisticated criminals; and guards treated prisoners brutally to compensate for lack of sufficient peaceful means to control the prison interior. Advances in many of the techniques advocated by nineteenth-century reformers, particularly behavior modification, gave rise to new hope that outside experts could rehabilitate prisoners.[8]

These techniques required a new kind of prison. Prisoners should have their own rooms, with minimal comforts not available in old-fashioned cells, so they could learn how to live under somewhat normal conditions. Treatment experts should assume control of the prison interior to end brutal treatment by guards and the lawless regime of prisoners. Programs and activities should be made available to prisoners so they could learn the skills necessary to function in free society. In accordance with this thinking, the second half of the twentieth century has been dominated by the construction of smaller "remedial prisons" with individual rooms for prisoners and separate facilities devoted to schools, libraries, job training, visiting, medical treatment, and recreation.[9] Some of these facilities and techniques were grafted onto the warehouse structure of KSR at various times, but these efforts had little impact on the prisoners' everyday lives.

Although progress in rehabilitation has occurred, the noble goal of the remedial prison has been frustrated largely because treatment personnel have been unable to assume final decision-making authority. From the advent of the remedial prison, treatment experts and security forces have struggled for ultimate decision-making authority. Security personnel generally perceived reform efforts as useless and dangerous because convicts were hopelessly dangerous, so such workers sought to undermine reform efforts. Because political authorities continued to give top priority to preventing escapes and riots, security personnel remained firmly in control of the remedial prison. Efforts at rehabilitation, though not doomed, were largely held in check.[10]

The enlightenment, warehouse, and remedial prisons largely failed. When Shorty filed his lawsuit in 1979, KSR was a classic failed warehouse prison, the product of discredited nineteenth-century thinking. Although genuine attempts had been made to develop some behavior-modification programs, the great majority of inmates were unaffected, and the reform phase that achieved dominance around 1950 largely bypassed KSR. Since U.S. courts, prior to the 1960s, had adopted a hands-off policy toward prisons, the executive and legislative branches of government made the decisions that produced warehouse prisons like KSR.

Old Guard and Reformers

KSR remained a warehouse prison because the prison system was known as the bastard child of Kentucky politics. The Bureau of Corrections had a $24 million budget in 1979, woefully inadequate to pay 1,700 employees, maintain ten prisons, and feed, house, and care for more than 4,000 prisoners. Kentucky was spending less than a dollar a day per prisoner for food, clothing, and shelter. The primary reason inmates lived in squalor at KSR is that the legislative and executive branches of Kentucky state government refused to provide sufficient funding for the Bureau of Corrections to improve living conditions. The prison system was last in line when it came time to divide up Kentucky's public money.

By tradition, Kentucky's governor was the most powerful figure in state government. The governor set overall public policy and formulated the state's budget, and the General Assembly usually acquiesced in the governor's budget. Carroll and his predecessors did not get elected by campaigning for better prisons, because the average voter was indifferent, at best, toward the fate of convicts. The general public had never raised an outcry for decent prisons, preferring—understandably—to use the bulk of tax revenues to pay for education, transportation, and other programs of direct benefit to the public. In addition, Kentucky had a long tradition of spending public money on pork-barrel projects such as dams. Because of public apathy about prisons, gubernatorial policy for the prisons could be summarized by an anecdote related by one of the state's attorneys in the LaGrange case. Upon appointing a corrections commissioner, one Kentucky governor had stated his penal policy succinctly: "I don't want no riots." Throughout this governor's term of office, those were the only words he spoke to the head of the prison system.

The state's lawyers were not alone in trying to buck this long tradition of neglect. The Bureau of Corrections itself was deeply divided over corrections policy. On one side were the reformers, mostly younger career professionals, who believed that the traditional policy was outmoded and that it was time to address problems like overcrowding, filth, and programs for prisoners to better themselves. The other side, the old guard, was content with the status quo and, like Bland, resisted any outside interference with the system.

Shorty's lawsuit became the focus of the policy battle. The reformers in the Bureau of Corrections agreed with much of what the prisoners had complained about and seized on the litigation as an unprecedented opportunity to pressure the governor and General Assembly to make funding available for long-overdue improvements in prison facilities and programs. The lawyers, firmly in the reform camp, wanted to negotiate a settlement that would require extensive improvements in living conditions, which in turn would provide leverage with the executive and legislative branches to increase funding for corrections to pay for the improvements. The old guard, led by Bland, did not agree and thought the state's attorneys wanted to give away the store. Bland and his compatriots believed that the state should oppose the lawsuit in virtually every respect. The result of this dissension was that Bland and the state's attorneys worked at cross-purposes. Thus divided internally, the state was unable to agree on its own negotiating position, so negotiations to settle the prison-reform litigation remained at a standstill throughout 1979.

In ordinary litigation, a client has the right to fire his lawyers, but Commissioner Bland was not an ordinary client because he lacked such authority. The Bureau of Corrections was a component of the Kentucky Department of Justice, so the commissioner of corrections was subordinate to the secretary of the Department of Justice. The lawyers worked directly for the secretary, and the corrections commissioner had to report to the secretary, a member of the governor's cabinet. The secretary, Jack Smith, was an ally of the reformers. Smith had an open mind about the prisons, was willing to listen to arguments for change, and was not willing to fire his lawyers. Instead, Smith gave the lawyers permission to seek to settle Shorty's lawsuit.

Another powerful political ally of the reformers was Robert Stephens, who had served with Judge Edward Johnstone on the advisory committee on the Eddyville penitentiary in the early 1970s and had seen the appalling living conditions. Stephens was now Kentucky's elected attorney general, and he believed it was time to reform the prisons because it was the right thing to do. The governor had to pay heed to the views of the attorney general on legal matters, including Shorty's lawsuit.

John Y. Brown

The climate in state government changed dramatically in favor of the reform faction in corrections with the November 1979 gubernatorial election, ten months into Shorty's lawsuit. The voters elected John Young Brown Jr. as the next governor. John Y., as folks called him, was not a professional politician. He was a successful businessman, a millionaire many times over. Years ago he had met an old gentleman who sported a white goatee, wore string ties, and ran a restaurant in a small town in eastern Kentucky specializing in "finger-lickin' good" fried chicken. An official Kentucky colonel, the old fellow was Harlan Sanders. Brown saw a business opportunity in the colonel's chicken and proposed the idea of selling it all around the United States in small franchise outlets. The colonel agreed, and thus was born Kentucky Fried Chicken, a business that made Brown extremely wealthy.

Though not a professional politician, Brown came by political ambition in a natural way. His father, John Y. Brown Sr., was a successful lawyer prominent in Kentucky Democratic politics. John Y. Brown Jr. turned his attention to the pursuit of power and easily won the Democratic nomination for governor. There was speculation that he intended to use the office as a stepping-stone to the U.S. Senate, and when he won the gubernatorial election, his political future looked bright.

Brown presented himself to the voters as an independent politician who had not risen through the ranks of the Democratic Party and who was not beholden to the party regulars who were accustomed to getting their friends elected and having their friends run the government based on the tenets of cronyism and political favoritism. Brown owed few political favors and based his campaign on bringing change to state government. Brown assumed the governorship with an open mind on the issues of the day.

The first important political event after the election was the prelegislative conference in late November. The new governor and newly elected members of the General Assembly did not take office until January 1980. The prelegislative conference consisted of orientation sessions for new legislators, selection of the legislative leadership, and assignment of legislators to committees. The conference sought to organize the General Assembly for the beginning of the official legislative session in January. The governor-elect attended the conference to discuss the major issues facing state government for the next two years, so it was one of Brown's first significant appearances in his new job.

The state's lawyers in Shorty's case arrived at the prelegislative conference as guests of their reform-minded ally, Attorney General Stephens. Stephens arranged for them to talk to legislative leaders and representatives of Brown's incoming administration about the prison system's needs. Never before had the bastard child of Kentucky politics commanded such attention from the politicians, and the reason was Shorty's lawsuit. The case was scheduled for trial in federal court in less than five months. If the case was not settled, the facts revealed in discovery and the opinions rendered by the experts indicated that Judge Johnstone would almost certainly rule the conditions unconstitutional and order sweeping change at KSR and the penitentiary. Not only was the state's legal position weak, but Stephens also believed the prisons should be reformed as a matter of sound correctional policy. As the state's chief legal officer, he had the standing to command the new governor's attention.

The state's lawyers made a presentation at the prelegislative conference about the policy implications of the prison litigation. They described similar lawsuits in other states, where the government had refused to settle out of court, gone to trial, lost, and been ordered to reform prison conditions. The costs of complying with the court orders in those states were staggering: North Carolina, $85 million; Oklahoma, $70 million; Louisiana, a whopping $240 million. The costs were high even in states that had settled such cases. In Georgia, for example, the lawyers estimated the cost of implementing a settlement at $96 million. Shorty's lawsuit, in essence, was a big-money issue that the legislature and the new governor would face. The lawyers told the legislative and executive leaders that approximately $50 million would be required to upgrade KSR and the Eddyville penitentiary: $25 million would build a new prison to ease overcrowding, $12 million would renovate buildings at KSR, $10 million would rebuild facilities at Eddyville, and the remaining $3 million would be needed to expand smaller, minimum-security prisons. The litigation was presented to the politicians as a dollars-and-cents proposition: it would be cheaper to spend $50 million to settle the case than to go to trial and risk having a federal judge order changes costing anywhere from $70 million to $240 million. The lawyers raised the further specter that the federal court might even assume control of the prisons, as Judge Johnson had nearly done in Alabama.[11]

The politicians balked in public. Outgoing Governor Carroll said inflation made it impossible to start any new spending programs. One legislative leader, Joe Clarke, said that he didn't know "where the money is coming from." Another legislator, Kenneth Gibson, said that it would be difficult for the prison request "to stand up against needs for roads, education and other things of interest and benefit to the public."[12]

The real business, however, was conducted behind the scenes. Stephens and the state's lawyers had direct, private conversations with Brown. The attorneys focused their efforts more on the new governor than on the legislature because if the governor's budget allocated more money for the prisons, then by Kentucky tradition the General Assembly likely would acquiesce. Moreover, it was important to make the lawyers' views known to Brown before Bland and the old guard presented their side of the case. This strategy worked: the lawyers found that the new governor had an open mind about the prisons and was receptive to new ways of running the prison system. Perhaps the founder of Kentucky Fried Chicken understood that it was bad business to invest millions of dollars in prisons and then watch the investment crumble under the weight of neglectful policy and to risk a court order that might cost up to $240 million when he might be able to settle the case for $50 million. The lawyers came away convinced the prisons would no longer be the bastard child of Kentucky politics, and that come January 1980, when Brown took office, prison reform would be a high priority in state government.

Commissioner Wilson

Back in his dormitory at KSR, Shorty read the newspaper reports about the prelegislative conference and the proposal to appropriate $50 million to upgrade the prisons. He was disturbed that $50 million might be added to the corrections budget while it was still controlled by Bland and the old guard, so he wrote a letter to all the state's major newspapers.

The reason for this sudden interest in prisons is a suit in the Federal Courts filed by prisoners here at LaGrange and at Eddyville.

It seems that the present and past administration have neglected the prisons in this state until they are unfit to house even the dregs of society.

Due to the negligence of the bureaucrats and other officials in the Bureau of Corrections, the living quarters of the prisons have deteriorated until they are unfit for occupancy. The overcrowding of the prisons creates tension and unrest among the inmates which results in murders, assaults, dope taking and homosexual rapes. Prisoners are afraid to go to sleep at night for fear that some psychopath will stick a knife in him while he is unable to defend himself.

This letter is to inform the public of the conditions of your prisons and to put you on notice that unless somebody cares about how your tax money is spent, you may pour fifty million more dollars down the same rat-hole. Where has all the money gone that was appropriated in the past for maintenance and up-keep of your prisons? Are you willing to place fifty million dollars more in the same hands that mishandled your money in the past?

Mr. Bland and the Bureau of Corrections seems to have access to the news media at any time. It's time the public heard the full story. This reformatory is maintained by your tax dollars. The public has the right to know what goes on here. Why don't you come in and look the place over? Don't take the Warden's guided tour. Let the inmates show you around. You will find that things aren't the way they should be.

Once the prelegislative conference ended, Brown turned his attention to the search for people to fill the top executive positions in his administration, including commissioner of the Bureau of Corrections. Bland was the incumbent, he expressed his desire to remain in the post, and he had the support of the old guard. The state's lawyers, however, saw the same problem with Bland that Shorty saw. Merely allocating additional money for the corrections system would do little to improve living conditions and the administration of the prisons as long as Bland was commissioner. The attorneys believed that it was time for reform-minded professionals to take over corrections, so they and other reformers pushed the governor to appoint a new corrections commissioner, a man named George Wilson.

Wilson and Bland were bitter enemies. Wilson was a career professional in corrections, but he fiercely opposed the old ways of running prisons. He had a bachelor of arts degree in history and political science from Kentucky State University and a master's of science degree in social work from the University of Louisville. As a licensed social worker, Wilson spent several years working in treatment centers for juvenile offenders, then held the post of deputy commissioner for institutions in the Bureau of Corrections for more than three years, working directly under Bland. Wilson had new ideas about prisons, ideas that did not sit well with the old guard. He believed that too many people were in prison and that the current prison system failed to make streets and homes safer for law-abiding citizens. If society wanted to continue the failed policy of putting too many people in prison, Wilson believed society ought to foot the bill for safe and decent prisons.

I've seen very few hotel prisons, country-club facilities. The only ones I know of are federal prisons, and those usually are for rich, white-collar criminals.

Prisons are necessary, but I think they have been overused. Prisons are about public safety. People have a right to feel safe and secure. To the extent that prisons serve that end, they are justified. To the degree they don't, they're unnecessary. Therein lies the rub. We use prisons for everything. They have very little to do with public safety.

Many people are in prisons for reasons other than that they are dangerous or that the community is in jeopardy. I'd say the only reason why we have prisons is for the security and safety of the community. And there are people in prison for reasons other than protecting the community. So that means there's a problem. Prisons have been overutilized.

Some people don't have any money. We know that people go to prison because they don't have money. That's about as factual as anything. Most people will agree that that's not right, but they go to prison anyway. If you don't have a good lawyer, your chances improve immensely to go to prison. Race, culture, and background have a lot to do with your chances of going to prison. And that doesn't have anything to do with the security and safety of the community.

There are people who are locked up who don't need to be. There are many people in prison that could be dealt with in other ways and should be dealt with in other ways.

That's one of the problems we're wrestling with today. Those issues are not very well delineated and very well separated. There is a tremendous amount of confusion in the minds of the public about their well-being and their safety.

There's a false security and a tremendous hoax going on in the country. The public thinks everybody who possibly is a threat or a risk to them is in prison or locked up in jail. And that's not the case. My philosophy is that people who are dangerous ought to be in prison. People who deserve to be in prison ought to go, and they ought to spend the appropriate amount of time. I just don't think that everybody who breaks laws and who [is] dangerous [goes] to prison.

I don't think the scale is balanced. I have two kids, and I'm as concerned about their welfare and safety as anybody. If somebody would maim or maul or rape or do something to my children, I [would] want justice. But it shouldn't be just certain people who receive so-called justice. That's why we have the problem we have today, is that there's not a good balance today in the justice system.

The public believes that there's a black killer-rapist behind every bush. That's how it's portrayed on TV. They all think killers and rapists are black, because that's how it's depicted usually. And if the public thinks they're being jeopardized by black killers, rapists, then they build up all kinds of defenses to it.

It happens every day. And there's an overreaction. Laws are passed and people are mobilized based on those kinds of images, and that's how public policy is made. That's what happens. People think if you can build more prisons, they'd be more safe. That may or may not be true. In most cases, it is not true. And that's not good public policy, and that's not good business.

You can't have it both ways. If you want more people locked up, you have to pay for them. . . . And the people are paying for it. They ought to know they're spending millions of dollars for it. Politicians don't communicate that to the public. And they just go about on their merry way and think that they are safe and secure if they spend millions of dollars. And in fact they're in as much jeopardy, if not more, than before. And that's wrong.

As deputy commissioner, Wilson disagreed frequently with Bland over policy and personnel. One of their fiercest conflicts concerned a warden at Eddyville named Donald Bordenkircher, the same man who told Wilgus to go file a "goddamn writ" if he wanted a bigger blanket. Wilson was convinced that Bordenkircher condoned brutality toward prisoners, and Wilson campaigned to have Bland fire Bordenkircher. The commissioner refused, under pressure from the old guard. The incident was a major defeat for Wilson and the reform faction in corrections. About the same time, Wilson suffered a terrible personal loss when his thirty-one-year-old wife died of illness, leaving him with two children, ages eight and five. Under the pressure of these professional and personal losses, he resigned as deputy commissioner in September 1979, two months before Brown was elected governor.

Wilson was gone, but corrections reformers had not forgotten him. They campaigned to have Brown appoint Wilson as commissioner of corrections, and the new governor agreed to interview Wilson. In the interview, Wilson expressed strong ideas about how the Kentucky prison system should be changed and said that he agreed with many of the improvements being sought in the prison litigation. Wilson was black, and no black person in Kentucky had ever held such a high position in state government. Brown, however, was interested in Wilson's ideas, not his race. The new governor liked what Wilson had to say, and race was not a problem for Brown.

Oftentimes in change of administration top-level positions are usually looked at, and in many cases are turned over. In this case I think the governor made the assessment that given my background and some things that he had heard about me, that I might be the best person for the job.

He first interviewed me for secretary of justice, but he wanted to combine that position with commissioner of corrections. After some discussion between us, I thought the dual role would mean maybe just a little bit too much, given the complexities of the Corrections Bureau and some of the problems that were going on in Justice. Those two roles together may be a little much. So I asked him which one could I help him the best in, and he

decided that it was the Corrections Bureau. Based on that I was made the
commissioner.

Wilson was now the highest-ranking black person in the history of Kentucky state government. As commissioner, he was the chief policy maker for a prison system that was in deep trouble. On the inside, it was deeply divided over policy. On the outside, Judge Johnstone had scheduled the class-action prison cases to go to trial in federal court on April 7, 1980, now less than three months away, and the prisoners' lawyers, aided by the U.S. Department of Justice, had built an apparently overwhelming case. In addition, Wilson faced a second deadline, also less than three months away. With the General Assembly now in session, the prison budget had to be completed and approved by April 15, 1980, when the legislative session ended. Wilson was determined to negotiate a settlement of the litigation but could do so only if money to renovate and reform the prisons was in that budget, so a bruising fight loomed in the General Assembly. The new commissioner was sitting on the hottest seat in state government.

The Kentucky prison litigation, within a year of its assignment to Judge Johnstone, thus provided leverage for significant change in Kentucky prison politics. The reform faction in the Bureau of Corrections, supported by the Justice Department secretary and the attorney general, persuaded the new governor to commit to budgeting for the estimated cost of upgrading prisoners' living conditions as a means of settling the case rather than risking a more costly defeat at trial. Once this money was in the governor's budget, the General Assembly would be under enormous pressure to approve the funding. Moreover, the reformers also convinced the governor to appoint a new commissioner of corrections, again using the need to settle the litigation as the focal point for the argument that the incumbent commissioner adamantly opposed the reforms sought by the plaintiffs.

The propriety of using institutional-reform litigation as leverage to influence executive and legislative decision making has been challenged by critics as usurpation of state authority. In particular, court orders that require substantial restructuring of prisons at great cost to states have been attacked as an illegitimate assumption of the power of the purse. Defenders of judicial power to issue orders that influence state politics and budgets argue that traditional notions of federalism should yield to judicial intervention where state officials have refused to use state funds to house prisoners in humane, civilized institutions. While this study of the Kentucky litigation does not attempt to resolve that debate, it is clear that, contrary to the findings of one empirical study, this litigation had a major impact on state government by providing the leverage by which the reform faction seized control of corrections and achieved a major victory in the battle to garner dramatically higher funding for corrections.[13]

Judge Johnstone Visits LaGrange

On January 24, 1980, the day before Governor John Y. Brown publicly announced George Wilson's appointment as the new commissioner of corrections, Judge Edward Johnstone held a pretrial conference at the federal courthouse in Louisville. The primary reason for this conference was that the state's lawyers had formally requested to delay the trial set for April 7. They argued that Kentucky had a new governor, and the new administration needed more time to formulate its policies toward the prisons and to lobby the legislature to approve the governor's proposed increase in corrections funding.

The prisoners' lawyers, unaware of the link between the political infighting in the Bureau of Corrections and the now-dominant reform faction's need to consolidate its victory by reformulating prison policy, opposed the request. The prisoners' attorneys thought that the state's lawyers had concluded that, based on the information produced in discovery, Judge Johnstone almost certainly would rule in the prisoners' favor at trial, and a delay in the trial might produce some unexpected good luck that would turn the tide of battle. The prisoners' lawyers calculated that what was at stake in the request for a delay was far more than merely putting off the day of judgment for a few months. Perhaps foremost, the Plaintiffs' Committee was adamant that no delay should be allowed, and it was vital to keep their trust. In addition, preliminary negotiations to settle the case had begun, and the trial date represented a deadline for the prison authorities to decide whether to agree to improve the prisons or face near-certain defeat at trial. The trial date maintained the pressure on the state to offer a reasonable proposal to settle, but if the trial were put off, the negotiations might lose momentum. The pressure on the General Assembly would also be reduced because, without a trial in progress as the April 15 budget deadline approached, legislative leaders might be tempted to reject the governor's proposed increase for corrections on the ground that there was no pressing need. The governor himself might even back off his commitment to seek increased prison funding. The prisoners' lawyers believed the April 7 trial date was one of the most important components of the leverage this litigation afforded to induce the additional expenditures essential to improving the lot of the inmates, so how the judge ruled on the request for a delay was a test of his commitment: was he serious about reaching a legitimate solution to the problem, or would it be business as usual at the prisons? Viewed in this context, the January 24 pretrial conference was likely to profoundly affect the litigation's outcome.

The prisoners' lawyers had an additional concern. They and the Plaintiffs' Committee were eager to have Judge Johnstone personally view the conditions at KSR. The lawyers and experts, the state's experts included, were well aware of the appalling conditions at the prison. Even the state's own experts had concluded that the living conditions fell so far beneath professionally accepted minimum standards that KSR was not fit for human habitation. One very important person still knew very little about KSR, however—the federal judge. Judge Johnstone was familiar with the overcrowding, filth, violence, and brutality of the maximum-security penitentiary at Eddyville. KSR, however, was new territory for Judge Johnstone, for he had never been there, not even as a member of the advisory committee which had, in any event, focused on the penitentiary. Moreover, newspapers had never carried shocking stories about guard brutality toward prisoners at KSR, although such reports had appeared about Eddyville.

The lawyers sought to encourage a judicial tour of KSR for several reasons. Shorty and the other members of the Plaintiffs' Committee were
pushing enthusiastically for such a visit because, as Wilgus put it, "We
knew if we could ever get him there that we had the case locked up." Not
only was it incumbent on the lawyers to respect their clients' wishes, but
also the prospects for settling the case on terms that would produce substantial benefits for the inmates would be enhanced if the judge became
sensitized to the living conditions at KSR: if he was appalled at what he
saw, he would be more likely to push vigorously for a settlement that would
eliminate such conditions. If the case instead went to trial, the prisoners'
lawyers were confident that such a tour would solidify an already strong
case. By 1980, it was well established that housing prisoners in conditions that offend civilized notions of human dignity and that serve no legitimate penological purpose violates the Eighth Amendment prohibition
against cruel and unusual punishment. A recent U.S. Supreme Court decision in an Arkansas case had decisively established as federal law the
pathbreaking decisions of federal district court judges in cases such as
Holt v. Sarver, Gates v. Collier, Battle v. Anderson, and *Pugh v. Locke* that
had adopted this interpretation of the Eighth Amendment.[1] Contrary to
the criticism that Judges Smith Henley, William Keady, Luther Bohanon,
and Frank Johnson had usurped authority in these cases, the Court in
Hutto v. Finney affirmed the district court's ruling that inmates could not
be sentenced to more than thirty days in punitive isolation on the ground
that "taken as a whole, conditions in the isolation cells continued to violate the prohibition against cruel and unusual punishment," so the thirty-
day limit was an appropriate remedy for the violation.[2] The conditions
at KSR and the penitentiary—particularly the overcrowding—were sufficiently similar to the conditions in the prison cases already decided that
the prisoners' lawyers were reasonably confident that Judge Johnstone
would reach the same conclusion that conditions in Kentucky's two major
prisons were unconstitutional, particularly if he personally viewed KSR.

The immediate problem confronting the lawyers was how to arrange
such a tour without tipping off the KSR staff. If the lawyers followed formal
procedure by making a written request, perhaps holding a hearing on the
request, and scheduling in advance a date and time for the judge's visit,
KSR authorities would certainly be notified ahead of time. With advance
warning, they might attempt to cover up some of the worst conditions:
mopping the floors, plugging the worst leaks, painting some walls, replac-

ing broken glass, dumping garbage, transferring some prisoners for a few days. The lawyers had heard stories from reliable sources that such efforts had occurred in other cases in other states, and the attorneys did not want this sort of thing to happen at KSR. The lawyers decided to use informal channels to communicate to Judge Johnstone the need for an unannounced visit. They spoke to his law clerk and to his secretary about such a tour and simply asked the judge himself whether he had ever seen KSR, without directly requesting that he visit.

On the afternoon of January 24, 1980, all the lawyers walked into Judge Johnstone's law library for the pretrial conference and sat at the huge table in the middle. The judge took his place at the head of the table, dressed in a dark business suit, and spoke and acted in a far more formal manner than in previous conferences. It was apparent that he also viewed the state's request for a delay as a critical turning point in the case. The lawyers told the judge what progress they had made in preparing the case, mainly gathering information in the discovery process. The prisoners' lawyers made it clear they fully expected to be well prepared for the trial and they were eager to try the case. The lawyers for the state explained their request for a delay in the trial. The two sides argued back and forth for a few minutes. Once the lawyers were finished, silence fell over the room, and it felt as if the case hung in the balance.

The silence lasted only a few seconds, but it felt much longer. Johnstone announced, in a deliberate and solemn voice, that there would be no trial delay. The April 7 trial date had been set nearly a year ago, he said, and all parties knew about it. The judge's manner was respectful to the state, but he stood firm and denied the request for a delay. Equally important, his action reconfirmed that this case was top priority for the federal court. The judge immediately stunned every person in the library. It was about 5:30 P.M., but Judge Johnstone said he was free that evening, and if no one minded he would like to drive out to KSR and tour the prison. All the participants dashed to their cars and made the half-hour drive up Interstate 71 to LaGrange. In the caravan were the judge, two federal marshals for security, and nine lawyers.

This delegation arrived at KSR shortly after 6:00 P.M. and walked up to the main entrance of the prison. The lead lawyer for the state told the doorkeeper that the federal judge was here to see the prison. The doorkeeper's eyes widened in apparent surprise, likely because a federal judge had never before toured the reformatory. His key unlocked the entrance door with a harsh metallic thump, and the door squeaked open. Judge Johnstone entered KSR for the first time.

It appeared to the prisoners' lawyers that, despite the surprise nature of the visit, somebody had notified KSR staff that the judge was coming. Though it was dinnertime, prisoners were busily mopping the floor in the entryway, and the smell of fresh paint along the walls of the entrance hallway was unmistakable. If in fact there had been an attempt to cover up the squalor of KSR, it failed pathetically. A half-century of neglect could not be concealed on a half hour's notice, so the remainder of the tour was all reality.

This was no warden's public-relations tour. Johnstone politely requested that prisoners escort him around KSR. The lawyers had Shorty, the lead plaintiff and acknowledged spokesman for the class members, summoned from the Yard. Shorty met the delegation on the other side of the entrance building, in the interior of the prison compound. Nearly a foot taller and a hundred pounds heavier than Shorty, the judge had to bend over to shake the prisoner's hand. They made quite a contrast, the tall judge in a dark business suit and parka and the short inmate in blue jeans and sweatshirt. The judge looked Shorty in the eye, cracked a big, friendly grin, and said, "Hi. I'm Ed Johnstone, and I'd like you to show me around."

It was suppertime for the prisoners, so Shorty first took Judge Johnstone over to the mess hall. It was a cold January night, well below freezing. Wind was blowing and snow was falling. Outside the entrance to the mess hall stood a line of approximately one hundred men wearing thin jackets and no gloves or hats. They hunched over against the wind, and all were silent. These inmates simply stood shivering in the cold, shuffling a step forward every thirty seconds or so. Shorty told Johnstone that it would take a man about a half hour to go through the line to get out of the cold and another half hour to pick up food and that this misery occurred because there were too many prisoners at KSR.

Shorty led the judge into the mess hall, which was very noisy, in stark contrast to the silence in the outside line. The moment the judge entered, however, silence blanketed the big hall, and everyone stopped eating. Every inmate in the mess hall, hundreds of them, stared at the delegation. The news about the federal judge's visit had traveled quickly through the Yard, and it was obvious that every prisoner knew who this big man was and why he was there. The two federal marshals looked around nervously, because their job was to protect the judge, and they feared that this crowd might contain vengeful convicts that Johnstone had sent to prison when he was a state circuit judge in western Kentucky. Johnstone himself, though, appeared utterly relaxed. He asked if he could try the food, so Shorty escorted him to the front of the line. If he had been a prisoner cutting in line, there would have been a problem, but the men at the front of the line understood the gravity of the occasion and stood aside for the judge. Johnstone picked up a tray and ate the same supper as the prisoners, except for the pudding, which had a cockroach in it. After supper, the delegation headed out into the cold, snowy night to dormitory 4. The judge walked in and saw trash, peeling paint, cracked walls, broken windows letting in the January wind, bunk beds crammed together about a foot apart, and leaking toilets. He sat down on beds and talked to some inmates: "Hi, I'm Ed Johnstone. What's your name? Where are you from? What are you in here for?" He had a way of getting these men to talk, perhaps because he spoke to them with keen interest and respect. Wilgus was in dormitory 4 that evening.

> Johnstone . . . was asking where the water fountain was at there in th' upper left o' 4. The guy told him, said, "Right thar's the only place where you c'n git any water." And the guy pointed directly at a sink where when you pushed the button the water'd shoot up in your face. And it was cockroaches ever'where.

The delegation moved on through the other dorms and eventually came to dorm 9, where Shorty lived. Shorty witnessed a strange but familiar incident.

> Judge Johnstone was coming through dorm 9. The deputy warden in charge of the physical plant was there—maintenance of the buildings and all that stuff.
> We'd been complaining about the heat, 'specially in upper right wing of dorm 9. We were out in the hallway there, second floor. I was telling Judge Johnstone about not having any heat up there. I told him that the return lines on the steam system needed draining, that they was waterlogged.
> The deputy warden said, "This dormitory don't have steam heat." He was standing right under the steam radiator. Johnstone looked at me, and

I pointed up, and he looked up and shook his head. And the deputy warden had said that these dorms are not steam heated. I felt me and Judge Johnstone was sharing something, that we had caught this high-ranking official in a lie, together.

The tour wound down to an end. Judge Johnstone had seen with his own eyes the conditions at KSR, and they surprised him. He had not known how desperate were the conditions at KSR. By sitting on bunk beds and conversing directly with convicts about how it felt to maintain their dignity in such squalor, the judge now had a context for understanding both the settlement proposals that might be presented in negotiations and the evidence that would be presented if the case went to trial.

Reflecting on his visit to KSR that cold January night, Johnstone thought that what he observed at KSR—bugs, human waste, overcrowding, and the like—was simply wrong. Just as with people, he believed it was important to probe beneath the surface of a prison, so he went to KSR to become educated about the reality of the prison. His strategy was to ask questions of the inmates, not the wardens. He was vividly impressed when an inmate told him there were bugs. Johnstone said, "Well, I don't see any bugs. Where are they?" The man pulled out his radio from under his bunk and removed the back, revealing cockroaches crawling throughout the interior. The judge realized that the prisoners had shown him living conditions of which very few people were aware, such as human refuse six inches thick flowing free under the dorm floors because the plumbing was broken. The judge suspected that even prison authorities were unaware of many of the problems, as in the case of the deputy warden for maintenance, who appeared not to know the dorms were steam heated.

While Judge Johnstone believed he was performing his judicial duty by viewing the prison for himself, critics of judicial activism might deride his visit as a departure from the neutral, detached attitude that judges ought to assume. Conversely, proponents of a more proactive model of judging as a legitimate response to the complicated process of addressing abuses of power in the modern bureaucratic state would probably applaud such a visit as a means of educating the judge about the underlying problems that gave rise to the litigation.[3] John J. DiIulio Jr., for example, argues that judges "are rarely in a good position to know the actual state of affairs inside prisons" and should not remain cloistered in their chambers if they anticipate the possibility of sweeping court-ordered reform. Instead, they should view the living conditions for themselves.[4] Within the context of this endless debate over the proper role of a judge and the legitimacy of judicial intervention into administrative functions, it is clear that Judge Johnstone concluded that key decision makers in state government, including key legislative leaders, would have to become educated about the living conditions at KSR to bring about change that would benefit the inmates.

This is a petition signed by only six prisoners. We hope that it will be treated as a class action petition.

If we were permitted to do so, we could get several hundred other prisoners to sign. However, it is our under-standing that it is against institutional rules to circulate a petition. Also, most prisoners feel that the administration would take reprisal action against them if they signed.

We hope that the Court will overlook any misspelling, bad grammar and punctuation.

We sincerely hope that the Court will investigate our complaint and that we can get some relief soon. Especially now that winter is coming on and our living quarters will be even more crowded because of bad weather and people will be staying inside more.

Respectfully yours,

James M. Thompson.

Original, handwritten petition by James M. "Shorty" Thompson
(signatures of five other inmates omitted). Source: United States
District Court for the Western District of Kentucky.

Overcrowding and
idleness at KSR.
Source: *The Courier-
Journal.*

Inmates waiting for lunch at KSR. Main tower in background.
Source: *The Courier-Journal.*

Some members of the Plaintiffs' Committee. Shorty is third from the right.
Wilgus is on the left. The author is third from the left. Source: author.

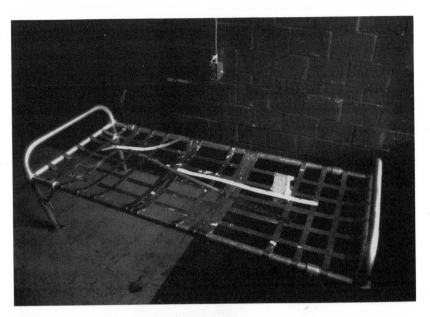

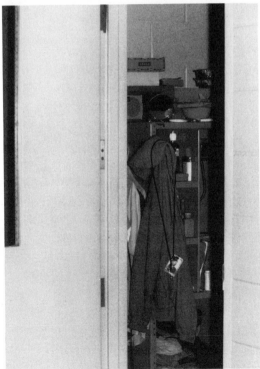

Above: Typical cot on which KSR inmates' mattresses were placed. Source: author.

Left: Inmate's single room in newly renovated KSR dormitory. Source: author.

Judge Edward H. Johnstone,
United States District Court for
the Western District of Kentucky.
Source: *The Courier-Journal.*

Kentucky Commissioner of
Corrections George Wilson.
Source: *The Courier-Journal.*

Negotiation and Settlement

All the participants in the litigation believed that Judge Edward Johnstone would attempt to encourage a settlement. Nearly a year earlier, when he appointed the author of this book to represent Shorty and the other named plaintiffs, the big man had pointed his huge right index finger at the lawyer and rumbled in his deep western Kentucky drawl, "I want a consent decree." Johnstone, likely influenced by his talk with Judge Frank Johnson in Alabama, believed the chances for true reform were greater if the state willingly agreed to change the prisons than if change was imposed from the federal courthouse. Johnstone sought to motivate all the participants—politicians, prison officials, prisoners, and lawyers—to work together to achieve a shared goal of better prisons, because he had a deep conviction that improvements in social conditions are best achieved when people work together toward shared goals.

Prospects for settlement looked bright when George Wilson was appointed commissioner of corrections. The lawyers took depositions of Wilson and the various wardens at LaGrange and Eddyville throughout the fall of 1979 and the winter of 1980, and all of these officials candidly admitted in sworn testimony that conditions at the two prisons were extremely undesirable and expressed willingness to work for change if they had enough resources. To obtain the needed funding, Wilson's staff prepared a budget request that the General Assembly authorize $50 million to finance prison improvement. The prisoners' lawyers began work on a proposal to settle the lawsuit. Shorty, Wilgus, Walter, and the rest of the Plaintiffs' Committee were not pleased with the prospect of settlement, because they wanted a trial in open court, not a backdoor deal that would entrench the status quo. The lawyers urged the plaintiffs to be patient, keep an open mind, and wait to see the state's first offer.

Signs of trouble began to appear in mid-February, less than two months before the trial date. Governor John Y. Brown Jr. made public statements that the state of Kentucky was running short of money, and he then froze all spending for capital construction. Perhaps the most powerful figure in the General Assembly, House Speaker William Kenton of Lexington, was reported as saying the actual price tag for prison reform was $200 million. Some legislators said Wilson needed only $17 million to fix up the prisons. The chairman of the key House Appropriations and Revenue Committee, Joe Clarke from Danville, said he had heard about the $17 million figure but denied that he knew where it came from.[1]

It appeared that the old guard in the Bureau of Corrections was behind this disarray. David Bland was no longer commissioner, but the old guard remained. Bureaucracies rarely change as quickly as their leaders, and the bureau was no exception. There were rumors that the old guard had plugged into the "good old boy" network of Kentucky politics and was lobbying legislators about the budget. There were even whispers that the old guard was pressuring the governor's top advisers to take a hard line in negotiations with the prisoners.

Judge Johnstone had his own contacts in state politics from his years of political campaigning in western Kentucky, so he was aware of the political maneuvering and took affirmative steps to influence the political process. He ordered the lawyers to appear before him on March 7, 1980, and present in open court their proposals to settle the case, a move designed to trump all the rumors and to pressure the Brown administration and the

General Assembly to make the hard decisions about what they were actually willing to do to alleviate the problems at KSR and Eddyville.

Sheldon Shafer, Reporter

By late February, with the deadline for presenting the parties' respective settlement proposals just a few weeks away, the prisoners' lawyers decided it was time for the general public to receive information about the conditions at KSR. In a case as politically charged as this one, where so much depended on what the governor and General Assembly were willing to fund, the lawyers surmised that it would be beneficial for the public to find out what KSR was like, because politicians are affected by public opinion. The lawyers found Sheldon Shafer, a reporter for Louisville-based *Courier-Journal,* the largest and most influential newspaper in Kentucky. His assignment was to cover the news in the small towns and counties east of Louisville, which included Oldham County, where KSR was located, so a story about KSR would be within Shafer's news beat.

The prisoners' lawyers were chary of approaching Shafer directly, out of concern that they would be accused of being unethical glory-seekers. They had a contact, however, Brad Casselberry, a prisoners'-rights advocate who worked for the Southern Prisoners' Defense Committee and had often provided liaison between the prisoners and the outside world. Casselberry's wife, Sonie, worked with Shafer, and the two men knew each other, so the lawyers asked Casselberry to speak to Shafer about KSR.

Casselberry called Shafer and described the lawsuit. Shafer was interested, but not because he was a crusader for prison reform. He believed that if a person committed a serious crime, the punishment should be time in prison and that the time in prison would make law-abiding citizens safer and might deter future criminal conduct. Shafer knew nothing about living conditions inside prisons. Moreover, there was little in Shafer's background to suggest that he would take an active interest in a major lawsuit and political controversy over prison reform. He was raised on a farm in a rural county in northeast Indiana, north of Fort Wayne, and went to Indiana University, where basketball, not social protest, is king. He majored in government and journalism and served as editor of the student newspaper, the *Indiana Daily Student.* During the Vietnam War, Shafer enlisted in the army, did a year's training, went through Infantry Officers' Candidate School, and received a commission as a second lieutenant. The Vietnam War was raging, but unlike Walter Harris, Shafer saw no jungle combat. He was not even sent to Vietnam but instead was assigned elsewhere to army intelligence. He was in Chicago during the antiwar protests at the 1968 Democratic National Convention and was then transferred to Iran and finally Turkey. Shafer finished his military enlistment and returned home to Indiana to start a career in journalism. He spent three years learning the trade with a newspaper in Fort Wayne. It was not social consciousness or political ideology that brought this Hoosier farm boy and military-intelligence analyst into the big-city newsroom. Shafer simply enjoyed the work.

Friends from school helped him land a job with the *Courier-Journal*, and Shafer headed for Kentucky. He now had experience in the business of reporting news, but more than the technique of news gathering, he had a philosophy about being a reporter that involved more than merely writing stories.

All reporters have to be editors. You're exposed constantly to a barrage of possible stories. People call you. You go to meetings, press conferences. You read the work of other reporters on other papers and other reporters on your own paper who will maybe mention something in passing that might be worth ferreting out as a full-blown story of its own. You follow up things that you've written previously. You spend an awful lot of time calling people who are on your beat just to see what's coming up. You're an observer. You have to sort out the wheat from the chaff. Unless he's given an assignment, it's up to the reporter to decide what is worth pursuing and then recommending or discussing that with your editor. . . . My idea of what's news is to tell people something that they don't already know about.

When the *Courier-Journal* first assigned Shafer to the suburban bureau, his beat included Oldham County, which was something of a prison colony. It had the huge reformatory, a nearby minimum-security farm prison, and the Kentucky Correctional Institution for Women near the town of Pewee Valley. In the fall of 1979 Shafer wrote a couple of routine stories on KSR that were typical of most prison reporting. One story was about plans to build yet another prison in Oldham County, with a psychiatric hospital for emotionally disturbed convicts and additional cell blocks to house regular prisoners. The other story was about plans to put prisoners to work making license plates. There was very little in those stories about living conditions, so Shafer and his readers remained in the dark about such conditions at KSR. Thus, when Casselberry asked Shafer to investigate KSR, the reporter was interested because it looked like he might be able to tell his readers something they did not already know. It was a business decision.

> This was obviously a very good, developing, unfolding story which I kind of latched onto. Another Courier-Journal reporter of long standing, John Filiatreau, had written many, many very good stories over the years about a variety of issues related to the Kentucky penal system. He wrote extensively about drug problems, gang problems, race problems, primarily at Eddyville. In the early 1970s there had been some racial problems at the Kentucky State Reformatory that had resulted in lockdowns and black-on-white confrontations among inmates. But it just had gone for a while where things were kind of quiet.
>
> Then it became evident that there had been some litigation filed on behalf of the inmates that raised issues about the type of conditions in the major Kentucky prisons. I had an interview with Brad [Casselberry], who was working with some of the inmates out there. It was pretty obvious from what had happened in a few other states that this issue was ripe for some sort of fairly drastic solution by the courts.
>
> I was detached from the newspaper's city staff. I was not in a position where the city editor could walk by my desk and come over and see what I was doing at that time. So I would have to consult with him by telephone once or twice a day. On Mondays we would map out two or three things that I would tell him I would be working on that week. In the course of that I said, "Well, there's a prison story that I've been alerted to." . . .
>
> The prison issue involved a lot of gut-wrenching issues. And it was the editor's belief, and mine too, that it would evolve into a major issue that would affect a lot of taxpayers, perhaps a lot of money being spent on correctional improvements. It involved a potential for major state expenditures. The Courier-Journal was the newspaper of state record in the state of Kentucky. We felt it was an issue that if we didn't report it, there'd be no one else who would.

The city editor gave his approval for Shafer to investigate KSR. Casselberry set up a meeting between Shafer and Shorty and the Plaintiffs' Committee.

Getting Down and Dirty

Shafer had already talked with the wardens and received, as he put it, "the typical once-over-lightly wardens' tour." Now it was time for the reporter to do as Judge Johnstone had done: get under the surface. Shafer intended to view KSR from the inmates' perspective and to talk with them about the living conditions. He arrived at KSR just a few days before the March 7 hearing, and the Plaintiffs' Committee gave him their perspective.

Being from a small-town, rural background . . . I had driven past the local jail a bunch of times, but I had never been inside the walls of a correctional facility.

I was a bit overwhelmed by the first time I took a tour of the Kentucky State Reformatory. It wasn't so much that the conditions were decrepit. I was more overwhelmed by just the starkness of the place, the hardness of the place. I've been in the army. The discipline wasn't really that new to me. It was just a bleak, damn big, depressing place. You could always hear the doors slamming. I was just kind of overwhelmed by it.

I spent a couple hours one morning with the Plaintiffs' Committee. Brad [Casselberry] and a lawyer were there. And we had kind of a round-table discussion. We talked about what the prison was like. I had toured the prison with the warden and written several stories. And I thought, "I'm writing about something I don't really have any firsthand knowledge of. I want to go out and find out who these people are, what their grievances are, and what they're really like, to try to get down and dirty with some of these guys who are making these claims."

Brad always referred to them as "the guys." And I thought, well, Brad is not some kind of idiot. He's a decent human being. His wife worked at the paper. And I thought, if Brad can get close to these guys, despite what they've done, they've got to be intelligent, well-meaning people who are trying to improve their condition, whatever it may be.

So I went into that meeting. I wasn't afraid of these guys. There were probably two or three murderers in the room, but I went in there more curious about what made these guys tick, really, than anything else.

I came away from it with an honest impression of some people who deserved at least humane treatment. And I came away with a belief that they felt that the conditions were less than humane. The thing that most struck me was the intensity with which they held their views. They were expressing passion. They felt very strongly about what they were being subjected to. I came away from it thinking that these guys are not a bunch of idiots being led down the primrose path by a bunch of ambitious young legal aid attorneys, that these are legitimate legal and constitutional questions that exist there.

They talked about contraband. They talked about assaults. They talked about drugs. They talked about illegal weapons. They talked about rat infestation. They talked about poorly prepared and polluted food and not having toothbrushes—all sorts of things like that that everybody else on the outside takes for granted.

These guys were sitting there and feeling very strongly and telling tales that maybe I wouldn't have believed unless I had heard them directly. They were the type of things that if I read them in a legal brief that had been filed in court, I would say, "Is that really true? I mean, is it really that bad?" But after I sat down and talked to them, it was clear that there were some serious problems within the walls of that place.

When we were done, each one of those inmates who had been in that meeting, before they could go back to their dorms, they had to be strip-searched. That made an impression on me. These guys had to stoop to something that would have been very demeaning to me, just to be in a meeting like that. And it seemed to me that was something they shouldn't be subjected to.

Believing that his story would have greater credibility with the public if he talked to all sides before writing the article, Shafer arranged an interview with state corrections officials at the state capitol in Frankfort. A day or two later, Shafer interviewed a cabinet officer, Commissioner of Corrections George Wilson, several central staff members, and the wardens at KSR and Eddyville.

I think they were aware that when the major state newspaper is bringing to them allegations of things wrong in the system, that they feel it's important to get everybody in one place at one time to try and respond to them.

I basically took each of the major points that the inmate committee had raised in the previous interview and asked their response, got their response to each one. Was point A true? Was point B true? Was point C true?

It went well. Wilson and his staff did most of the talking. They were very up front about it. I came away from that meeting with a respect that I still have to this day for George Wilson. He's a good man.

Wilson and his top aides confirmed most of the information the inmates had given Shafer, although there was disagreement on a few details and the officials knew nothing about several of the claims. Now that Shafer had verified most of the facts, he was poised to write the story, but one more step remained in the process. Johnstone's settlement pretrial conference was on March 7, just a few days away, so Shafer decided to witness the proceedings in the courtroom to learn the status of the negotiations before writing the story.

A Couple Pages of Nothing

The negotiations were going poorly. On March 5, two days before the hearing, the prisoners' lawyers had received the state's proposal for settling the case. It contained plans to build new facilities to house prisoners, a very slow timetable for reducing the population at the two prisons, and essentially a restatement of current prison policy. It was basically a proposal to maintain the status quo, except for new construction and gradually moving prisoners to the new facilities.

The prisoner's lawyers were perplexed and disappointed with this first proposal. They had come to believe that building new prisons to ease overcrowding in existing facilities would do little to improve the men's daily living conditions and that the new facilities would themselves become overcrowded within a few years unless drastic changes occurred in corrections policy. Unaware of the disarray caused by the power struggle within the Bureau of Corrections, the lawyers could only wonder what had happened to Wilson's new, reform-minded ideas and Brown's open-minded philosophy.

The lawyers had a scheduled meeting with the Plaintiffs' Committee the next day to decide how to respond to the state's proposal. The prisoners' lead counsel (the author of this book) was designated to present the state's proposal to the committee and give whatever advice they asked for but then leave the decision about whether to accept or reject the proposal to the committee, since the lawyers believed it was their ethical obligation to leave the ultimate decision to the plaintiffs. The lead counsel was certain that the prisoners would turn the plan down. In February the prisoners had resisted any thought of negotiation, and the lawyers had worked hard to persuade the committee to work out a settlement proposal. Day after day, for hours on end, the prisoners and lawyers had sat in their stuffy conference room at KSR, arguing, fighting, cajoling, and generally getting on each others' nerves. The prisoners wanted to spell out detailed standards for classification, maintenance, food, hygiene, medical care, and every other area of prison administration. They wanted arcane and intricate rules for parole that were incomprehensible to the lawyers. They wanted reforms for which there was no case-law precedent, that were not of constitutional magnitude, and that Johnstone surely would not order if the case went to trial. The prisoners threatened to walk out en masse a few times. Wilgus lost his temper at one meeting and was walking out the door, but Shorty talked him into returning. The prisoners eventually agreed on a thirty-six-page settlement proposal and sent it to the state's lawyers. Thus, when the state's largely status quo proposal came back, the lawyers knew their clients would be frustrated and angry.

They were unprepared, however, for the magnitude of the anger, and the March 6 meeting at KSR was a disaster. Shorty, Wilgus, Walter, and the rest of the plaintiffs were furious over the state's offer. They believed that they had advanced a good-faith proposal to settle the case. The offer the state had sent back was an insult as far as Walter was concerned.

[The state's settlement proposal] basically told us that the way things were was the way they wanted to keep 'em. We all got real hot about that. We didn't want to talk anymore.

The prisoners' lawyers were in a difficult and delicate situation. Although their clients were furious, wanted no more talk of settlement, and were insistent on a trial in open court, Judge Johnstone wanted the case settled without a trial. The lawyers' professional judgment was that it would be better to settle out of court than take a chance on a long trial because, although it was clear to them that the totality of conditions at KSR and Eddyville were unconstitutional, it was not clear how much authority the federal court had to order improvements. The lawyers also disagreed with each other about how to respond to the state's offer. Lead counsel wanted to reject it, another lawyer thought the prisoners should accept it, and a third was uncertain. Thus, the prisoners' lawyers had to motivate the prisoners to keep talking about settlement when they were too angry to do so, yet the lawyers had their own differences of opinion. Walter had been distrustful of the lawyers all along, and now Wilgus felt some suspicion.

> *We never actually trusted but one of the lawyers. It came down the lead lawyer was the one that we were depending on in a pinch. We knew that the other guys would fight like hell, but they never did seem to come to a good conclusion about what we wanted. The first proposal that was sent back sort of soured us on them.*
>
> *The lawyers brought that proposal back, and one lawyer read it. He throwed it on the table and said, "There it is, gang. That's what they said. I'll tell you from my point of view, from my part of it, it's a pretty good deal. My advice is you'd better take it. Yeah, take it. It's the best you're gonna get."*
>
> *That proposal was a couple pages of nothing — of nothing. Never said anything in 'ere. It was wrote on back and front and it was just nothing. Nothing. It didn't say anything, and I thought, "Boy, who's this guy?" We never could get him to understand how we felt about some things. Him and Walter had some terrible, terrible arguments.*
>
> *The lead lawyer . . . advised us not to take that proposal. He never did say anything like, "It's the best you're gonna get." And we agreed with him. He was always the slowest one in the bunch. He would set around and smoke his pipe and he had a big beard. He'd think things out. He always seemed to be on our side whether it was good or bad.*

The lawyers were exhausted and depressed. It seemed that months of legal wrangling, endless meetings, and mountains of paperwork had come to nothing. Their clients were in open revolt, the settlement hearing was the next day, and trial was only a month away. No matter how much Johnstone wanted the case settled or the lawyers believed that doing so was in their clients' best interest, settlement could not occur unless the prisoners agreed. They were the plaintiffs in the lawsuit, and this was perhaps the only situation in which they had any final, insurmountable authority, for there could be no settlement without their consent. The prisoners' lawyers left the March 6 meeting and drove along two-lane country roads back toward Louisville instead of taking the usual route on Interstate 71. The drive was more relaxing that way, rolling up and down hills past quiet farms. Tomorrow promised to be a dramatic day.

Sixty Square Feet

On March 7, 1980, Shafer walked across the street from the *Courier-Journal* building to the federal courthouse, up to the second floor, and into the courtroom for the settlement hearing. The lawyers filed in and sat down at counsel tables. The lawyers had asked Judge Johnstone for permission to have prisoners present in the courtroom, which the judge had granted. The prisoners—Shorty, Walter, Wilgus, and several inmates from Eddyville—walked in, handcuffed and accompanied by stern-looking guards, and took seats at counsel table next to their lawyers. The court bailiff entered the courtroom and cried, "All rise!" Everyone rose, and Johnstone came through a door at the front of the courtroom and sat down behind the long wooden bench. Court was in session.

In open court Johnstone was all business and formality, a stern expression on his face. The lead attorney for the KSR class rose first and described the prisoners' proposal for settling the reformatory case. It called for sweeping change in living conditions at KSR, most importantly a swift end to overcrowding. The lawyer advanced a formula for eliminating the overcrowding, which was called the American Correctional Association–rated standard capacity. This standard stated that there should be only one prisoner per cell and that open dormitories should have sixty square feet of space per inmate. To figure out the total capacity of a prison, one simply added up all the square feet in the dorms and divided by sixty, then added in the total number of individual cells. At KSR that formula yielded a capacity of 1,200 prisoners. In essence, then, the plaintiffs proposed to reduce the population at KSR from nearly 2,100 to 1,200, and they wanted it done in twelve months. Judge Johnstone asked only one question during this presentation: what was that square-footage figure? The lawyer repeated the sixty-square-foot figure, and the judge scribbled some figures on a yellow pad. The judge appeared to be giving serious consideration to this proposal, and he, like the experts who had inspected KSR, seemed to sense that overcrowding was the root problem at KSR that exacerbated all the other problems.

After the lawyer for the Eddyville prisoners presented a similar proposal, the state presented its proposal. The state's lead attorney rose and went to the podium. He agreed that the prisons were overcrowded. He proposed to reduce the total population at both prisons by 200 within six months but said that the total rated capacity at KSR was 1,472, not the 1,200 calculated by the plaintiffs. The state would build new prisons to address the problem, but only if the legislature voted the necessary funding. With respect to all the other problems at KSR, he proposed a few changes but mostly promised to do some studies and write up some plans.

Shorty, Wilgus, and Walter were furious. Behind the state's proposal, they felt, there was no real promise to reduce the population at KSR. They believed that the entire proposed reduction would occur at Eddyville, leaving KSR unchanged. In addition, the capacity of KSR was much lower than 1,472, and there was not even a promise to reduce the population to that level.

The two sides were so far apart that settlement looked hopeless, and Johnstone knew it. He needed to find a way to motivate these people to find common ground. With the trial just a month away, time was running out to settle the case. He needed to apply some pressure, particularly to the state, but he sensed it would not be helpful to do so heavy-handedly. Instead of criticizing or praising either proposal, Johnstone chose a gentler approach. He announced in open court that if either side asked him to step into the negotiations, he would offer his services as a mediator. The bailiff cried, "All rise!" everyone rose, and the judge walked out of the courtroom. The hearing was over. There was no noticeable progress in negotiations, but at least the proposals were out in the open and the judge had agreed to act as mediator.

Back Channels

Some maneuvering out of the public eye commenced immediately after the hearing. After leaving the courtroom, Johnstone called the lawyers into his chambers, where, off the public record, he told the lawyers that any negotiated settlement must have "strict standards." The judge did not specify what those standards ought to be, but it was clear he was not impressed with the state's vague proposals. He wanted clear and definite statements of what changes would be made in the prisons, not the indefinite possibilities of the state's proposal.

After the conference in chambers ended and the lawyers left, the judge resorted to a time-honored practice in government called the back channel, a private, unofficial communication through a third party. In his days as a country lawyer and political campaigner in western Kentucky, he had developed a large network of political connections. His own politics were moderate to liberal. He had great compassion for unfortunate, underprivileged people and believed that government should lend a hand to them. Strangely enough, Johnstone's political allies were conservative Democrats. His personal mentor in politics was reported to be a man named Smith Broadbent, a wealthy farmer from Trigg County in western Kentucky and a conservative Democrat. Nevertheless, Broadbent liked Johnstone and trusted him to give sound advice. As a liberal whose most powerful friends were conservatives, Johnstone had learned not to push his liberal views through open politics very often. He used the back channel for many years in western Kentucky. People knew Johnstone had liberal ideas, but they also knew he had good judgment.

Now as a federal judge, Johnstone resorted again to the back channel. He knew the state's negotiating offer would not lead to a settlement of the case because the proposal failed to address the living conditions at KSR and Eddyville in any substantial way, and the governor needed to be told. At the same time, Johnstone was leery of saying publicly that the state's offer was not good enough, because then opponents of prison reform like the old guard would charge him with playing favorites, coddling prisoners, and prejudging the case. It was time to send word privately to the governor, who was not a party to the lawsuit. The back channel might have been his law clerk. It might have been a mutual friend. It might have been several people. Whoever it was, it was somebody the judge knew and trusted.

One of the back channels was a man named Edward "Pritch" Pritchard. A Kentucky native, Pritchard went to Harvard Law School and subsequently went to work in the Roosevelt administration during the New Deal. He then took a job as law clerk to Felix Frankfurter, associate justice of the U.S. Supreme Court. Pritchard eventually returned to Kentucky to practice law and Democratic politics, but the old tradition of vote fraud in Kentucky politics—the same tradition some of Wilgus's forebears followed in Appalachia—landed Pritchard in trouble. He was caught stuffing a ballot box, was charged and convicted of federal vote fraud, and spent a few months in federal prison. His old mentor, Frankfurter, interceded on his behalf with President Harry Truman and urged him to pardon Pritchard. President Truman did pardon him, and Pritchard returned to Kentucky, where, because of the pardon, he resumed the practice of law. Through the sheer force of his intellect, Pritchard became a valued behind-the-scenes adviser to Kentucky Democratic politicians who favored progressive politics. He came to know Johnstone through work on political campaigns in western Kentucky. Pritchard was now a trusted unofficial adviser to Governor Brown. Since he knew both the governor and the judge, Pritchard was one of the people in a position to provide a back channel between the federal judge and the governor. Through the back channel, Johnstone conveyed to Brown that the state's settlement was unsatisfactory and would not help settle the case.

Ironically, Judge Johnstone's initiative provided important leverage for the state's lawyers. Unknown to the prisoners' lawyers, the state's first offer represented a standoff between the reformers and the old guard. It was not a product of Wilson's thinking, and the lawyers had presented it with reluctance. When Wilson had taken office in January, he was unable to give the prison-reform litigation his full attention. He had many other priorities, such as appointments to key positions in corrections. That situation gave the old guard an opening to lobby the legislature, meet with gubernatorial advisers, and pressure Wilson not to move quickly on reform issues. The old guard's lobbying efforts in the early days of Wilson's administration prevented an offer of settlement that would have represented true reform. The state's initial settlement offer was thus primarily a product of Bland's administration, not Wilson's. The state's lawyers themselves felt the first proposal was undesirable, but they lacked authority either to dump it or to present a better offer. Now that the governor had been told through the back channel that the federal judge was dissatisfied with the Bland proposal, all participants in the litigation knew what was essential to settle Shorty's lawsuit: running the prisons according to modern professional standards. The state's lawyers had sought this outcome throughout the litigation. In their long battle against the old guard, their single biggest ally turned out to be the federal judge.

Page 1

At about the same time as Johnstone was working the back channel, Shafer was writing his stories about the litigation to reform KSR. His first story appeared on page 1 of the *Courier-Journal* the day after the settlement hearing, March 8, 1980. The headline read, "NEGOTIATIONS START IN PRISONERS' LAWSUIT." Shafer gave a brief history of the lawsuit and described the contrasting settlement proposals. He gave special attention to the most important part of the hearing:

> An important issue in the dispute is when the number of inmates will be reduced and by how much—especially at the reformatory.
>
> U.S. District Judge Edward H. Johnstone decided yesterday to help mediate the differences in the two sides' proposed settlements. Attorneys in the case hope to reach an agreement so the case won't have to go to trial. They fear that a trial might take a long time and they believe both sides might fare better if they can negotiate their differences.[2]

The paper ran a picture of the judge with the caption, "Will help mediate in dispute." This story sent an important message to the state capital: the federal judge was stepping into the negotiations.

Shafer's second story ran in the *Courier-Journal* three days later, again on the front page. The paper printed a huge photograph of a crowded dormitory and five additional pictures, such as one showing a long line of men waiting outside for lunch. The story told about Shafer's interview at the prison with Shorty and the Plaintiffs' Committee and about the reporter's conversation at the state capitol with the top corrections officials.

> Payoffs for haircuts. Payoffs to ensure that laundry isn't lost or damaged.
>
> Bunks crowded so close together that inmates must stand on foot lockers to let someone through. Trading cigarettes for shoes—as well as drugs, liquor and other contraband. Widespread sexual harassment.
>
> And tension—constant tension.
>
> That's how inmates of the Kentucky State Reformatory describe conditions at the medium-security prison near LaGrange. More than half of the state's prisoners are kept there.

The state reformatory had nearly 2,100 inmates. It was designed for about 1,250.

"We're packed in the dorms like sardines," one inmate said.

State corrections officials agree that overcrowding is a problem. But they disagree sharply on the severity of the conditions.

The inmates said that, "At least 30 to 40 percent of the prisoners have been assaulted sexually." They said the percentage of inmates who have participated in homosexual activity is much higher. "We've got plenty of guards who like it, too," Haddix said.

One time last year, 12 inmates were in isolation with gonorrhea, they said.

Feb. 29 was a typical day. "There were three pipings, two stabbings and two robberies," Haddix said.

But Steve Smith, reformatory superintendent, had other figures for Feb. 29. "I am aware of one stabbing and one robbery," he said.

In 1979, eight staff workers were either fired or asked to resign for various offenses, including one corrections officer charged with having a sexual affair with an inmate. That year there were only eight reported cases of sodomy or sexual abuse between inmates, Smith said. The number of reported assaults in recent years has declined, despite a rising inmate population, said Corrections Commissioner George Wilson.

"The reformatory is almost unmanageable," said Dewey Sowders, former reformatory superintendent and now warden of the Kentucky State Penitentiary. With the reformatory's open-dormitory housing, instead of single cells, "you can't tell what's going to happen. That's how gang rapes occur," he added. . . .

The Kentucky State Reformatory near LaGrange houses about 2,100 inmates, or more than half of all the prisoners in Kentucky's corrections system.

The inmates and corrections officials agree the prison is overcrowded and that fact affects nearly every aspect of the prison's operation. It means long waits in line to eat. It means double bunking in many dormitories. It means about 400 prisoners don't have jobs, and it means that the reformatory's staff, including corrections officers, is spread thin.

The state says that millions of dollars will be spent to improve the reformatory's conditions. Meanwhile, state officials say they are trying to make the best of the situation.[3]

The day after this story hit the newsstands, the state offered a dramatically different proposal to settle the case. The new proposal was nineteen pages long and, amid a variety of new promises and more concrete proposals for change, stated that the leadership of the executive and legislative branches of the government had approved the plans for prison renovation, which would be funded by the state even if the General Assembly did not vote to spend the money. This offer signified that the most powerful people in state government—the governor and the leaders of the General Assembly—were publicly committed to spending the money it would take to settle the case.

It is unlikely that Shafer's articles caused Brown to approve this new proposal. Instead, shortly after the March 7 hearing, when Johnstone's back-channel message got through to the governor, he had met with the state's lawyers, with his own legal counsel present. Brown had brought flexibility and a willingness to consider new ideas to the office. Shorty's lawsuit was simply an issue with which he had to deal in a businesslike manner. However, $42 million over two years for population reduction and prison renovation was a great deal of money, and this amount would only pay for a portion of the cost. More money would be needed in later years to renovate other portions of the prisons. Thus, the governor and his lawyers had a long discussion and thorough review. In the end, Brown said he would think it over. He then consulted a few trusted friends, among them Pritchard, who told Brown that he would be a fool not to settle the case. It wasn't so much the right thing to do, Pritchard said, as the appropriate thing to do. Brown eventually agreed with Pritchard and he put the $42 million into the proposed budget for the next two years. As a result of the commitment to find funding outside of the budget if necessary, settling Shorty's lawsuit was no longer subject to a veto by the legislature.[4]

There is also no evidence that Shafer's articles caused a surge of public opinion in favor of improving prison conditions. Shafer had extensive contact with the public and was well aware that the average citizen had little sympathy for convicted criminals. Shafer also believed, however, that his stories on KSR probably did have an important impact on the General Assembly. Legislative approval of funding for prison reform remained important despite the governor's agreement, because it would be far less disruptive to state government if the General Assembly appropriated the $42 million than if Brown obtained the money by other means, such as selling state property. Experience had taught him that politicians are sensitive to public opinion. In this case, it was unlikely that politicians were worried about public sympathy for convicts. A scenario that appeared more likely, however, was that if the state failed to settle the lawsuit and the case went to trial, the federal judge could rule that conditions at KSR and Eddyville were unconstitutional, take over operation of the prisons, and close the doors to new prisoners to end the overcrowding. In that event, the voters were virtually certain to vote out the legislators who lost control of the prisons.

Shafer thought his articles had another important impact in that they probably preempted any attempt by politicians to whip up a public outcry against spending their money to build "country-club prisons." He had witnessed ambitious politicians advance their careers by manipulating the public's fear and anger about crime with rhetoric about the crime issue, feeding the public misinformation about crime, and telling voters that the solution to the crime problem was to stop coddling criminals and get tough on crime. Such attempts could well have engendered a public outcry against efforts to settle Shorty's lawsuit. That absence of such events likely occurred in part because Shafer communicated accurate information to the public, thus preempting any attempt to spread misinformation.

[*The newspaper has] a full-time research department that does public-opinion surveys on the types of material that we print and publish — what's important, what's not; what's getting read, who's getting read; what types of stories are of interest, what comic strips are of interest; that sort of thing. You can also tell by letters that you get to the editor, phone calls you get, what kind of complaints you get about what articles you're writing. . . . There are other gauges, too, like what the legislature does. . . .*

Failing the state's willingness to settle the case, I think there was some political fear that the judge would take over the system and maybe let inmates walk, to get within the population limit. At that time there was a fairly recent precedent in Alabama, where a federal judge almost did take over the state prison system and release hundreds and hundreds of inmates. There was a great public outcry about the state administration allowing that to happen.

I think there was a political fear that no matter how much money they would spend, [settling] would be a better political alternative to having that happen. If the judge had released people, and said these people have to be freed, and turned convicted felons loose on the state roads and state streets, the political figures feared a great political outcry. The response

from the electorate to that would have far exceeded the electorate's re-
sponse to having to spend $40 or $50 million to improve the condition
of the prisons. The thought was that they could avoid this happening
by spending $40 or $50 million.

Three days after the state's new settlement proposal came out, the
Courier-Journal ran an editorial about the prison-conditions litigation.
Shafer did not write the editorial, but his stories provided its foundation.

It was the lead editorial of the day, headlined, "COURTS RIGHT IN DE-
MANDING THAT PRISONS MEET STANDARDS."

> Governor Brown's budget for Kentucky's prison system includes $17 million
> for renovation and $25 million for new construction over the next two years.
> While he deserves praise for trying to make up for the deficiencies of past bud-
> gets, this sharp rise in spending is not the product of idealism: it's bowing to
> the inevitable.
> The same thing is happening in nearly all states, and the reason is judicial.
> Simply put, the states are on notice that if they won't bring prisons up to stan-
> dard, the courts, particularly federal courts, will force them to do so.

The editorial described how federal courts had abandoned the traditional hands-off doctrine toward prisons that had contributed to night-
marish living conditions and bloody riots and how federal courts were now
interpreting the U.S. Constitution to mean a prison had to be a decent
place in which human beings could live. The editorial then focused directly on the Kentucky litigation.

> Attorneys are working actively on an out-of-court settlement of a consoli-
> dated suit, based on complaints by convicts at Eddyville and at LaGrange. But
> the Commonwealth is not alone in having to face long-deferred costs.
> The Kentucky Department of Justice recently surveyed eight other states
> that are under court order to upgrade prison conditions or that face active
> prisoner litigation. Alabama, it found, has spent $20 million on prison con-
> struction in recent years, and has another $28 million under way. Georgia has
> spent $96 million. Louisiana's bill for new construction has been an astound-
> ing $240 million.
> The list goes on: Mississippi, $26 million; North Carolina, $85 million;
> Ohio, $30 million; Oklahoma, $70 million; and Tennessee, $32 million.
> While the courts are determined to compel prisons to meet minimum stan-

dards, one theme that has emerged from the civil-rights rulings might offer the states, including Kentucky, a way of lessening the staggering costs.

This would involve better classification so inmates wanting to improve their skills through training or schooling could be kept apart from those dangerous to others. Similarly, as planned in a new hospital wing at LaGrange Reformatory, mentally disturbed prisoners need separate quarters. Accurate classification could go a long way to reducing the crowding in maximum and medium security institutions.

But until experiments with classification, work release, counseling, probation and minimum-security facilities are better tested, Kentucky will find the bill a stiff one to pay. Yet even if we had no constitutional requirements, the barest commitment to what's right and human would leave us no alternative.[5]

The names of the state's largest newspaper and its publisher, Barry Bingham Jr., were now behind the effort to settle the case, obtain funding, and improve the prisons to minimum standards. With the governor and the leaders of the General Assembly also on board, the last remaining potential holdouts were the rank-and-file members of the General Assembly. The vote on Brown's budget was coming up, and the trial was only three weeks away. In Shafer's view, the editorial's message that the appropriate policy for the state was to approve the governor's request for prison funding was primarily directed at the legislators.

Settlement

The state's lawyers moved quickly on the opportunity provided by their greatly expanded authority to settle by asking the prisoners' lawyers to meet once more. The exhausted prisoners' lawyers decided to give negotiation another try but first met with their angry clients. Tempers had cooled since the disastrous March 6 meeting. The members of the Plaintiffs' Committee were willing to listen to their lawyers one more time before trial. After the lawyers explained the new political configuration, the plaintiffs approved another effort to settle. Walter believed that this enterprise was a game but a very important game.

The lawyers persuaded us to give it another try. All we had to do was continue to use whatever leverage we had and things might work out. That's when the expression game *came up. I said, "This is a game, and we're not*

*the real players. This is really a contest between the federal government
and the state of Kentucky. Federal government has decided it wants to
revamp the prison system of the United States. And the state of Kentucky
has decided that it wants its prison system to stay the way it is. The question is who is going to win and how far it's going to go in terms of actually
improving the lives of the inmates that are affected."*

*We had to figure out how we could manipulate our fragile position in
the middle to our advantage, to get what we were constitutionally entitled
to, and not to wind up with substantially less than we were constitutionally entitled to. I was just glad Governor Brown came along when he did.*

The prisoners and their lawyers worked together to formulate a negotiating position. Shorty's lawsuit involved nearly every aspect of living conditions at KSR, but everyone agreed that by far the most important problems were overcrowding and filthy, crumbling housing. Agreement with
the state on the housing problem was nearly certain because Brown had
already agreed to renovate the dormitories and cells, starting with $17 mil-
lion for renovation during the next two years. That left overcrowding as
the top issue in the upcoming talks.

The plaintiffs agreed to a three-part negotiating strategy proposed by
the lawyers for the overcrowding problem. First, based on the American
Correctional Association standard, they would propose that the combined
populations of KSR and Eddyville be reduced by 600 inmates within six
months and then reduced by another 400 inmates within twelve months.
If the state's lawyers rejected this initial proposal, the fallback position
would be to propose a total population reduction of 750 within six months.
The third and final position would be to reduce the population by 600
within six months and by another 400 within eighteen months. The Plaintiffs' Committee chose their lead attorney to present those proposals to the
state's lawyers.

On March 19, 1980, the designated negotiator arrived at the state capitol with thirteen separate items to discuss with the state's lawyers, but
overcrowding remained the key issue. The lawyers shook hands, sat down,
and the prisoners' representative immediately advanced the crucial proposal for population reduction. He did not expect the state to agree and
was willing to settle for one of the lesser proposals, but the state's lawyers
stunned him with their immediate response. Their latest calculations in-

dicated that the state would be very close to reducing the population by 1,000 in just over six months, well ahead of the plaintiffs' schedule. A new prison was already under construction and scheduled to open within six months, and state officials had plans to implement procedures to release prisoners on parole at a faster rate. The prisoners' lawyer casually said, "Well, looks like we're going to settle this case."

The other twelve items on the agenda passed by quickly. Parole, pre-release programs, maintenance, education, grievance procedures, food, and visiting, though vitally important in the day-to-day existence of the average inmate, were matters of detail in the context of negotiations in which population reduction was the key to settling Shorty's lawsuit. The lawyer went home with the deal it seemed that his clients wanted. All he had to do was give them the good news at the next day's meeting.

The March 20 meeting with the Plaintiffs' Committee did not have the result the lawyer expected. The inmates were pleased with the progress on agreement to eliminate overcrowding but found the supposed details of the agreement insufficient. A barrage of new demands ensued. The inmates wanted a promise that job-training programs would be kept at full capacity at all times. They wanted a meaningful job for every prisoner who wanted one, increased meal hours to reduce time spent in the waiting line, and so on. The prisoners were in no mood to celebrate, and the lawyers felt ambushed, so it was a rocky and contentious meeting. Once again, the lead counsel sat quietly, took careful notes, and scheduled yet another meeting.

On March 21, 1980, the lawyers met at KSR with the Plaintiffs' Committee for the third time in four days. The inmates presented demands to expand the law library, include hobbies and crafts in the recreation program, hire only qualified social workers, give guards a 20 percent pay increase, hire only licensed plumbers and engineers, improve emergency medical care, lower prices at the prison store, and the like. By the time the inmates were finished, the lawyers had a list of twenty-one more demands to present to the state's attorneys. The prisoners had no constitutional right to any of these demands, a fact that mattered little to them. Improving daily life in prison for the average inmate was what counted, and they said they would not agree to settle the case without these concessions. Thus, the possibility of settlement lay in the details.

Putting all these demands in writing was a nightmare for the lawyers.

Expressing clearly, in exact detail, precisely all the changes the prisoners wanted was impossible under the pressure of time. The lawyers had to do their best, however, because their clients wanted these changes and would not settle without them. As finally written, much of the proposal was vague and ambiguous. The lawyers suspected that there might be problems of interpretation when it came time to implement the settlement, but it was the best they could do given their time constraints.

The lawyers on both sides met again. The state's lawyers read the new proposal and, instead of accusing the prisoners' lawyers of negotiating in bad faith, said they would talk to their client, Wilson. By this time, Wilson was devoting full attention to the prisoners' lawsuit. He had come to see the lawsuit as political leverage, an opportunity to bring new methods of management to the prisons and to obtain funding to pay for the changes. He wanted to get the lawsuit behind him so he could get to work on making Kentucky's prisons a professional operation.

The department's attorneys were the lead people in the actual negotiations. Based on their contact with plaintiffs' attorneys, and what the issues were, they were able to compile a list of the issues that the plaintiffs' attorneys felt needed to be looked at. Based on that they got back with me to find out what part was acceptable and what part wasn't and on what basis could some of the issues be adjusted so that they could be acceptable, both operationally and philosophically.

My attitude on some of the issues was different from my predecessor's. I felt that some of the issues had some substance and could be accomplished. I think there were some differences there. I know that some of the things that may have bothered him didn't necessarily bother me.

Coming in at that time, recognizing some of the systemic needs of the prison system, I saw an opportunity to take some of the thrust of the consent decree and achieve some departmental, systematic impact from it. My overall strategy was how could I have systematic impact—living-condition issues, the issues of confinement. We had life-safety issues. We had policy and procedure issues. We had mental-health issues, medical accessibility.

Early on, I recognized an opportunity. Corrections had difficulty attracting the kind of support—monetarily, resource-wise—to get anything accomplished. And I knew it was somewhat unique, that we were in a pos-

ture that we would possibly garner some support that we wouldn't otherwise get.

Wilson listened to the list of demands and asked the lawyers for their recommendation. The lawyers knew that the Constitution did not require states to abide by the detailed administrative requirements the prisoners were demanding, so the judge was unlikely to order these modifications, and the state's lawyers were unhappy with much of the wording because, like the plaintiffs' lawyers, they believed it was vague and ambiguous. Conversely, these new demands generally entailed minor changes that could be made without great effort, and the ambiguities could be resolved as the need arose during implementation. Reducing the population and renovating the housing constituted the broad package, the big picture, and Governor Brown had $42 million in his budget for doing so. It seemed silly to argue about details when agreement on the major issues made sense to Wilson because, from a professional standpoint, approximately 80 percent of the prisoners' demands represented sound prison policy. It was good policy, for example, to have better-paid guards and to have licensed plumbers and engineers. More broadly, Wilson perceived that the American Correctional Association standards were the foundation of the prisoners' demands, which were in effect a blueprint for KSR and Eddyville to be run by professional, modern standards. The idea behind the standards was that a prison should be run according to written plans, binding on prison staff, that would provide the impetus for achieving decent living conditions for the prisoners. Wilson did not see the demands as a threat but rather as an opportunity to force the prison system to change for the better, so Wilson gave the lawyers his approval to agree to most of the prisoners' demands.

The state's lawyers met again with the prisoners' lawyers. They worked out the final wording of the settlement. The final document was a proposed consent decree, an agreement between the parties that, if approved by the court, has the force and effect of a court order.[6] The lawyers—thirteen in all—signed the proposed consent decree and shook hands.[7]

On March 26, 1980, negotiations were not yet complete, since the plaintiff-class representatives still had to sign the consent decree. The prisoners' lawyers thus headed off to yet another meeting at KSR. The Plaintiffs' Committee grumbled that Wilson had accepted only 80 percent of their demands and did not believe that the state would comply with the agreement. Walter was one of the most suspicious plaintiffs. He said he would not sign anything until a lawyer from the U.S. Department of Justice, one of the amicus curiae lawyers, came from Washington, D.C., to KSR and told the prisoners what he thought about the proposed consent decree.

> *My position might have been born out of desperation. What I was doing was weighing all of the factors against each other. I was weighing and playing both ends against the middle, in the sense that the United States Department of Justice had its own reasons for getting involved in the case and our lawyers had their own reason for getting involved in the case.*
>
> *While our lawyers were telling us some things, Justice was telling us some things in addition to that. While we didn't always agree with either position, there was a certain amount of latitude there that enabled us to reach a better position, a better position than the one at times we thought that our lawyers wanted us to accept. It was through that sort of thing that we got the type of flexibility that we needed.*

On March 31, 1980, a U.S. Justice Department lawyer, Shawn Moore, met with the prisoners and their lawyers at KSR. He dressed like it was an appearance in court: dark blue pin-striped suit, white shirt, striped tie, black polished shoes. By this time all the lawyers in the case and all the inmate representatives at Eddyville had signed the consent decree. Only the members of the KSR Plaintiffs' Committee were withholding their signatures. Shorty, Wilgus, Walter, and the other men left their dorms and trudged across the yard. They entered the Administration Building, were frisked by guards, and entered the meeting room. Everyone shook hands and sat down.

Shorty was the leader. The tenant farmer's son got right to the point: what did the lawyer from Washington think about the proposed consent decree? The lawyer's answer was just as direct: he had worked on many lawsuits over prison conditions, and this was the best agreement for prisoners he had ever seen. The state was promising the prisoners more than the federal judge had the authority to order. He also said that the federal government was prepared to go to court to enforce the agreement if the state did not comply with it.

That was enough for Shorty. He signed the consent decree. Others followed. Walter was next to last. The ghetto refugee still did not trust the state to live up to its promises, but he found a way within himself to place some trust in the lawyers who were on his side. He signed the consent decree, although he still had misgivings.

On the day that we signed off on the consent decree, I had some reserva-
tions. I said that I wasn't signing it because I agreed with everything in it
but because of the trust that I was placing in all of our lawyers at that point,
that the lawyers thought that that was the absolute best deal that we could
come up with at that particular point in time.

And I went with it. I said if we got screwed, we wouldn't get screwed by
the corrections cabinet or the court. We'd've gotten screwed by all of our
lawyers who were there.

That left Wilgus. The Appalachian hillbilly was the most stubborn of the inmates. During the negotiations he had been most adamant about adding new demands, always pushing for more. Now Wilgus again was the last to go along. He grumbled a bit, looked around, and allowed as how he ought not to hold things up. Wilgus signed. It was a big moment for everyone, especially for him.

The thing that I'll always remember about the conclusion of the lawsuit is
the day we signed it. Nobody knew what anybody was gonna say to any-
body or anything, but we signed it. I was sitting on one end of the table in
the conference room. The lead lawyer got up and scooted his chair back.
Ever'body, they was shaking hands and carrying on and congratulating
one 'nother. The lawyer turned away from all of 'em and ran and hugged
me and said, "By God, we did it, Haddix." And put his arms around me.
I've always remembered that. I thought, "Well why did he say that to me?"
Well, he could have shook hands and said that to anybody in the room. But
as soon as it was signed and as soon as that was over with he turned to me
just immediately and said, "By God, we did it."

April 3, 1980, was a big day at the federal courthouse in Louisville, the day for the final conference before the scheduled start of the trial on April 7. Shorty's lawsuit was a class action, and federal procedural rules require that the judge must approve a class-action settlement before it becomes effective to assure that the lawyers and representative plaintiffs have acted in the best interests of the members of the class and achieved a settlement that is fair, reasonable, and adequate.[8] Thus, Johnstone had to approve the proposed settlement before anyone could be assured that there would be no trial.

Johnstone scheduled a public hearing in open court to review the proposed consent decree. All sides would state in open court what the settlement required the state to do. Present were all the lawyers, Wilson and all the other top prison officials, and Shafer and a group of other news reporters as well as other spectators. The last participants to arrive were Shorty and the other inmate representatives from KSR and Eddyville. Prison guards had put them in handcuffs early in the morning, escorted them to a prison van, driven them to the federal courthouse, placed them in a special holding cell, and brought them out just before the start of the hearing. They remained in handcuffs until entering the courtroom, when at last they were removed and Shorty and the other plaintiffs walked in and sat down with their lawyers.

The court bailiff entered the crowded, hushed courtroom and cried, "All rise!" Everyone stood up, and the judge entered the courtroom in his black robes and sat down. Johnstone opened the hearing by saying that he wanted the lawyers to describe what was in the proposed consent decree. Lawyers for the prisoners spoke first, and then the state's lead attorney rose and started to talk. The judge broke in. Wilgus listened very carefully and remembered how it went.

"Do you realize what you've agreed to here?"

"Yes, we do."

"Do you realize that if this case had gone to court, these guys may not have gotten this much?"

"Yes, I realize that."

"And do you realize that you've made an agreement to more here than I would have probably agreed to?"

"Yes."

"You know, this is a lot of money here."

"Yes, sir, we know that."

"Well, my concern is how is the state going to pay for this?"

"Judge, I left the governor's office this morning—Governor Brown—and he assured me that if you asked that question to tell you that we'd sell some state property if necessary to comply with this decree."

That was enough for Judge Johnstone. If the General Assembly eliminated the $42 million for prison renovation and construction from the budget, Brown had committed to finding the money some other way. Johnstone had already read the entire consent decree. He knew that parts of the document were not well written, and he could tell that much of the language resulted from the prisoners' input. The document read as if a committee had written it, full of the kind of vague and ambiguous provisions that only a committee is capable of generating. Like the lawyers, the judge suspected that this language would cause problems during implementation of the agreement, but he was loath to reject the entire settlement for that reason. The overcrowding and dilapidated housing were by far the most important problems, and the consent decree addressed those problems in unmistakable, clear terms, so Johnstone signed the consent decree.[9]

The judge's approval of the settlement was only tentative, however. The thousands of other prisoners still had a right to be notified of the settlement and to file objections. Johnstone ordered the state to give a copy of the consent decree to every prisoner at KSR and the penitentiary, and he gave the prisoners forty days to object to the settlement. Nevertheless, all the parties believed that Johnstone would not reject this settlement because of prisoners' objections because the agreement benefited them substantially.

The document itself was less important to Judge Johnstone, however, than the spirit of consent that made it possible. That spirit was everything toward which he had worked for more than two years. He believed that change in Kentucky's prisons depended on the state's desire for change, on its willingness to do whatever was needed to have decent prisons, not on how this word or that word was used in the document and not on orders from the federal court. All his efforts had been directed toward achieving that consent. He thought that if state officials were educated about the prisons, with accurate information about the living conditions, the officials would see the need for change, and all participants could work together, voluntarily, toward a shared goal of decent prisons. He believed that there was good in the most hardened criminal, the most brutal guard, the most insensitive warden, the most cynical politician and that it was possible to bring out the best in all of them. His belief had been tested in the process of settling Shorty's case and had been confirmed by the spirit of consent that now existed.

Respect for the Law

Within a week, the General Assembly approved a budget containing the promised money for the prisons. The news media reported the settlement all over the state, billing it as a $42 million settlement, though in truth $42 million would be expended in just the first few years. One paper called it a "historic day" in Kentucky prisons. Shafer wrote a story for the *Courier-Journal* in which he reported that the state would have to spend $42 million just over the next few years, reduce prison population by more than one thousand inmates at the two major prisons, and offer many new programs for the prisoners. The article said that everyone on all sides was pleased with the settlement.[10] There was truth in what Shafer wrote, but few observers at the time anticipated that it would take many years for the state to live up to the agreement, and only a few participants realized the actual cost of the settlement would far exceed $42 million.

All those concerns, however, lay in the future. For the time being, everyone knew sweeping changes were coming to Kentucky's two major prisons. Although case-law precedent provided some of the impetus for change, the litigation gave reform-minded professionals, both inside and outside the corrections bureaucracy, powerful leverage to change policy in the prison system. From Shafer's perspective,

I think the thing that affected the political decision was the federal judge. It's just my own one person's belief that if there's one thing that people— the housewife and the factory worker—probably don't really feel sorry for, it's somebody that's a felon. And I think if 75 percent of Kentuckians had their say about it, they wouldn't have spent $40 or $50 million in taxpayers' money to improve the conditions in the state prisons.

If there's any single person who corrected what was wrong with the Kentucky penal system, it was the judge. It may have been a case of affecting a very few key opinion makers. It did fall heavily on the governor. It did fall heavily on some state legislators. It did fall heavily maybe on elected officials in the counties where the prisons were located.

But more than affecting and moving and swaying thousands and thousands of people to feel sorry for Kentucky prisoners, I think it was more of a case of John Y. Brown having to comply with a federal court order and budgeting money to improve conditions in the prisons in response to a federal court order.

Back at the barbershop in Judge Johnstone's hometown of Princeton, Kentucky, Herby listened to people talk about the settlement of the big prison case. Just as Shafer suspected, most people did not agree with spending large amounts of money to upgrade the prisons or feel sympathy for the plight of the prisoners.

This prison case isn't popular around here. People won't say it to Ed's face, but they'd criticize his orders to me. And I'd defend him. Now if I were the judge, I'd probably be a lot harder on the prisoners than he is. I came from a poor background, but I worked hard and never stole someone else's property. But Ed helped me to see things a different way, not so black and white. Before I knew Ed Johnstone, I thought of everything in black and white, maybe [because of] my lack of education. He taught me that things aren't always so clear. He broadened my thinking.

He just has a lot of compassion. He took a lot of flak around here for that prison case. People around here figure if it's not their grandson convicted of crime, just throw 'em in the dungeon. But if it is their grandson, well, they want him to be treated well. Now, this is the way it was told to me by Ed. So I'd tell these guys who say they ought to just throw convicts in jail and forget about them, "Well, if it was your grandson in there, you'd want that prison to be a decent place!"

Judge Johnstone doesn't make the law. He just interprets it. Nobody used to think prisoners had any rights. But some of those guards at Eddyville treated the prisoners pretty badly. So that's why the law is that prisoners have the right to be treated like humans.

Shorty's Faith

To Shorty, this case meant respect for the law, which was a new conviction for Shorty. He had started to see the law from a different vantage point, as an instrument that could help people rather than merely as a device for sending people to prison. When he filed his lawsuit in the federal court, he was placing a great deal of faith in the Constitution and the federal courts. The results made Shorty feel he finally had made a good choice in a life previously strewn with mistakes.

As far as I'm concerned, everything that we had, every proposal or every complaint we had was a valid complaint. I believe we got what we asked for. We got just about everything we asked for.

It tickled all of us when the United States Justice Department come in on the case. We felt that was an important thing and that's when we really got confident. I don't have too much faith in state law, but I have a lot of faith in federal law. I have a lot of faith in federal courts and the United States Constitution. When the Justice Department come into the case I felt like we was gitting somewhere. I knew the conditions that we were living under were wrong, and I was positive that the United States Justice Department would agree with that. And I felt like we had our case won right then. I knew that we would win the case.

It comes from studying case law. Federal courts are for the most part consistent in their rulings. In other words, they won't rule in one case one way and then the exact same situation rule another way.

I really don't know what gives me faith in the Constitution. I've studied history a lot, and I admire the people that drawed the thing up and signed it. And although I don't agree with the Supreme Court of the United States on a lot of things, the Constitution is there, and in most cases they enforce it. I look at the Constitution just like I do the Kentucky Statutes. It's a law. And for the most part the Supreme Court upholds that law, where the State of Kentucky don't uphold the statutes. They rule one way one time, one way another time. I don't have no faith in these state people.

But Shorty was obliged to trust one of those state people, George Wilson. The state now had to live up to its promises, and Wilson was facing a formidable task.

Compliance: Obstacles and Impact

Prison-reform litigation in America has been marked by major obstacles, both purposeful and unintended, to full compliance with federal court orders. In the Texas case, for example, state officials fiercely resisted any changes that limited the discretion of security personnel.[1] Recalcitrant state officials in Alabama erected similar obstacles to compliance with Judge Frank Johnson's orders.[2] The Georgia litigation, while also dogged by delays in implementing the consent decree approved by Judge Anthony Alaimo, featured state officials who were largely willing to comply with the order but were hampered by unforeseen events and the complexity of achieving systemic reform in a prison system.[3] The process of implementing the prison consent decree in Kentucky bore a great resemblance to the Georgia experience, in that state officials who were prepared, even eager, to comply with the order met obstacles almost immediately.

In the first few weeks after Judge Edward Johnstone signed the consent decree, Commissioner George Wilson moved quickly to begin complying with the state's agreement because he believed the decree's requirements were appropriate policy for the prison system. The new budget contained sufficient funding to pay for the first two-year phase of renovation. Wilson also directed corrections personnel to begin work on the other, nonconstruction aspects of the decree.

Just as in anything, nothing works any better than the degree of support it gets from the top. The bureau at that time recognized that they did have my support, and that we were going to do it, and we were fully committed to it.

We set about putting in place a mechanism that would be ongoing in terms of monitoring and contact with the lawyers, making sure that when disputes or conflicts would occur that we would get a handle on it on the front end rather than letting it turn into a major issue. We had the person in charge of monitoring working out of our lawyers' office. Through his contacts and his ongoing involvement, he gave the system a degree of sensitivity that caused it to respond and react appropriately. He knew many of the issues affecting the inmates. He had a sensitivity to some of those issues that the average person wouldn't have.

The administration embraced the idea that the consent decree was necessary under the circumstances, that a higher level of commitment was necessary to put the system in constitutional compliance. The governor was aware of all the circumstances. Governor Brown was sensitive to correctional issues. [Funding for compliance] was built into the budget, which the legislature also recognized as an area of considerable need.

Wilson set the policy for Kentucky prisons: the consent decree is the law, and we will obey it. He told his top administrators to treat it as a road map to steer the prisons. Despite all the complexities of the thirty-five-page document, Wilson's central message to corrections personnel was clear: they were merely implementing the law. In budgeting, managing, and hiring, all decisions were driven by the decree. Wilson and his top executive staff—budget director, legal counsel, and deputy commissioners—broke the consent decree down into areas and set priorities according to agreed timetables. Among the first obligations to be met were a 20 percent salary increase for guards and the hiring of additional guards and program staff. The executive staff members checked off all the people who had to be hired, position by position, then allocated funding from the budget for those new positions. Wilson and his advisers immediately set in motion the implementation of these priorities.

Written plans were also a necessity. One of the major problems at Eddyville and KSR was the lack of plans for prison operations, so that response to problems was often tardy or nonexistent and was never preventive. The consent decree mandated written plans for proper building maintenance, fire prevention and evacuation, provision of meals with adequate nutrition, proper medical care, and so forth.

Wilson also set major construction projects in motion. The dorms and cells at KSR and Eddyville were in a state of ruin, and a centerpiece of the consent decree was renovation of both prisons. The consent decree required the state to renovate one of KSR's eight open dorms per year over the next eight years, divide the dorms into single rooms, and provide each inmate with his own room. Renovation of the first two dormitories was estimated to cost more than $2 million. The money was in the commissioner's budget, so he opened the projects for bidding by construction firms.

The most pressing problem was to reduce the number of inmates at KSR and Eddyville. The state was required to reduce the combined population by six hundred inmates by November 28, 1980. Wilson developed several strategies for complying with this deadline. First, Wilson's records indicated that many men, especially at KSR, presented very little risk of violence or escape and thus qualified for reclassification to minimum-security status. Once reclassified, they could be transferred to one of the minimum-security prisons, which had empty beds.

Wilson's second strategy for meeting the November 28 population deadline was to speed up paroles. The state parole board had jurisdiction over decisions as to whether eligible prisoners' records of behavior indicated that they were ready to be released from prison on a trial basis. A number of inmates, especially at KSR, had model records demonstrating readiness for parole, so Wilson obtained the parole board's agreement to expedite grants of parole to those men.

An additional strategy was to establish a more flexible policy on parole violations. Once released on parole, people could be returned to prison if they failed to meet any of the conditions of parole, which were imposed by law. Fully one-third of the prisoners at KSR—nearly seven hundred men—were there because of parole violations, many of which were technical in nature. A technical parole violation occurred when a parolee violated one of the noncriminal conditions of parole, such as failing to report to his parole officer, losing his job, or leaving the county without permission. Since technical parole violators had not committed any new crime, Wilson decided such parolees presented a sufficiently low risk to society to justify keeping many of them out of prison, so parole officers were instructed to treat technical violations on a case-by-case basis.

The state calculated that transfers to minimum security, speeding up parole, and easing up on parole violations would reduce the population at KSR and Eddyville by less than 200 in the next six months, however, leaving more than 400 men to go. Thus, the most important strategy was to rely on the opening of a new prison that had been under construction since 1977, predating Wilson's tenure. The new Luther Luckett Correctional Complex would have cells for 480 men and a ninety-six-bed psychiatric hospital for mentally ill inmates. Luckett was scheduled to open in October 1980, so if all went as planned, enough men would be transferred from KSR and Eddyville to Luckett to easily meet the November 28 deadline. Unfortunately, obstacles soon arose.

Bad News

The bad news began in June 1980, two months after the historic consent decree had been signed. Carpenters went on strike at Luther Luckett for seven weeks, delaying the opening of the new prison. Prison officials informed the news media that the strike made it unlikely that they could comply with the November 28 deadline. Luther Luckett would not be open until December at the earliest, so officials hinted that they might ask the federal court for a delay in population reduction.

More bad news—primarily an outgrowth of the breadth and complexity of the reform process mandated by the consent decree rather than prison officials' recalcitrance—emerged in the summer meetings between the Plaintiffs' Committee and their lawyers. The prisoners had not seen any substantial changes in their living conditions at KSR, despite the consent decree's promises. The prison was still filthy, open sewage still flowed under the floors of the dorms because of holes in the sewage pipes, and guards continued to mistreat prisoners. Prisoners claimed that female guards continued to order male inmates to remove their clothing and submit to nude searches, prisoners were still placed in isolation cells without hearings, long lines remained at the mess hall, one unarmed guard still was assigned to cover all four wings of a dormitory, and guards continued to ignore fire alarms, leaving them ringing for as long as forty-five minutes until prisoners finally cut the wires because they could not bear the noise.

The written plans required by the consent decree also ran into problems. Prison officials had been attempting to write plans, as ordered by Wilson, for the operation of the prisons, but the officials were untrained to write useful plans, so the process degenerated into a pattern of, as one official put it, "We'll do this, we'll do that, we'll do this."[4] The plans were mere memos with no clear guidelines to follow.

There was some good news, however. Guards received a 10 percent raise, with another 10 percent committed, and the state organized an improved inmate-grievance procedure. Back at KSR, though, the Plaintiffs' Committee was frustrated with the lack of progress on living conditions. On September 23, 1980, the prisoners' lawyers filed a motion to hold the defendants in contempt of court for failing to obey the consent decree, charging the state with twenty-six violations.

Wilson was in a difficult position. Having started out with the best of intentions and having ordered corrections personnel to comply fully with the consent decree, he was now being charged with contempt of court and, though it was not yet part of the contempt motion, he was facing a November 28 deadline that he probably could not meet. Wilson could have responded with a strategy of intransigence such as characterized the Alabama and Texas cases, because the provisions concerning living conditions were sufficiently ambiguous to find loopholes. Wilson had a mission, however, to reform the prison system, and compliance with the consent decree was only one facet of this mission. He wanted to foster more professional behavior in corrections personnel and to create treatment programs that incorporated the latest research and trends in the field of corrections. Wilson thought he could obey every part of the decree in a technical sense and still have little impact on the prison system, but he sought to use the decree to advance his larger goal of achieving systemic reform. In this sense, Wilson's response to the early obstacles of compliance foreshadowed DiIulio's observation that "[c]ourts and corrections are permanently linked, and the question is how each can help rather than hurt each other."[5]

Wilson launched an attack on the problems in the fall of 1980. His first order of business was the contempt-of-court question. Judge Johnstone stepped in at this point and ordered the parties to meet, discuss the twenty-six contempt charges, and attempt to find solutions. Johnstone had a general philosophy that it is better for parties to a complex lawsuit to settle their own disputes than to have a judge order a solution, and especially in this case, he wanted to keep the spirit of consent alive. For his part, Wilson thought that most of the charges were legitimate inmate complaints and that finding solutions to them would result in a better prison. He saw no reason to oppose the majority of complaints, so he directed his lawyers to find solutions. Government lawyers met with the prisoners' lawyers, and together they reached agreement on most of the charges.

It remained for the judge to rule on the few unresolved complaints, the most important of which was filth and open sewage underneath the dorm floors. Judge Johnstone scheduled a hearing for October 22, 1980. The day before the hearing, he made another unannounced visit to KSR. He had the Plaintiffs' Committee show him around. In one of the dorms, Shorty said, "Look here, Judge." Inmates lifted up some floorboards. The judge peered down and saw raw sewage, including human waste, floating beneath the floor. One inmate pulled back his mattress and pointed to the underside, and Johnstone saw swarms of cockroaches crawling on the mattress. Just as on the first visit, another man pulled off the back of his radio, and cockroaches swarmed out. In another dorm, inmates politely asked the guard to open the fire emergency escape door. The guard fumbled with his key chain and tried key after key in the lock, but nothing worked: it was obvious that the guard could not open the door in case of fire and that he was unaware of that fact. Johnstone came away from this visit with the overall impression that KSR continued to suffer from filthy, dangerous conditions of which the prison administration was completely unaware. As the judge saw it, the problem was not that Wilson and his team were backsliding on the consent decree but rather that they needed to be educated about these problems.

The next day at the hearing, Johnstone ruled that sanitary conditions at KSR violated the consent decree and constituted a state of emergency; he ordered immediate improvements. He stopped short of holding the state in contempt of court, but his message was clear: the judge would enforce the consent decree if the need arose. A few weeks later, he also ordered the state to eliminate long lines for meals, provide fireproof trash barrels, and double the number of guards in the dorms.

The entire contempt controversy was a major success for the prisoners. Wilson cooperated with Johnstone's order. He ordered plumbing and other improvements to begin immediately, and the work was completed by late October.

By this time the deadline for reducing the population at KSR and Eddyville was only a month away. The combined populations had already been cut by three hundred men, leaving three hundred to go. The new Luther Luckett Correctional Complex certainly would not be open by November 28 because of the carpenters' strike. Wilson saw that he simply could not get another three hundred men out of KSR and Eddyville by November 28.

Wilson decided to take a proactive approach to the problem instead of waiting for the deadline to pass and then offering excuses to the court. He decided to generate some publicity, just as the prisoners had done prior to trial. He arranged an interview with Sheldon Shafer, the *Courier-Journal*'s reporter on the KSR litigation. Wilson wanted to be sure that Judge Johnstone was aware of the problem and was not surprised when the deadline was missed. He also wanted both the judge and the prisoners to know, well ahead of time, that the cause of the delay was beyond his control and that he was doing all he could to find another solution.

Shafer had a long talk with the commissioner and then wrote another front-page story, this time about the population problem. The story hit the newsstands on November 10, 1980, less than three weeks before the deadline.

With several thousand inmates and a federal judge looking over his shoulder, state Corrections Commissioner George Wilson admits a "sense of urgency" in reshaping Kentucky's long-neglected prison system.

Wilson's most pressing problem is reducing the population of the Kentucky State Reformatory near LaGrange by about 300 inmates in less than three weeks.

That could mean reaching for some unusual solution. For example, he has looked into housing prisoners at closed schools in Jefferson County.

The settlement calls for the state to have reduced the combined populations of the reformatory and penitentiary by a total of 600 by November 28.

Nearly all the reduction is to be at the reformatory; its population has fallen from about 2,150 last spring to 1,850.

Some inmates have been transferred to federal prisons, others have gone to Kentucky's minimum-security prisons, some are in new halfway houses and the release of a few has been expedited.

The hitch is that the state had hoped to move about 400 inmates into the new medium-security Luther Luckett Correctional Complex being built near the reformatory. It was to be open by now, but construction was held up by last summer's strike by carpenters, and it may not open until February.

Wilson said he plans to "exhaust every resource" to meet the deadline, but he doesn't want to rule out the state's right to ask the court for an extension.

Wilson is checking on old schools, abandoned treatment centers, unfilled halfway houses, even Army bases to find a place to house, at least temporarily, about 300 inmates.

He won't speculate on what will be done but said he is negotiating on several fronts. He said he won't put prisoners in places where they and the community aren't protected.

Wilson has looked at the old juvenile-detention center and the abandoned Ormsby Village treatment center in Jefferson County, but neither is available.

He has also talked with Jefferson County public school officials about using abandoned school property. And he's looked at Fort Knox and Fort Campbell.

A good bet may be one or more old schools in Western Louisville owned by the Roman Catholic Archdiocese. Father Pat Delahanty, coordinator for the West End Catholic Council, said some properties probably could be made available.

Wilson said that, eventually, he hopes to get the reformatory population below 1,400, or near its ideal capacity.[6]

The editors of the *Courier-Journal* followed Shafer's story two days later with an editorial. The state's leading newspaper threw its influence behind Wilson and called on the prisoners to back off on the November 28 deadline.

Prisoners Should Bend a Little, Too, in Seeking Their Greater Goals

Kentucky prisoners, having won a monumental lawsuit in April, are right to keep pressure on the state to live up to its agreements. But they'll fare better in the long run if they'll be reasonable when unforeseen circumstances keep the state from sticking to its timetable.

That has happened at the badly overcrowded Kentucky State Reformatory near LaGrange. The state faces a November 28 deadline to reduce the number of inmates there by about 400 from 2,087 last spring. It planned to move them into the new medium-security Luther Luckett Correctional Complex nearby. But a carpenters' strike last summer delayed construction; the opening is off until perhaps February.

Corrections Commissioner George Wilson, as the Courier-Journal's Sheldon Shafer reported Monday, has worked hard to find temporary quarters elsewhere for inmates who must be moved. It's possible he may have to ask federal Judge Edward Johnstone for an extension; the prisoners' attorney responds that they might ask, instead, for a freeze on admission of new inmates until the goal is reached.

We suspect that the judge, if push comes to shove, will side with Commissioner Wilson. The state once lagged as badly as most in making its prisons habitable and humane. It is now getting good marks from even its severest critics for making a conscientious (and costly) effort to improve. But public backing is vital, especially since some of the improvements will include more halfway houses and other programs that require community understanding and support.

So it would be foolish of the inmates to unnecessarily alienate the public, during a difficult period of major reform in custody and rehabilitation, by not voluntarily bending a bit if the state is delayed by circumstances it can't control.

There is no excuse, either in simple human fairness or in the long-term interests of society in reducing crime, for some of the past conditions and treatment in Kentucky prisons. But the Brown administration and Commissioner Wilson are showing strong interest in going beyond the letter of the law. The inmates who had so much to do in forcing overdue reform won't want to jeopardize that state interest—and the public support that makes it possible—by making the job unnecessarily harder.[7]

The editors' message to the prisoners was clear: we are on your side for prison reform, but you will put the reforms in danger if you try to hold Wilson to the November 28 deadline. The editors probably agreed that Wilson had no place to put the prisoners at that time, so the only option left within the terms of the decree was to release hundreds of prisoners onto the streets, in which case, the editors believed, a public outcry would ensue and higher authorities would abandon Wilson's reform program.

November 28 arrived, and, as expected, the state missed the goal by about two hundred men. The state's lawyers filed a motion in federal court asking the judge to extend the deadline until Luther Luckett opened. On the same day, the prisoners' lawyers filed their second motion asking the judge to hold the state in contempt of court, this time for failing to meet the population deadline. The prisoners had decided to stick to the deadline, not because they were ignorant of the problems at Luther Luckett but because they simply did not trust the prison system or the state. The prisoners believed that agreeing to a delay at this point would lead to more delays and more backsliding on the consent decree. The next crucial population deadline, May 28, 1981, was only six months away, at which time the state was required to have reduced the population of KSR and Eddyville by more than a thousand inmates. Compliance with that requirement would bring the two prisons into conformity with the American Correctional Association's design-capacity standards, so that overcrowding would at last be eliminated. The way Shorty put it, if the prisoners let the state off the hook on the November 28 deadline, they would be doing the same for the following deadline; consequently, the prisoners felt an obligation to oppose every request for delay. Judge Johnstone held a hearing on December 22 at the federal courthouse in Louisville. Shafer was in the courtroom, and he reported the result the next day, again on the front page of the *Courier-Journal*.

State to Get More Time to Cut Prison Populations

U.S. District Judge Edward Johnstone said yesterday that he will give the state more time to further reduce the populations of its two largest prisons.

But he indicated that he will probably grant only one extension of the deadline.

Last May, in settling an inmate lawsuit over conditions at the Kentucky State Reformatory and the Kentucky State Penitentiary, the state pledged to reduce the number of inmates at the two prisons by 600 by November 28. As of December 16 the number of inmates was down 414.

In federal court in Louisville yesterday, attorneys for the state Bureau of Corrections asked to be given until April 15 to meet the goal.

By then the state is to have moved about 400 men to the Luther Luckett Correctional Complex being built near the reformatory in Oldham County. The state says the new prison is to open by March 1 and will take 30 to 45 days to reach full capacity.

A construction strike that delayed work on the prison about two months was one reason the state missed the deadline.

The inmates' attorneys had asked that the state be held in contempt for violating the settlement sanctioned by Johnstone. The attorneys had also asked that Johnstone prohibit the two prisons from accepting new inmates until the inmate-reduction goal is reached.

When Johnstone indicated midway through final arguments that he would grant the state more time, the inmates' attorneys asked for a February 1 deadline. That date was also suggested by the U.S. Justice Department's Civil Rights Division, a friend of the court in the case.

In the end Johnstone postponed setting a deadline. At one point he hinted it may be March 15.

Pointing a finger at the state Justice Department's general counsel, Johnstone said: "The court will grant an extension. The Bureau of Corrections has made a good faith attempt" to comply with the settlement.

But he added that he wants the new deadline to be the final one.

Johnstone also said he didn't want to tie the reduction to the opening of Luther Luckett because it would get the court "involved in corrections decisions."[8]

Judge Johnstone thus let Wilson off the hook for missing the November 28 deadline. Some questions were left unresolved, however, such as how much additional time Wilson would have to get another two hundred prisoners out and, once he did so, whether he was prohibited from inching the population up again. On January 14, 1981, Judge Johnstone made his final decision on the six-hundred-man population-reduction controversy, giving the state until February 28, 1981, to meet the target population. That was a month more than the prisoners' lawyers had suggested but was a month and a half less than the state's lawyers had wanted. Johnstone also capped the population, so that if the state failed to meet the six-hundred-man figure by February 28, it could not put any more prisoners into KSR or Eddyville until it met that goal. In the event of failure to reduce the population, the prison doors would close on March 1, 1981. The judge had handed down a compromise decision. The state received what it most wanted, a delay in meeting the initial population-reduction deadline. At the same time, however, Johnstone had made it clear that he would not bend if the state asked for any more delays in ending overcrowding.

The decision gave Wilson a little room to maneuver. He did not dare rely on opening Luther Luckett to meet the new February 28 deadline; Wilson had to find other ways that were more in his control. Over the next month, he ordered more prisoners transferred to federal prisons, minimum-security prisons, halfway houses, and county jails and achieved a new agreement with the parole board to expedite paroles. By mid-February, Wilson was confident that he would meet the February 28 population deadline. He was only forty-five men short and was certain that he could further reduce the population in the two remaining weeks. It was a difficult process that involved making enemies in the state government and spending a good deal of money, but Wilson was determined to comply with the revised deadline. Wilson and Shafer met again and talked about these efforts, and the reporter wrote his ninth major story about Shorty's lawsuit.

State Expects to Meet Deadline for Prison Cuts

The state will meet a February 28 deadline for reducing the number of inmates at two prisons, but the effort has put "immense pressure" on finances, staff and smaller jails, Corrections Commissioner George Wilson said yesterday.

To meet the federal deadline, the Bureau of Corrections needs to move about 45 more prisoners from the Kentucky State Penitentiary at Eddyville and the Kentucky State Reformatory near LaGrange.

Yesterday the reformatory had 1,604 and the penitentiary about 715, said Al Parke, a bureau deputy commissioner. That was about 555 fewer than last May.

To reduce the prisons' populations, inmates have been reassigned to minimum security and transferred to federal prisons, halfway houses and county jails.

In addition about 40 have been released since November through intensified reviews by the Kentucky Parole Board.

To meet the deadline, inmates will be moved to minimum-security prisons or furloughed. Furloughs are sometimes granted to prisoners who have made parole and need to look for work.

The effort to meet the deadline means that the state's three largest minimum-security prisons are packed.

Blackburn Correctional Complex in Lexington, for example, had 170 inmates two years ago; it now has 325.

The populations of the state's two prison farms are also up sharply, mainly from taking reformatory inmates.

Roederer Farm Center, the Western Kentucky Farm Center and Blackburn "are certainly pressing their upper capability," Wilson said.

Wilson said the strain on minimum-security prisons will be relieved when the new medium-security Luther Luckett Correctional Complex opens.

Luckett, which is near the reformatory, may receive its first 100 inmates by mid-March, Wilson said. Construction delays were a main reason the state missed the November 28 deadline.

Wilson said that some probation and parole officers have doubled their workloads lately to help meet the deadline.

He said the crunch has come from transporting more prisoners to job interviews, increased supervision at the county jails housing state inmates and intense screening of inmates' records to find out which ones might be released or reassigned.

But Wilson was confident that he isn't turning loose dangerous men.

"I won't put dangerous people on the street. I won't do it, even if it means missing the deadline," he said.

Wilson said state officials will soon have to make some hard decisions about money. He wasn't specific, but he said complying with the court order had caused severe financial problems for the Bureau.[9]

Wilson did meet the February 28 deadline, but he was still facing the May 28 deadline. Luther Luckett was scheduled to open in mid-March and would hold more than four hundred men, thereby, in theory, enabling Wilson to meet the next deadline. Once again, however, unforeseen obstacles, created by the enemies Wilson had made in meeting the February 28 deadline, threatened the implementation process.

Power Struggle

Soon after the judge's deadline, a vicious bureaucratic fight broke out between Wilson and his superior, the secretary of the Kentucky Department of Justice. The secretary of justice was a new man in town, a former FBI official named Neil Welch. Governor Brown had recruited Welch for this job in 1980 because Welch had a strong reputation, based on his involvement in a famous FBI sting operation known as ABSCAM, for rooting out government corruption. Welch and Wilson clashed almost immediately. Wilson thought Welch did not know how to administer a prison system, yet, in Wilson's view, Welch decided to demonstrate that he was in complete charge of the Department of Justice, including setting policy for the prison system.

Without first asking Wilson, Welch moved Wilson's handpicked deputy commissioner, a reform-minded professional from Oklahoma named Al Parke, into the warden's post at Eddyville and moved Eddyville warden Dewey Sowders into the deputy commissioner's post.

Welch made a couple of administration changes without consulting me. They moved my deputy commissioner to Eddyville and moved the warden from Eddyville to central office. He called me, then gave me a letter and told me that he wanted me to send it out, send a memorandum ordering that change.

I suspected it had been done in his office. I refused to do it. I told him that he had to do it himself if it was going to happen. If I wasn't involved in the decision making, I wouldn't send it out.

He did send the memorandum out. In the meantime I was in consultation with the governor. The governor agreed with me that Welch should not have done that, but it then hit the media.

I had to make a professional decision about whether or not I wanted to have him retract it after it had been announced and cause a whole lot of disruption among the inmate population about not knowing who was in control. It was a very heavy decision—I mean, one minute there's an announcement that a person had been made warden, and then I go and get it reversed, and he's not the warden? The implications of that on the prison population could be fairly grave.

So I chose instead to register a protest with the governor that I would not continue to operate under those circumstances. If it happened again, I'd leave.

Secretary Welch's next move was to clamp a freeze on hiring any new people in the prison system. Brown had ordered his cabinet secretaries to find ways to cut spending, because the state was experiencing a revenue shortfall. Welch in turn had decided that one way to cut spending in the prison system was to order Wilson to stop hiring new people.

Welch's hiring freeze caused a legal problem with the consent decree, which contained the state's commitment to open up the psychiatric hospital for mentally ill prisoners at the Luther Luckett Correctional Complex. Once the psychiatric hospital was open, a notorious unit at Eddyville, proven to be a horror chamber of abuse and neglect of mentally ill men, would be shut down. Luckett was by now nearly ready to open, but staff still had to be hired to operate it. In the face of Welch's hiring freeze, the hospital could not open as promised. Thus, the hiring freeze became a crucial test of the state's willingness to live up to its commitments in the decree.

Wilson again used the media to demonstrate that obstacles had arisen to delay compliance with the consent decree. He had another talk with Shafer, and the result was Shafer's tenth major article about the Kentucky prison litigation.

Prison Upgrading Could Be Delayed by Budget Problems

State budget problems apparently will indefinitely delay the opening of a psychiatric hospital for inmates and put off compliance with a federal court order to improve Kentucky's prison system.

Justice Secretary Neil Welch has ordered a hiring freeze in the Bureau of Corrections, and the new $50 million hospital in Oldham County can't open, Corrections Commissioner George Wilson said yesterday.

The hospital's opening is required under the court order and Wilson said the state probably will ask the court to give it more time to get the facility operating.

Wilson said Welch directed the hiring freeze about three weeks ago. He said he didn't fight Welch on the matter, but "I explained to him what the implications were—that part of the (court order) can't be fulfilled with the existing staffing level."

The two officials have had differences lately, stemming in part from the amount of money needed to comply with the court settlement.

And last week, Welch ordered Dewey Sowders, who had been the penitentiary warden, and Al Parke, a deputy corrections commissioner, to exchange posts. The transfers came over Wilson's objections.

Wilson had considered resigning, but he said yesterday: "I am going to stay on. We talked and got some understandings. That is all I am going to say" about the difference between himself and Welch.

Governor John Y. Brown Jr. recently met with the two on their differences.

Welch could not be reached for comment yesterday.

Wilson said yesterday that he didn't know when the hospital might open.

Wilson said he can't staff the hospital because of the hiring freeze. He said, "I need about 100 more people for the hospital, and I can't open it with what I've got." If it opened with too small a staff, the hospital would violate state certification rules, he said.

The hospital is completed except for some finishing touches. It is to have 96 beds for mentally and emotionally disturbed inmates.[10]

Wilson abstained from discussing what he felt were the underlying problems. Wilson thought that Welch's hiring freeze involved more than a problem of obeying the court order. Judge Johnstone had granted a delay on the first population deadline, and he might grant more time to open the psychiatric hospital as well. The larger issues for Wilson involved power and race. Behind the hiring freeze and the legal issues lay the question of who was in charge of the prison system. Wilson believed that Welch did not understand prison administration and that some other officials resented having a black man in charge of corrections policy.

When you get a new administration, you get a shift of the players. Some of them understood the prison issues, and some didn't.

There was an unprecedented amount of resources going into corrections. At the same time, there was a tremendous revenue shortage in the state, so corrections stood out because we were getting additional resources where everybody else was being cut back. So there was some clamoring or some pressure as to why we were adding personnel and everybody else was cutting people.

We had to educate the people that the state had made a commitment to do those things, and if it didn't, we would possibly have to go through continued litigation. And that litigation may not be to our advantage. It could cost us more, like the Alabama case and some others, where states had fought litigation and had taken somewhat of a licking. So it was a teaching process with higher-ups in government as well as my superiors.

The situation came about that there was just a clear difference of philosophy about what was correct as far as corrections was concerned. I felt like that professionally I had as good a grasp on correctional issues as any of the other players and that as commissioner, I should not give up my position, that I had to argue what I thought was right, and based on the issues as opposed to just giving in.

That caused a conflict. It came down to whether or not I would be in control and, if I was going to be responsible, whether or not I'd be able to make the decisions that I thought were appropriate. The problem was communications and not understanding what the issues were. I was forced to articulate issues in a very forceful way, which was in conflict with what was going on in other sections of the government. In some cases they didn't understand what corrections was about, and there were people trying to input the area who didn't know anything about it. And I would not allow that. I wasn't going to accept that somebody, perceived to be more powerful than me, could just come in and tell me that I was going to have to do it a certain way, and then hold me responsible for it.

And I think there was an issue subtly lurking about. In Kentucky prior to this, there had not been a black serving at the commissioner or secretary level. Although it was not said, I think there was some underlying concern about (1) whether or not I was capable, and (2) whether I was strong enough to make the case, or whether or not I was a token black. I had to make clear that I did not take the job for the sake of the salary and that I believed in what I was doing and expected to be treated that way.

Kentucky now had a high-level governmental power struggle. There were rumors that Welch had ordered undercover state police units to follow Wilson around, wiretap his phones, and bug his offices. According to these rumors, Welch was seeking to obtain information with which he could force Wilson out of government. These rumors were never proved, but in politics perception can have more impact than fact, and many people in Kentucky believed that the secretary of justice had the corrections commissioner under surveillance.

Judge Johnstone was disturbed by these conflicts because he was certain that Wilson was committed to complying with the consent decree and that the attacks on him were, at bottom, attacks on the effort to reform the prisons. Once again, Johnstone intervened by the back channel, this time in an effort to influence the political struggle between Welch and Wilson. The judge's law clerk, Phil Shepard, had worked for influential lawyer Ed Pritchard during law school. Pritchard was going blind by the 1970s and hired Shepard as a reader. The two men got along well, and Shepard went to work in Pritchard's law firm after graduation, subsequently clerking for Judge Johnstone. When the Welch-Wilson struggle broke out, Johnstone let Shepard know that it might be a good idea if Pritchard and the *Courier-*

Journal were made aware that Wilson had the federal judge's full support. Shepard conveyed Johnstone's views to Pritchard and to the newspaper.

The *Courier-Journal*'s editors jumped into the conflict. They opined that Welch was at fault in the conflict and called for the governor to back Wilson.

Conflict in Kentucky's Justice Department Dims a Great Potential

The apparent conflict between state Justice Secretary Neil Welch and Corrections Commissioner George Wilson is painful to anyone interested in good state government for Kentucky.

Governor Brown considered it a triumph to attract Mr. Welch, a former F.B.I. administrator, to Kentucky. And indeed, his reputation as a law enforcer looked like powerful insurance against the kind of corruption that has infected some past state administrations.

Mr. Wilson appeared to be an equally fine choice. Experts in the field consider him outstanding as an administrator and an authority on corrections. His record in Frankfort confirms that confidence.

Nevertheless, Mr. Welch, without Mr. Wilson's approval, has just shaken up the top-level command in the Corrections Department. Al C. Parke, a Berea native whom Mr. Wilson brought back from Oklahoma to serve as deputy commissioner, has replaced Dewey Sowders as warden of the maximum-security prison at Eddyville. Mr. Sowders moved into the deputy commissioner's chair.

Both of those men also have excellent reputations. But on the surface, at least, both seem better qualified for the jobs they had than for the new ones. Mr. Sowders has done impressive work at Eddyville, but he lacks the broad background in corrections that Mr. Parke has. Mr. Parke, though he has experience as a warden, has never run a maximum-security prison.

The shift is billed as a cross-training exercise. But the timing is odd. And Mr. Welch, who has had no experience in corrections at all, seems in the process to have badly undercut Mr. Wilson's authority. The root of the problem, some observers say, is last year's $42 million settlement of a lawsuit demanding an overhaul of the state's prison system. The state faces the task of complying with this agreement at a time when sagging revenues are causing severe cutbacks in other essential services.

Some say personality conflicts also may be involved. But the money seems more important. Mr. Welch is said to feel that Mr. Sowders may be more effective in finding ways to trim expenses.

In the final analysis, U.S. District Judge Edward Johnstone, who is supervising the prison reform settlement, may have the most to say about the money issues. In the meantime, there's disarray in an area of state government that should be a source of pride to this administration. The Governor should do his best to calm the troubled waters.[11]

The prisoners' lawyers also intervened in the power struggle because it was clear that Welch's hiring freeze would delay the opening of the new psychiatric hospital and because, despite the prior contempt issues, they believed that Wilson was genuinely committed to complying with the consent decree and that Welch was undermining Wilson's ability to do so. The lawyers decided to take Welch's deposition so that they could question him, on the record, about the hiring freeze and other policy conflicts. Welch demanded that the deposition be sealed from public view, so that no one could read his testimony except the lawyers and the judge. Judge Johnstone agreed.

The lawyers took Welch's deposition, during which it became clear that he had been quietly trying to undermine Wilson. The lawyers decided to ask Johnstone to unseal the deposition and make it available to the public. The judge scheduled a telephone conference call with the lawyers. Shafer found out about the sealed deposition and arranged to be present in a lawyer's office for the crucial conference call.

> *Welch gave a deposition that said some very harsh things about George Wilson. And for some reason the deposition was sealed. Several people, including the newspaper, raised the question of how comments about a public issue by a public official could be sealed.*
>
> *The lawyer applied to unseal it. He had the deposition. He gave it to me, embargoed. That's kind of a buzz word, which means you have information that you can't print until the source of the information gives you permission to do it. It's frequently embargoed if somebody is having a press conference at 10:00 in the morning. A lot of times they give us the information beforehand if you don't print it, just so you can background yourself. So I couldn't publish anything in this case until the judge says it's OK. If the judge had never unsealed it, well then, we never could print it.*
>
> *The lawyer had a conference call among a couple of attorneys and the judge. I was sitting there listening on the speakerphone in his office when Johnstone gave the word to unseal it.*

I thought it was a very bold decision to unseal the deposition. And at that time I already had the document, and I took it back to the office and wrote it up. It was a very interesting deposition because, more than anything else, it revealed a lot of personal insights about what kind of man Welch was.

Once Welch's deposition was made public, the decisive confrontation between Welch and Wilson was unavoidable, because one of them had to go. Wilson obtained a copy of the deposition. He was not surprised by what he read, and he knew the time had come to go straight to the governor, who could no longer smooth things out between the secretary and the commissioner. Brown sought Pritchard's advice. Pritchard presumably told the governor that Judge Johnstone supported Wilson. According to the commissioner,

Welch had a whole list of things that he had alleged in federal court that I was involved in, that in some ways had illegal connotations or criminal connotations—that I was spending money unwisely, that I'd had several parties. He never did accuse me of it. He did it through innuendoes. He testified in federal court to some of that stuff and then asked that the records be sealed.

In fact he was trying to impugn my credibility so that my credibility in arguing the issues would be undermined, and I would not be able to carry out some policies.

The governor supported me. There were others that didn't, but in that case you only need the vote of one. After many discussions with John Y. Brown, he was convinced that I knew the field. I had his confidence that I was making decisions that were in the best interest of the department and the commonwealth. I think ultimately that bore in the decision to separate us from justice, and make us a cabinet [department].

Ultimately, when he made the decision, one of the things that weighed in my favor is that he knew a couple things had occurred that were wrong and incorrect. . . . Obviously he believed in what I was doing, otherwise he wouldn't have elevated me to cabinet status, given that backdrop of events, and made me secretary.

Brown's decision appeared neutral at first. In July 1981 he separated the Bureau of Corrections from the Department of Justice and renamed the bureau the Department of Corrections. Corrections was now part of the governor's cabinet, and the secretary had cabinet rank. Brown named Wilson as the first secretary of the new department. Welch remained secretary of justice. On the surface, it looked like a mere cabinet shuffle. A crucial power shift lay behind the formal changes, however. As a secretary in the governor's cabinet, Wilson would have far greater authority and prestige than would a commissioner reporting to a secretary. He would, it appeared, report directly to the governor, not to another secretary. Welch lost his authority over the prison system.

Respect

Wilson's struggle for authority over the prison system was not quite over. Welch's accusations still hung over Wilson's head, making the governor uneasy. Consequently, Brown shuffled the cabinet again. He named his secretary of transportation, Frank Metts, as vice chairman of the cabinet and ordered Wilson to report to Metts, even though Wilson had equal rank in the cabinet. Wilson was the only cabinet secretary who reported to another secretary instead of directly to the governor.

Wilson went along with this unusual arrangement for a few months, but it failed. Metts had no background in prison administration, yet like Welch before him, Metts attempted to dictate prison policy to Wilson. Wilson came to feel that he was reporting to Metts because he was the first black person ever to reach cabinet level in the state's history and people were uncomfortable with that development. By July 1981 it was again time to confront the governor.

> Brown's way of handling Welch's allegations was to say that "until we get the cloud resolved, I want you to work with Metts, because this thing is still in the air. Report through Metts until we can get this thing resolved."
>
> I agreed to do that for a period of time. And that period of time, he said, was "three or four months, until we can get this thing resolved."
>
> As experience dictated it, Metts got very involved in the operations.
>
> I confronted the governor again: "I'm the only secretary reporting to a secretary, and I won't do that. Now, you make your decision: if you don't have confidence [in me], say so and I'll be gone, and you don't have to worry about it." . . .

Brown didn't want to do that, I don't think. But there was that last little bit of trusting me to make decisions. I can't say that it was racist, [but] there was a racist strain to it. No black had ever operated in the state at that level. . . .

When I talked with the governor the final time, he understood what I was saying.

Brown discontinued the arrangement and made Wilson a full-fledged cabinet member, reporting directly to the governor for the first time. Wilson was the first black person to reach that level in the state's history. His struggle for authority was over, and he was in complete control of the prison system by July 1981. Years of hard work lay ahead: he had to comply with the consent decree's many promises, and he was committed to bringing new treatment programs and modern professional standards to the Kentucky prison system. It would take eight years to complete the job, and education, roads, and other more popular programs would compete for public funding. More unforeseen and unintended obstacles would continue to hinder his efforts, yet the most crucial battles for prison reform were fought from June 1980 to July 1981, the first year of implementing the consent decree, during which time Wilson faced contempt-of-court motions, missed a critical population deadline, and became locked in a power struggle with his cabinet secretary. He overcame every challenge.

I think it was a period of teaching some people that I am serious about this and that I'm going to be treated like everyone else. And I tried to do that without flag-waving, but by the same token it was clear I would not take it.

There were two or three times that I offered my resignation. Not a lot of people know that. They know something happened, in order for the thing to happen as it did, but they don't know what. But it happened because I was willing to put it on the line, to get control as I should have, and I was willing to accept the responsibility. I said, "I'll take the lick. If I do something wrong or have to be held accountable for something, that is my responsibility. I'm a man, and if I do something wrong, fire me. Treat me like everybody else, but give me the stick. I'm not going to let somebody else call the shots and then hold me responsible. And I mean it."

It could be no other way, particularly in this field. It has to be clear where the signals are called. In corrections, uncertainty of command and unrest and instability is a frightening thing. People, particularly inmates

and staff, need to know where the signals are, who's calling what. . . .
These people's lives are really dependent on who's making decisions every
day. Who's at the top is very significant to them. They get cues from that.
If they trust you, and your credibility is good with them, they'll generally
follow through. But if there's instability, if they're confused, if they get a
feeling that somebody is not dealing in their best interest, it causes unrest.
They don't have to agree with me. They just have to know that the person
is credible.

Most of the time, if they know, they'll live with it. You come in and say,
"Listen, I'm going to punish you for this, this, and this," and they do it,
and you punish them, they accept it. If you go in and change the rules on
them every day, and they don't know who or what, it causes us a problem.

After a rocky start because of political infighting, the way was now clear
for true reform to occur at KSR. A cabinet secretary who had staked his
career on reform was fully in charge of the prison system, and he had a
federal judge for support. Wilson and his staff, unlike recalcitrant prison
officials in Texas and Alabama, embraced the consent decree as their
means of achieving systemic change but were not always able to adhere
to the decree's scheduled requirements. During this first year of both
progress and frustration in implementing the decree, however, Wilson
used the news media, the support of Judge Johnstone, a plaintiffs' deposition, and the force of his own personality to overcome the obstacles and
strengthen his administration's position for the compliance struggles that
lay ahead.

Prison Reform and Gender Discrimination

The KSR-Eddyville litigation also had a major impact on the state's
women's prison. Perhaps because of the early problems encountered in
complying with the consent decree governing the men's prisons, the state
refused to settle separate litigation over conditions at the women's prison,
the Kentucky Correctional Institution for Women (KCIW) in Pewee Valley, not far from LaGrange. The ensuing 1981 trial set the stage for Judge
Johnstone to render a decision on gender discrimination at KCIW in which
the men's consent decree was a major factor. Furthermore, his decision
was a pathbreaking precedent that reverberated throughout the nation.

Female inmates brought suit in U.S. District Court, claiming that conditions at KCIW were unconstitutional, but on a different legal theory than the male inmates had advanced. Whereas the male inmates had claimed that the conditions in the men's prisons constituted cruel and unusual punishment in violation of the Eighth Amendment to the U.S. Constitution, the women alleged that conditions at KCIW violated their rights under the Fourteenth Amendment to equal protection of the law. Their theory was that, largely (though not solely) because of the reforms at the men's prisons mandated by the consent decree, vast disparities had arisen between female and male prisoners' living conditions and opportunities for vocational training and education. Repeating his proactive approach in Shorty's lawsuit, Judge Johnstone quickly certified the case as a class action entitled *Canterino v. Wilson* and permitted the U.S. Department of Justice to intervene as amicus curiae.

The trial lasted four weeks and focused on three areas of concern: the "levels system" at KCIW, which was designed as a behavior-modification program to promote positive behavior but which the plaintiffs contended had become merely a tool for punishment with harmful effects on inmates; vocational education, training, and jobs, asserted by the plaintiffs to be inferior to opportunities available at the men's prisons; and the totality of living conditions at KCIW, including overcrowding and unequal provision of services such as legal assistance, recreation, and grievance procedures. In his findings of fact, Judge Johnstone ruled that the levels system, in which a female inmate's opportunity to live in the more desirable areas at KCIW was determined by her ability to adhere to rules of conduct, had degenerated into a demoralizing method of punishment in which women were treated like children and every detail of their lives was controlled by their ability to avoid disciplinary charges. Comparing this system to the classification system in the men's prisons established by the consent decree, he further found that the levels system resulted in "massive disparities within Kentucky's penal system between male and female prisoners in the availability of privileges and the opportunity to fulfill basic human needs." With respect to vocational education, training, and jobs, Judge Johnstone found that "[s]imilar inadequacies and disparities are pervasive in the areas of on the job training, work assignments, academic opportunities, and opportunities for community release and recreation." Finally, he found that living conditions at KCIW were inferior to those at the men's prisons, and again the consent decree had an important impact on his analysis. For example, Judge Johnstone emphasized that the state had agreed to abide by American Correctional Association minimum standards for housing male prisoners, yet conditions at KCIW fell well below such standards.[12]

Whether these disparities between the treatment of female and male prisoners amounted to a violation of equal protection of the law presented Judge Johnstone with a difficult problem, for, unlike the men's case, which was guided by precedents from the Arkansas, Mississippi, Oklahoma, and Alabama cases, there was only a single reported case, *Glover v. Johnson*, pertaining to women's prisons.[13] Moreover, the *Glover* decision was limited to the issues of classification and vocational training and jobs, so that Judge Johnstone had no direct precedent on the totality-of-conditions discrimination issue. Nevertheless, he chose to follow the reasoning of *Glover* and concluded that the disparities between female and male inmates wrought by the levels system and the lack of adequate education and jobs were not justified by any important government interest and therefore violated the female inmates' right to equal protection of the law. Acknowledging the lack of direct precedent on the totality-of-conditions issue, Judge Johnstone drew analogies from nonprison cases such as university education and took the unprecedented step of extending equal-protection guarantees to prison living conditions. Having done so, Judge Johnstone ruled that the disparities between male and female inmates with respect to housing, recreation, grievance procedures, legal assistance, and personal-hygiene supplies—disparities that had been brought about primarily by the consent decree in the men's litigation—deprived the women of equal protection of the law. In conclusion, Judge Johnstone connected the wide variety of issues decided in *Canterino* to a central theme: "The Court has been guided by a general principle in this case: male and female prisoners must be treated equally unless there is a substantial reason which requires a distinction to be made."[14]

Judge Johnstone's decision in *Canterino* became a leading precedent for other cases across the United States in which federal courts ruled that disparities in treatment of female and male prisoners constituted illegal gender discrimination.[15] Thus, the judge's efforts to mediate the settlement that produced the consent decree in Shorty's lawsuit, along with the efforts of all the other participants in that case, had a broad impact beyond the immediate effect on Kentucky's male prisons.

Personal Struggles

During the corrections administration's struggle to implement the consent decree, the lives of the three inmates who played key roles in the litigation followed a similar mixed pattern of progress and setback. Wilgus Haddix and Shorty Thompson ceased active participation in the litigation because they left KSR, and Walter Harris emerged as the prisoners' designated leader in their effort to enforce the decree. The lives of all three, however, remained entwined with the litigation as they continued their individual struggles to rise above the squalid conditions to which they had been subjected and to achieve a measure of human dignity.

About the same time George Wilson was appointed secretary of corrections, Walter became eligible for parole after eight years behind bars. He had compiled a good prison record, stayed out of trouble, done well in the prison school, and held steady jobs. He had a plan, if he were granted parole, to pursue a college degree at the University of Kentucky. The parole board was impressed and granted Walter parole in July 1981.

But Walter was not ready for parole. He went to Lexington, rented an apartment, and enrolled in the university, lasting less than seven months.

I started having woman problems. I started resorting to the same things that led me to be incarcerated in the first place, only not to the extreme this time. My parole was violated.

He was convicted of robbery and sentenced to ten years in prison. Walter was back at KSR by February 1982.

Walter: No More Mr. Loner

In the early days of his return to KSR, Walter tried to retreat back into the woodwork, stay out of trouble, avoid being noticed, attend prison school, get an innocuous job, and wait for his next parole eligibility date. He wanted nothing to do with the consent decree or with trying to improve conditions at KSR. Walter wanted to be Mr. Loner again. The inmates on the yard refused to leave him alone, however. The prisoners were unhappy with the pace of implementing the decree. The carpenters' strike and the power struggle between Wilson and Neil Welch had slowed everything down. Nearly two years had passed since Shorty's lawsuit was settled, and the men believed that life for the average prisoner was little improved. Most of the dorms remained in shambles, the food was still filthy and lacking in nutrition, inmates were idle most of the time because the school and job-training programs had too few positions, and prison jobs remained a pretense of meaningful work. Shorty had served out his sentence and gone home, so the prisoners had no leadership. To the prisoners, the consent decree looked like a mere piece of paper with no substance. As Walter recalled,

Everybody was wondering what I was going to do, even guards. I never thought my role initially was that prestigious or influential. Apparently they thought I had wielded some influence on the Plaintiffs' Committee, so they would come around and just ask me, here and there, what I was going to do. I was taking a low profile, trying to work on my own case. After I got done, I started working on other cases.

They just came and got me out of the woodwork again—figured that

I wasn't being fair to the guys since I had signed my name to the consent decree and represented it to be about the best deal we could come up with at the time. It got to the point where guys were saying that I sold 'em out.

I was telling them that anything I signed my name to, I would stand by. And if it turned out that it was actually a sellout, I'd own up to it. I wasn't convinced at that point that's what it was. And since I was back in prison, I just said, "What the hell."

About that time, a new warden came along. I thought he was a good guy, but he could only go so far. He needed somebody to antagonize him a bit. So I elected myself, got back on the committee.

The Plaintiffs' Committee by this time consisted of all new members who understood very little about the consent decree. They were bickering among themselves, and the bickering bothered the men on the yard. The general prison population was well aware of the decree. When the case was settled, every prisoner had received a copy of it, so the men knew what was in it and wanted it enforced.

The perception of the population changed. At the time the negotiations were going on, you could have told the guys out in the yard anything you wanted to tell them. Based on your charisma, they would either go with you or against you. If they liked you, it didn't make any difference whether they understood what you were saying or not.

But as things went along, especially when you started talking about visiting and living conditions, they developed a genuine interest in the consent decree. When they saw interest just didn't die off after a couple of months and that people weren't getting money, they started taking us more seriously and watching us a lot more closely, especially after the trip we made through the yard explaining the consent decree to everybody. From that point on, when they had a gripe, they were not going to sit back and hold their peace. They didn't get involved in the mechanics of it because they didn't understand what was going on and were intimidated by it. But they definitely became interested, and they began to question us more insistently than they had earlier on.

When that change came about it wasn't a matter of you just, "Well, this is how I feel. This is what we are going to do." You couldn't do that anymore because you were affecting the lives of thousands of people and not just at the reformatory, but at Eddyville. The guys wanted something constructive to come out of the consent decree. For better or worse, we were saddled with the responsibility for that.

If we advanced a particular position, we were going to be questioned about it when we got out on the yard. And if the guys who were capable of grasping the issue thought it was a bunch of hot air, they would tell us.

These weren't the type of guys you could just push and shove around. These type of guys, they gave you their opinion. If they thought you were full of shit, they'd tell you that. And if you didn't like it, they'd be prepared to take it to the next step.

When you deal with people like that, you have to be more thoughtful about what you say as well as what you do. You don't tell them one thing and then go do another.

They sized us all up. They began to realize that there were certain people on the committee that they could take gripes to, and to deal with other people on the committee, they had to give them something in exchange for what they wanted. I guess I fell in the category of a guy they could come to and get what they wanted without having to give anything up.

We couldn't hide anymore. We had to deal with the interests of the other guys in the population. It's kind of hard to be a loner when people you don't even know walk up on you at the darnedest times—while you're eating, while you're getting ready to go to bed—and they ask you about this, that, and the other. And you know there is no way you can whip every single person in the prison that wants to fight you. So when someone comes to you in an awkward moment, the best thing you can do is answer their question as quickly and honestly as possible and as satisfactorily as possible so they'll go on and let you do what you want to do. And that's what I started doing.

I sometimes had difficulty expressing myself with less-educated inmates. All I had was a general education degree at that point. I was talking with the vocabulary that I had picked up through the law books and some reading I had done. I was going over guys' heads. I had to make it a point to be simple.

Somehow I made myself understood. I think they detected my sincerity. But they always questioned our motives, one day to the next. Plus, they was always wanting to know more about the consent decree. It was hard.

Walter found chaos on the Plaintiffs' Committee when he returned. With the departure of Shorty and the rest of the original leadership had gone their knowledge and understanding of the consent decree. The new members had copies of the decree and had all read it, but they did not understand it and were unable to grasp how all the components fit into a broader pattern. In addition, Walter thought that the presence of more than twenty men on the committee made it impossible to have a focused discussion. One inmate would start complaining about the food, another would complain about not being granted parole, then two or three members would start talking at once, and the whole discussion would fall apart. The meetings resembled gripe sessions back in the dorm, and they did little to address the central problem: enforcing the consent decree. The men at least understood that there was a need to restore order so that the voices of the prisoners could once again be heard on the issues of implementation. They turned to Walter and elected him committee chairman.

This leadership role put him in a position to learn personal responsibility for his own choices and actions. He needed to get the committee working again toward its common goal of enforcing the consent decree. It was a difficult task, partly because he was a black man from a northern urban ghetto and most of the other members were whites from the rural South and partly because of the internal dissension.

My perspective changed when I was overseas in Vietnam. I was serving with some whites. When you're in a situation where your life is literally in the hands of someone else, you need help. And when you need that sort of help, you don't look up for somebody black or somebody white—whoever is closest is the person you want to help you, and you hope like hell that they won't hold race against you in terms of deciding to come to your aid or not. While we had our racial differences over there, all that was set aside when we went out in the field. We worked together as a team with the best relations possible, the most efficient military operation. We needed each other and we worked together.

I thought that on the Plaintiffs' Committee that could be achieved, which is what I attempted to do when I became the chairman of the committee. Finding the common ground and voicing it as a common concern, rather than just, "Well, this is what we want. Give us this, and you guys can do whatever you wanna do."

I called it the game. What I was referring to was the perspective of the situation. In spite of all our efforts, we didn't have any real control of the situation. We were just the witnesses. We were called forward to give testimony when the corrections cabinet decided that they wanted us to tell the truth. So in essence we were nothing more than puppets or pawns on the chessboard. If some of us told our stories, we wound up being reprimanded despite the sanctions against them.

I called it the game because the real contest, to my point of view, was between the federal government and the state. And it just so happened that Judge Johnstone represented the federal government and the wardens represented the state. So it was a question of the federal government bringing the state into compliance with federal law and how it was going to go about doing it.

I read that case out of Rhode Island where the warden had said you never give prisoners everything they want, and I felt that was pretty much going to be the end result of the consent decree.

But I still didn't quite understand it—what real control we would have of the situation. And not just in terms of manipulating the document to our personal satisfaction. But actually to the advantage of the majority of guys in the institution. So I started looking around.

I had to play games that I didn't like playing with guys to get them to do what needed to be done. They didn't want to come to the meetings regularly, and when they came, they wanted to run off at the mouth. They didn't want to deal with the issue that was before the committee at a particular point in time so that we could progress from one issue to the other and cover all areas of the consent decree and do it on a continuing basis in an effective manner.

So I just sort of elected a steering committee of five people out of all the guys that were on the committee at that time. I said, "Well, these are the guys who will meet with the attorneys. Other people will be placed on the steering committee as they demonstrate the ability to deal with the issues that are covered by the consent decree, in the interest of the entire class and not just selected members of the class."

I made a lot of enemies over that, but I'd had enough of it. Some guys saw the advantage of it and went along with it. Gradually, I put more and more people on that steering committee until all but five of the remaining members were actually interacting with the attorneys.

Things slipped back and forth. One minute we were going ahead, then
a while later we would be slipping back to the same routine again, and
I'd have to kinda put the foot down again.

Wilgus: Twenty More Years

Soon after the consent decree was signed, Wilgus was transferred to a
minimum-security farm prison and then to Blackburn Correctional Center near Lexington. Inmates who achieved parole had access to educational opportunities at the nearby University of Kentucky. When Wilgus
arrived at Blackburn on September 15, 1980, he had a new opportunity.
He would become eligible for parole in nine months, so he started making arrangements to attend the University of Kentucky in case the board
granted him parole. Accused of smuggling a pet dog into the prison, however, he was transferred back to KSR in December 1980 and subsequently
transferred to the adjacent Roederer Farm Center a month later. Wilgus
was in trouble again, however, by the summer of 1982. He had been at the
Roederer Farm Center near KSR for more than a year and had been a
model prisoner. For his good behavior, he was granted furloughs, short
trial release periods designed to help determine whether he should again
be granted parole. Wilgus spent his furlough time in Lexington, where he
found employment and married an old girlfriend, which turned out to be
a mistake that led to a new twenty-year sentence.

Right after we settled with the consent decree and the newspaper articles
was flourishing, an old girlfriend of mine had seen the articles. We made
contact, and she came to see me a couple times. And she said, "Hey, you
get out, you come to me." We set all this up. So I go there—Lexington.
I got a job. . . .
   One day she said, "Wudda you think about marrying me? When do
you think we could get married?" . . . I put all the pluses and minuses to-
gether. And I need to stay away from the area that I came from. I have lost
contact with Breathitt County and all of its people except my daughters.
I don't want to ever return there. My aunt is there, and I talk to her and
my daughters on the phone. I write to them. But I don't wanta ever return
because there has been so many things in my life that's went wrong. A lot
of bad memories comes from my early childhood, and I don't want to be

*tied to that 'cause it's gonna be the same thing as before. My reputation—
somebody'll lay in wait 'n kill me. If I go back there, I've got to carry a
pistol in every pocket. And I can't do that. I've got to go somewhere where
I can just blend right in and become a ever'day person, and in Breathitt
County I couldn't be an ever'day person 'cause I'm a household name in
that part of the country. So I thought, "Well, this'll work out fine." So we
got married [in January 1982]. . . . I . . . made parole on April 1 of '82 and
went back to her.*

Wilgus soon discovered, however, that his wife was having an affair.

*This guy comes to the house and demands that I leave. He's gonna call the
parole officer and tell the parole officer places I've been, which he couldn't
have told anything because I haven't done anything.*

*Well, one word led to another, then a fight. After I did what I wanted to
do to him, I still wasn't satisfied because he ran and got away from me. . . .
With all the frustration I had left, I just kicked her ass. We did tussle.
I believe she grabbed the butcher knife out of the kitchen and we tussled
over that.*

*And the first thing I know the police was at the door. This guy or some-
body had called the cops. They come in. They handcuffed me, they kicked
me, they beat me bad. They drug me in the car and they took me downtown. They put me in jail.*

*Boy, I was heartbroken because I was beginning to reestablish myself
with the community and I was moving on to a better job and I was reesta-
blishing my contact with my daughter.*

*They charged me with second-degree assault and being a persistent
felony offender (PFO). So then I'm trying to bargain with 'em. I told the
prosecutor I'll plead guilty to a small PFO—ten years. No, no deal. I said
I'll plead guilty to twenty years, first-degree assault. No deal. I'm going
through the courtroom telling the judge. The judge said, "Hell, that sounds
like an excellent deal to me. That'll save the state some money." The prosecutor, she said, "Your Honor, we're gonna save the state some money in the
long run. We want him tried."*

*So they went on and tried me. They found me guilty of second-degree
assault and give me ten years. Then they read my record. Therefore, I was
destroyed. Nothing on 'ar but gunplay. Boy, those people on that jury,*

*they went in the jury room—the last one was going in when the first one
was coming back out the door. I thought they was going to hit me with a
life sentence. They give me twenty years. They give me ten on the assault
and enhanced it to twenty on the PFO.*

On December 27, 1982, Wilgus returned to KSR, where he went
through the classification process. His mistakes in free society and demonstrated propensity for violence prompted a maximum-security classification and so, on January 27, 1983, Wilgus returned to the penitentiary in
Eddyville. His first opportunity for freedom had ended even more poorly
than Walter's first attempt. Wilgus was back in prison after only three
months on parole, with a new twenty-year sentence: added on to his old
twenty-year sentence that meant his prison term would not expire until
the year 2017. If he compiled a good prison record, he might accumulate
enough good time credits to gain release by 2007. The earliest possible
date he would again become eligible for parole was 1992, nine years away.
Even then, his chances for parole would be poor because of his status as a
PFO and his multiple convictions for violent crime, one of which was committed while on parole.

Wilgus's major challenge was to find a way to occupy his time. He first
sought to obtain a transfer out of the penitentiary.

*No one with a PFO had ever been transferred to Northpoint Training Cen-
ter from Eddyville. So a bunch of guys around Eddyville said, "Haddix,
put in for it. See if you can get this thing." So I put in for a transfer. And
bam! They transferred me to Northpoint.*

*So I went up there in April of '84. A couple of months later they done
sent some more guys up there from Eddyville. Well, they had a racial riot
at Northpoint. It come up over some Coca-Cola. They claimed I was the
major issue, and I had nothing to do with it whatsoever. So they transferred us all back to LaGrange, locked us in the hole, investigated it, and
put us back on the Yard.*

*So I said, "OK now, let me see if I got this straight. I was a clerk at the
Northpoint prison industry, making forty-two cents an hour. I was an
honor-status inmate. I had a room. Now your internal affairs has vindi-
cated me of all involvement. Now let me see if I can't get all the things back
that I had." So I threatened to sue 'em.*

> *In order to keep from setting a precedent and gitting everybody re-*
> *stored to their former status, they agreed to put me back. And I said, "OK,*
> *let's go with it." So I went into dormitory 4 at LaGrange, into a room.*

Wilgus returned to KSR on September 7, 1984, his ninth transfer in three years. Despite the general inmate dissatisfaction with implementation of the consent decree, Wilgus encountered significant improvements in living conditions. Overcrowding had been eliminated. Two dorms had already been renovated, and work on other dorms was under way, although the pace of renovation lagged behind the schedules in the decree. Security was tighter, with more guards on duty, so the atmosphere was more orderly and less tense.

Wilson, in his enhanced capacity as a cabinet secretary, had campaigned for three years to obtain from the General Assembly continued funding for prison reform. He had requested a great deal of money and run into opposition from legislators who preferred to fund improvements for services such as roads and schools. Such legislators gave Wilson's budget requests the lowest priority in allocating public money. These legislators' rhetoric accused him of trying to take money away from schoolchildren, and his budget hearings were riddled with hostile questions and silly political posturing. Wilson was the messenger of bad news that the prisons had to change, and it was going to cost millions of dollars. The secretary of corrections had to make the case for prison funding over and over again. Carl Collins, one of Wilson's chief assistants, watched his performance over the years.

> *When Director Wilson directed all the powers that be that worked with the*
> *consent decree to seek compliance, there was hesitancy at first, because*
> *I think a lot of people kept thinking there was no way we ever were going*
> *to be able to conform really to the dictates that were set out. The taxpayer*
> *and all the people that sit on the outside are against doing anything for*
> *inmates, to the degree that they would want to be billed for it. Right now,*
> *if you walked up to ten people in the state of Kentucky, I doubt if you'd*
> *find one that knew there ever was a consent decree. You might walk up to*
> *ten legislators and get that same answer.*
>
> *The thing had to be pushed along, with the help of Judge Johnstone,*
> *once it was settled, and Director Wilson. . . . The director says to us, "Well,*
> *you and the group here's got to work. You've got to build around this con-*

sent decree. That's not the only thing you're going to do, but you have to do this first. It's the law. The judge ordered it." It was a law as far as we were concerned.

But a lot of legislators and some of the executive branch said, "Well, why in the hell are we putting money into that?" Director Wilson had to fight that all the time. And he was the only one. . . . We had a package that had to be done, and we were under the gun to get it done, and it was going to take money. Sometimes they kill the messenger, whoever brings you the bad news. . . .

Wasn't anybody there but the director pushing forward and trying to explain it. He had to prove he needed the money and double-prove it and triple-prove it. A large percentage of the budget that the cabinet in Kentucky works under today is a direct outgrowth of nothing but the consent decree requirements.

Wilson won the budget battles, so that money continued to flow to fund the reforms mandated by the consent decree. With implementation of the decree progressing reasonably well from his perspective, Wilgus decided to pursue an education.

Wilgus: College Education

Wilgus had two daughters, and Shannon Dawn, the older one, was close to her father because they had remained in frequent contact while he was in prison. Shannon Dawn came to visit her father at KSR one day and persuaded Wilgus to enroll in the prison's college program, in which teachers from a community college came at night to teach college-level courses for credit.

My daughter . . . said to me, "Dad, I've talked to a lot of people who know you, and the first thing they all say about you is that you're intelligent. Well, why don't you take advantage of some of the educational opportunities that's offered to you?"

Then I got to looking around and I thought, "Well, why not? She wants me to do that, I'll do it." So I got into the college program. . . .

When I got into this college program, in walks a preppy that had graduated valedictorian from North Carolina State in English and had a master's degree in English and had a master's degree in engineering and was working on a master's degree in Divinity at Southern Baptist Seminary. And he started th'owing all this stuff around about onomatopoeias and personifications and symbolism. This was 'fore anything—the very first minute! English 101. First night.

I didn't know what the hell he was talking about! It's been twenty-six years since I've been to a classroom! This was a frightening experience for me. . . .

So he said everybody'd write a paper right now, in class, on the most influential person in your life. . . . I wrote about my grandfather. I told the things that I could remember about him, about he bought me a watch, a big hand watch that was $1.98. It would be an antique worth $100 now if I had it. The most outstanding thing that I remembered about him was the day he didn't eat his gingerbread. . . .

He said, "Class is over." Next Monday he come back, he passed out the papers, he said, "Everybody with a red check, you stay with me on Monday night. Everybody that doesn't have a red check, I will come back on an extra night and do you on Friday night. I'm gonna have to bring you along a little slower than these other guys."

Well, I looked at my paper and I had a red check, which meant that I was in the guys that made it. He told me, he said, "You've got a good writing style. You need to develop it." And I thought, "Well, oh boy, that's great. That sounds good." . . .

[After I wrote several more papers, the teacher] says, "Look, Haddix. You're not culture-bound. If you want to learn about the English language, if you want to learn the rules, then you're gonna have to come away from your cultural background. You're gonna have to come away from eastern Kentucky. You're gonna have to quit writing about eastern Kentucky. Come out of those hills of eastern Kentucky. Don't write me papers about coal mines and timber wolves and that kind of thing. Let me know that you can tell me something besides this. You need to expand your horizons. If you want to write well, you've got to be able to write about a lot of different subjects." . . .

So I got to digging into Socrates and hunting up all the Greek mythology I could, and I just started reading ever'thing I could get my hands on. . . .

I got an A out of that course. Now he said, "I'm coming back to English 102. And we're gonna teach a course next semester—along with 102—for you men who like a challenge. We're gonna teach a course called 'A Survey of Western Literature from the Greeks to the Renaissance.' This is Norton's Anthology of World Masterpieces.*" He pointed directly at me. He said, "Mr. Haddix, you're the first man on the list to sign up."*

I said, "Wait a minute. I don't know anything about Greeks."

He said, "But we're gonna teach ye something about 'em."

So I signed up. There was eight of us signed up out of fifty men. And we did the English 102 class. I did a critique of Robert Frost and got an A. All my papers was bringing As. . . .

Then I wrote my term paper on the Decameron, *Boccaccio's* Decameron *tales during the black death. Got an A. And he presented it to the English Department at Jefferson Community College and the University of Kentucky. So now my writing skills, people are beginning to reco'nize it.*

A legal battle erupted over one part of the consent decree while Wilgus was taking his English courses. Back in 1980, during the negotiations in Shorty's lawsuit, one of the prisoners' demands was to expand the college program so that a prisoner could receive a bachelor's degree while still in prison. Prison officials preferred to maintain a more limited program in which prisoners could gain college credits and only an associate's degree. The negotiators eventually compromised on a sentence in the decree that read, "The defendants agree to establish a college level program which leads to the acquisition of a Bachelor's Degree."

After the court approved the consent decree, corrections officials continued to refuse to offer a bachelor's degree program. They argued that the consent decree only required them to offer courses in which prisoners could earn college credits that could be used to obtain bachelor's degrees after release from prison. The prisoners contended that the words of the decree meant that a prisoner had the right to obtain a bachelor's degree while he was still in prison. The prisoners' lawyers filed a motion to require the state to establish a prison bachelor's program, but Judge Johnstone ruled against them. Wilgus was furious, but the defeat motivated him to further his education in the English language.

The language that was written in the consent decree was ambiguous. It was filled with words in meaningless language, a language that didn't mean anything—superfluity.

And that's another thing that made me do this English as hard and as diligent as I did. I thought that I need to know more about the English language. . . .

If I'd had the benefit of English 101 and 102 during the negotiations, I would have said, "Oh, now wait a minute, gang. Shorty, Walter—uh, uh. No."

When you break the English language down, it's all sentence structure, from capital letter to period. The mechanics of the English language, the commas, the semicolons, the colons. . . . If I had'a known [grammar] then, I coulda said it. Or I coulda used it to our advantage. But see, we agreed to it and if you agree to a contract that's got bad language in it, hell, you've got trouble.

That'll never happen to me again. I developed one of the damnedest complexes that ever was. I said, "That'll never happen again. Never again." If there's ever a contract laid in front of me, you can believe I'll take it home and diagram the goddamn sentences!

Wilgus took political science courses along with the English courses. What he read in the political science textbooks taught him a broader way of thinking about government than what his grandfather had taught him.

[In international relations,] most of the class took America's point of view. So I took Russia's point of view and did all the research that I could, 'cause we were gonna debate these issues in the last week of the term.

So I had to learn all I could about Russia's foundations. I had research material coming from the Department of the Air Force, from Leningrad University, from the University of Kentucky, from Stanford University, the foremost, formidable political science department in the world. I had it coming from ever'where. I read ever'thing I could on Lenin and Stalin. . . .

So, I took their point of view and at the end of class we squared off. And I ate 'em up—ate 'em up. . . . I took it from their point of view and presented it and come out on top.

The midterm consisted of a question about a period of time in American history that affected the social, political, and economical structure of this country, and it had to be tied to foreign policy. So I took Lyndon Johnson's Great Society program and the Vietnam War and the expenditures. I put it together and knocked 'em dead again!

The outside world found out about the prison college program during Wilgus's third semester. Colleges in the region held a competition called the College Bowl. Each school fielded a team of four students, and the winner, Jefferson Community College of Louisville, was invited to compete against a team of prisoners from the KSR college program in a special playoff. Wilgus was selected for the prisoners' team.

> We competed [against] a team that had never been defeated before. There was a crack engineering student and a top-notch electrical engineering student headed for the Speed School of Engineering in Louisville and another guy that was a English literature man and another guy was a political science person. They picked 'em from Jefferson Community College. They beat everybody. . . .
>
> There were fifty of us in the college program, and they took eight with the highest grade-point average and we competed against one 'nother and they narrowed it to four. So we went into this competition. . . .
>
> I held my own in literature, political science, and history. We come within twenty points and the score was 465–445. We were ahead with just seconds to go.
>
> The last question that was asked was the name of the earliest fourteenth-century Florentine writer who was a government official and his father worked for it. And they said, "He was the author of—." I thought that they was gonna say that he was the father of political science, Machiavelli, and I thought, "Well, they're gonna say The Prince." And I hit the button. Bam! I called it Machiavelli. But it wasn't. They're hunting for Dante, the author of The Inferno. You know, their lives are so similar. OK, I missed it. Hell, I'm eliminated. Couldn'a been but two people, Dante and Machiavelli. Those guys guessed it—Dante. And then they got the bonus question. That defeated us. But we got lots of airplay, and lots of newspaper play out of that.

Wilgus finished his third semester and moved on through the fourth and fifth semesters. He took courses in math, algebra, Greek, and anthropology, which was his favorite course.

> This professor come along and said, "I'm gonna teach a twenty-six-weeks course in Greek. You want it?" I said, "Why not?" So I took a twenty-six weeks course in Koine Greek and was examined in Greek.

*When you git to learning the plurals and the singulars and all this
in Koine Greek, I mean, my little world turned upside down again. But
I understood the English language much better by doing it—where a lot of
our root words comes from and a lot of the meanings. You get a much better, much more precise meaning of what's happening.*

*Then this professor come along with this cultural anthropology. . . .
I fell head over heels in love with anthropology. My first love is anthro-
pology. I'm in love with the stuff. Physical and cultural anthropology
I love. . . .*

*The final exam, we had no idea what we was gonna do. We walked in,
and he said, "OK, you're in a void world. There's only two species of life
on the planet. You're one. Tell me about the other. I want this species to be
homologous. Tell me about the species' given trait, genotype. Tell me about
the chromosomes."*

*I laid it out. I'm telling you, I went to where my biology skills and my
writing skills come in handy when I got to talking about the limbs and
how species and speciation would change and become other species and
where they can't mate back to one another. I used Australopithecus. My
species had a catastrophe, is what I said. I had a part of this earth split.
The species got separated and the terrain and environment was different.
These over here had to develop special skills in order to survive. I went
through the natural-selection process and showed how the environment
over here changed these people. They became different. Later on, years and
years, millions of years later when the migration started and the different
species got together, they could mate, but they couldn't produce offspring.*

*My anthropology professor said, "In all the years I've taught anthropol-
ogy—twenty-seven years—I don't believe I've ever read a more exciting
paper." Gave me an A+ on it.*

*And in social anthropology I did the same thing. And I got into physical
anthropology. I got into acquired characteristics, where we developed hair
and lost hair—the whole bit, Homo habilis and his tools. My biology—
I got with Darwin and Morgan and Tyler. All this stuff in anthropology,
boy, it just tied right in for me.*

*Then I tied it into political views. . . . I've connected all my subjects'
themes. Man has been described as a tool-using animal. That's the first
sentence in all anthropology books, just about. So, if I'm a tool-using
animal, the most useful and the most absolute tool known to mankind*

*would be language. All of our history, all of our oral history, all of our
messages, man's whole life all the way back has been traced by that one
tool—Language, when we stood up and our larynx developed and we began to speak. . . .*

*To me, everything connects to the English language. If I write an an-
thropology paper, I use my English skills to get it on. If I write a history
paper, I use my English skills.*

Wilgus was nearly forty years old by the time his college education
was well under way. At long last, a true rehabilitation through education
seemed within reach, but because of his long criminal record and disastrous first attempt at parole, many years would have to pass before he
would have another opportunity for freedom.

Shorty: Reincarceration and Personal Tragedy

Shorty served out his sentence for stealing cattle and was discharged in
February 1981, a free man for the first time in four years. He returned to
eastern Kentucky and went to work for Larry Stebbins at Larry's Body
Shop in Mt. Sterling. On weekends Shorty helped a friend, Henry Collins, farm fourteen acres of tobacco. His first wife, Phyllis, was living in
Mt. Sterling. They started seeing each other again, and he also started
seeing his daughter, Teresa, now a twenty-one-year-old woman. Shorty
and Teresa were strangers after so many years apart, but he wanted to
establish a father-daughter relationship. Nearly three quiet years ended
on January 3, 1984, when Shorty was arrested.

*A friend of mine from Rowan County, close to Morehead, he asked me if
I would drive a tractor back to Morehead. . . . It was snowing and drizzling
rain. I drove the tractor just across the Rowan County line. I drove it probably thirty miles. The State Police pulled me over and—"stolen tractor."
He'd just stolen the tractor sometime that morning. I got on at 7 : 30 in
the morning. This was on January 3, 1984. 'Course, I didn't know it was
stolen. If I'd known it was stolen, I wouldn't of drove it in daylight on the
main highway.*

Shorty was charged with three crimes: stealing the tractor, illegal possession of the tractor, and PFO, first degree, because, like Wilgus, Shorty
had committed earlier felonies and was now charged with committing

an additional felony. Shorty claimed he was innocent, but he knew his chances at trial were poor because he indisputably had been driving a stolen tractor.

I plea-bargained with 'em for a five-year sentence—reduce the charge to second degree, and I plea-bargained the five-year sentence. When I went to court, the judge sentenced me to eleven years: five years for the PFO, five years for stealing the tractor, and one year for possession of the tractor. I pled guilty and didn't get what I plea-bargained for. I got a illegal sentence.

Illegal sentence or not, Shorty was back at KSR for classification after nearly three years of freedom. He was classified medium security and sent to Northpoint Training Center in Burgin on July 10, 1984. Acting as his own lawyer, however, he filed a motion to vacate his sentence based on the state's failure to abide by the terms of the plea bargain. The judge agreed and Shorty was released from prison. Since the plea bargain had been nullified, he still faced trial on the charges, but the trial was seven months away. He was free until then.

Shorty took this opportunity to remarry his ex-wife, Phyllis. He moved into her house in Mt. Sterling, right across the street from Shorty's mother, Anna Mae. Shorty also had a long talk with his daughter, Teresa.

I knew she was into drugs and alcohol, but I didn't think she was smoking cocaine or anything like that. I talked to her about it two or three times. She didn't want to talk about it to me.

Last time I seen her I talked to her about it. . . . She wasn't drinking or on anything then. Only thing I'd ever seen her do's drink beer, but her mother told me she was on some kinda pills, smoking grass.

So I sit with her and talked about that stuff and told her it wasn't any good. I said, "It's for fools, and the only thing grass is good for is to sell. Not to smoke." I don't smoke it myself. I don't take any kinda pills myself.

We talked about an hour. She denied taking any pills, and she said she didn't smoke no grass. And of course I knew she drank. She was her own woman. She was twenty-six at this time, couldn't make her do anything. I just tried to tell her.

Shorty stood trial in January 1986 on the three charges stemming from the stolen-tractor incident. The jury found him guilty, and the judge sentenced him to a total of ten years in prison on the theft and PFO charges, only one year less than the sentence that had been vacated, so his success in overturning the prior sentence produced little net gain. Shorty returned to KSR on February 4, 1986, for classification and was again assigned to Northpoint Training Center. The stubborn little man immediately filed a petition for a writ of habeas corpus in federal court, claiming his conviction on the PFO charge should be vacated on the ground that evidence used at the trial to support that particular charge should not have been admitted by the judge. While his habeas corpus petition was pending, Shorty and Phyllis were divorced for the second time, an amicable parting designed to assist her with mortgage payments.

On the night of October 11, 1986, Shorty was watching the 11:00 news. He heard the worst news a parent can ever get.

My daughter, Teresa Thompson, got killed. They haven't found out who done it. It was in Morehead.

It was a mistake, that's what I thought, maybe. The name an' all— something. The next day I got a call from my mother, she told me. I tried to get hold of my ex-wife, her mother, the next morning, but she wasn't home. I guess she was in Morehead or someplace. . . .

I believe the state police handled most of the investigation. That's where my ex-wife, Phyllis, [Teresa's] mother, been getting most of her information—what little she's got. The local coroner and the state police.

I haven't talked to any police official at all. From what I could find out from my ex-wife, the coroner said there was bruises on her neck and on her wrists and ankles. It looked like where somebody had held her down, and she died from an injection, overdose injection of cocaine. . . . She was twenty-seven. She had been married, but she was divorced. No kids.

She was taking drugs, and my ex-wife, her mother, thinks she was dealing drugs. I don't know, but that's what my ex-wife thinks. And she seems to think that [Teresa] owed some money for drugs, and she was trying to rip somebody off, and they come 'ere and killed 'er. Or else somebody come 'ere and killed 'er trying to find drugs.

They don't think it was an accident. She had marks all over her wrists and ankles where two people—it took two people—held her down, and bruises on her wrists and ankles where they held her. . . .

I don't know what happened. Nobody seems to know. . . . During the investigation they found out one of her cars was missing—the Mustang was missing and some of her jewelry. She had some jewelry missing. . . .

Her car was stolen during the robbery and it showed up three months later 'bout two miles from the house. Looking for it all over the state, showed up 'bout two miles from the house. . . .

I have nobody to talk to. I'm not religious, so I can't talk to the chaplain. I don't feel like talking to the chaplain. It's something to get over— not completely over it, but I'll get over part of it.

The thing that bothers me is they never did find out who killed her. I can't explain it. The case is on hold or dead file or whatever you call it. My ex-wife calls up the Morehead State Police post, and asks about it, and nothing developed. I haven't heard anything at all.

I just like to know the truth. I would like to know who done it. I'll probably find out one of these days. I'll check into it when I get outa here, that's for sure.

I didn't want to go up 'ere to her funeral with handcuffs and leg irons and all that stuff, you know. I tried to go, I asked to go without leg irons and handcuffs and they told me I had to have handcuffs and leg irons. So all the family was there, her grandmother and of course her mother. And I didn't want to embarrass the family.

Shorty did want to find out why his daughter had died. The police report on Teresa's death eventually provided an explanation: Teresa had been arrested on October 10, 1986, for drunken driving. On the way to jail in the police car, she said she had already been in jail too many times, could not go back again, had nothing left to live for, and was going to kill herself. She produced a small knife and tried to cut off the handcuffs, which explained the cuts on her wrists the night she died. Teresa was released the next day and hosted a party at her house the same night. According to witnesses who attended the party, a wide variety of drugs was available, and Teresa inhaled cocaine and swallowed various pills. She abruptly ordered the partygoers to leave because she intended to kill herself. One man remained with her. The next morning, Teresa did not wake up. The man rubbed her face with a wet washcloth, trying to wake her up, but she remained still. A man from a furniture store arrived to measure Teresa's wicker tables for new glass tops. Teresa's friend let the furniture man in and told him what had happened. The furniture man went into the bedroom, looked at Teresa, said she was dead, and left. Someone finally called the police, who found Teresa in bed, her mouth partly open and her face ashen gray. The police found a note, scrawled in barely legible handwriting.

> $100 in the first dresser door. In the 3rd dresser door is your pills. If anything should happen to me the money is Faye's . . . and everything.
> Signed
> Teresa Laverne Thompson

The police sent her body to the morgue. The coroner's autopsy report came to a brief conclusion.

> Patchy Cutaneous Abrasions and Contusions of Arms, Legs and Abdomen.
> Acute Combined Drug (Amobarbital, Secobarbital, Diazepam, Ethyl Alcohol and Cocaine). Toxicity by Injection, Ingestion, and Inhalation.
> Suicide.

The investigation continued for several weeks, but the police found no evidence of murder. Teresa had brass objects in her house worth about twenty thousand dollars, but none of them was missing, so the investigators ruled out murder committed in the course of robbery. Later on, some of her jewelry showed up at a pawnshop, and her Mustang was found at the side of a road, but the police had no explanation.

Shorty received this information but remained unsatisfied. Questions lingered about the bruises on her body, the jewelry, and the Mustang. He wanted to find out for himself. Even if it was suicide as the coroner and police said, why did she do it? Shorty had had little contact with his daughter for a quarter century during his fugitive and prison years. He probably did not know much about her thoughts and her feelings. He could not know what was going through her mind the night she died. Maybe Shorty would never know the truth of what really happened to his daughter. Maybe with time he would come to accept it, but he would never forget it or get over it completely. He would have to live with it, like any parent who loses a child.

Shorty filled his time in prison by working in the body and furniture shops. He enjoyed working and was glad to have a job at the prison.

I started out doing mechanic work here. We worked on State Highway Department vehicles, Department of Military Affairs vehicles. We have had a couple of school buses in here. And for the State Police.

Then they closed the body shop where I was working and made a chair factory of it. They brought in a chair factory. We make office chairs. . . . I do just about ever'thing. I'm a lead man out here, and if a guy don't show up for work or a guy goes home on parole or discharges, then I sorta take over his job until we get a replacement, then I train the replacement. . . .

We also make mattresses. Last week we turned out more than twenty-five thousand dollars worth. We been making mattresses for Luther Luckett. We'll probably make mattresses for Blackburn when they decide whether or not they're gonna put a fence around it and increase the population up there. We made five hundred new mattresses for Eddyville. . . .

I feel I'm overworked and underpaid—actually, not overworked, really, but I don't believe I get paid enough for the work I do. Now, I enjoy working. I like to keep my mind occupied while I'm in here, I'd better do something. I can't lay on the Yard in there and loaf around. I'd go crazy, I guess. But we made five hundred mattresses and five hundred pillows last week, and the state paid somebody over twenty-five thousand dollars for 'em. And I made fifteen dollars for my part of it. And these chairs I make, I could put four of these chairs together in a day and they sell them for $297 each, and I get paid $4. So I put out over $1,000 work, and my part of it is $4. So I believe I'm underpaid.

They expect you to be to work ever' day, and sometimes the work is hard. If a guy goes home and leaves a spot, then I have to pick up the slack 'til they get a new guy in.

We work 7 ½ hours a day. It's too much for the money. I don't expect to make minimum wage or wages like a person would on the street, but I expect the state to recognize my work, compensate me pretty good for my work. I don't expect minimum wage, but I think a dollar an hour would be fair. Money and the meritorious good time are the only two things I work for out here.

Shorty also performed legal work for other prisoners. Shorty's interest in the law and working on criminal cases had begun during his earliest days in prison, because he met numerous inmates whose legal rights had been violated during the prosecution of their cases. Shorty had become a first-rate jailhouse lawyer, known for his ability to get a conviction vacated.

I got to be doing something. If I'm on the Yard and not working, I'm usually helping guys out with their legal work, filing writs and motions, and helping 'em get divorces and get credit for their jail time. . . .

*I sorta pick my cases. I look at a guy's case, whether he's got a chance.
I research the case law and the statutes on the issue, and if there's case law
on it in his favor or if they didn't follow the statute when they tried him or
sentenced him, or if the crime didn't fit the statute or something like that,
that's what I base it on, if there's been a constitutional violation. . . .*

*First of all, I gotta have his record, the transcript, or record of the po-
lice, and all the court records. I look at that and listen to his story, and
I base my decision on that. If I don't think he's got anything, I'll just tell
'im. I'll just tell what I think about it, and he can take it somewheres, or
whatever. If I think it's not a good issue, I'll try and explain it to him why
it's not, 'cause he's free to take it to anybody, to somebody else.*

*They don't ever pay me. I don't ever charge nobody nothing. I've had a
couple to buy me a box of cigars or a bag of coffee, something like that.
I never charge nobody. It's just something to do and keep my mind occupied and help me do my time.*

Walter: A Learning Experience

Walter continued at KSR with the work of enforcing the consent decree. By mid-1985, overcrowding no longer existed at LaGrange and living
conditions were vastly improved because newly renovated housing units
had reopened and work was under way on others. Walter turned his attention to the racial makeup of the prison staff. Black prisoners complained
that there should be more black guards and social workers. Walter knew
the decree required efforts to both hire additional minority staff and create a more effective procedure for prisoners to file grievances, so Walter
fused the two provisions and filed grievances demanding that prison officials hire more black staff to work at the prison. He also urged other prisoners to become involved in the effort to improve living conditions by using
the grievance system established by the consent decree.

*At the point where I left the reformatory, it was a hell of a lot better than
the way we started out. I think it kinda woke the majority of the guys
up, because as a result other people became more interested in their own
cases and more aware of what was going on in the institution and stopped
thinking as individuals.*

*When problems came up, they started doing things like through the
grievance committee and stuff like that. They started—I don't know—*

developing a collective consciousness that enabled them to deal with the prison officials more effectively to have programs, improvements.

For example, it was through the consent decree that we got the recreational program improved. At one point — despite them having put a new floor in the basketball court, put in a handball court, put the track up, and the outside weightlifting — there were no real programs 'cause the outside entertainment really had stopped. And guys weren't really frequenting the gym as often as they had before.

And I thought it was because the people who were running the gym were telling the inmates what they should be interested in and what programs were good and what programs were not good for them.

I voiced my opinion to the Plaintiffs' Committee. After we kicked it around for a while, somebody asked me for suggestions. I told 'em I thought the suggestion was for them to put out questionnaires to ask guys what type of programs, recreational programs, they were interested in and for the administration to choose the programs that were most feasible and that the most interest was demonstrated in and to start those programs.

Were we surprised when they did it without us having to go to court! We started a recreational committee with inmates and caseworkers.

We started doing the same thing with a number of programs throughout the institution. I don't think that would have come about without the consent decree, because if it hadn't been for the consent decree, someone of the new warden's caliber would have never arrived as the warden.

Walter was transferred to Northpoint Training Center on September 19, 1985, marking the end of his tenure on the Plaintiffs' Committee. He served more time on the committee than any other prisoner, nearly five years, including three as chairman. KSR was a vastly improved prison by the time Walter left. Wilson had appointed a new warden, John Rees, with the mission of complying with the consent decree. Rees listened to the prisoners' complaints and made changes when he thought the prisoners were right. Prisoners had become involved in organizing programs for other prisoners. The largest construction program in the history of Kentucky prisons was in full swing. Four of the old dorms were completely renovated, and each man in these dorms had his own room. One old dorm was torn down, and a new dorm rose in its place. The mess hall was renovated. New buildings were constructed for visitors and for meetings with social workers. The academic and vocational schools had been expanded. The electrical system, heating system, and fire-fighting equipment were repaired. Security was tighter, so that life was much safer for the average prisoner. There had been many delays and other failures to comply, but on the whole the progress at KSR far outweighed the setbacks.

It took a great deal of hard work by many different people to remake KSR. Wilson endured endless budget battles in the General Assembly to obtain funding for all the changes. Judge Johnstone monitored the decree-implementation process and occasionally resorted to the back channel to make legislative leaders aware that Wilson's budget requests were necessary to comply with the consent decree. Wardens and guards had to learn new professional standards of conduct toward prisoners. Walter made his own contribution by leading the prisoners away from battling the old system and toward using the new system to improve their living conditions. In the process of helping to change KSR, Walter changed himself.

It was a learning experience, I think for everybody. It was worth it. Maybe it brought me to the realization that I have now, that enabled me to get my life in order: quit pursuing that endless dream of the fast buck.

I started something, and I completed it. It made me feel good. Up to the time I got arrested in the '70s, I had started a pile of things and I hadn't completed one of those things satisfactorily. I screwed up in the service and high school, jobs I had were menial, my life wasn't really going anywhere. I was basically the type of person I really didn't want to be.

The school principal at LaGrange kinda got me pointed in the right direction when he made me get my general education degree before he gave me the job as a clerk. My exposure to him and the other teachers kind of broadened my horizons to why I couldn't do a lot.

I found I could expand my mind to some extent. That's why I started reading things that I probably wouldn't have attempted before—just reading poetry, nonfiction, things of that sort, studying.

It's funny how things work out. I'd never thought of myself as a patient person. Before I got involved in the lawsuit, it was just Walter Harris doing his thing, and Walter Harris was very naive in terms of what was actually going on in the corrections cabinet and in terms of what we as a group could do to improve the situation. We didn't have to accept things the way they were because that's the way they were. And we did just that. We just in a rut passing time. No place to go and nothing to do.

I was reading a book and it's talking about psychological outsiders. And I kind of fancied myself as a psychological outsider because I couldn't identify with anybody. I wasn't into penitentiary hustle, trying to make a little money from day to day to make things a little better while I was in there.

I tended to look at things a little differently, but it didn't really focus until after I got involved in the lawsuit and started finding out who was actually running the show and reassessing my opinions on my position from one day to the next and where I wanted to go.

I was wondering what I would do after I got out. I sure as hell wasn't interested in coming out and sweeping somebody's floors and washing dishes. But short of having a skill, there was nothing else I could do.

So it became a challenge of me finding whatever talent I had for the law, and obtaining some recognition for being relatively good at it. . . . I [started] wondering if there was a way that we could have a legal-aid program formalized and becoming a professional program where professionals would come in and teach these courses, so that it would become on-the-job training for when we got out, so that we could go somewhere and say we had formal training and at least get something like a legal secretary position on the outside. . . .

Later on, after I became chairman of the Plaintiffs' Committee, I tried to realize that, to actually put proposals to the corrections cabinet, to establish it as part of the college program. Well, we didn't have much success with that. But it went along and I started checking out paralegal programs.

All of this came about through my continued involvement in the lawsuit and through the broadening of my horizons. I wasn't content to accept things the way they were anymore. I knew they could be changed, but change had to begin with me.

I had to want something and to go after it. And I couldn't go after it the same way I had gone after everything else. So I not only had to start something, I had to follow up on it. And if I didn't follow up on it and it didn't work out, I couldn't blame anybody but me. 'Cause it was past the point where I could conveniently say, "Well, if you had put me in this position, I would have did this."

Once I got started, it was just like research. You interested in something

but you don't know what the law is with respect to that issue. You have
to start somewhere. You have to define a topic and then start jumping all
over the place if you have to, until you can reach a point where you can
say with some satisfaction that this is the law on this issue. And then argue that position convincingly, because you have convinced yourself that
is what the law is or should be. Hopefully, you're right. By doing that it
became a habit. . . .

My perspective changed. My values changed. I became closer to the type
of person I ultimately would like to be, someone that is not self-centered,
just concerned with their own welfare or gain. And money is not the bottom line.

It wasn't easy getting there, coming to that realization. Perhaps all
those years in isolation did more for me than anything else since it forced
me to deal with myself and my situation.

I feel damn good. I haven't gotten to where I want to go, but I'm a hell
of a long way from where I was in '73—unskilled, not looking forward to
anything promising in terms of a career or a family, things of that sort.
That was just out of my reach because I didn't have the basic tools to live a
normal life. Violating the law was not a luxury. It was a necessity because
of the situation—the environment I had grown up in and the conditions
I had imposed on myself and my own way of thinking. . . . I came to the
realization that I had to make sacrifices. I had to dispense with some
things in the hope of winding up with more at a later point in time.

Through all the rigors of the consent decree—the negotiations and the
enforcement part of it—we had to see that it was rigidly enforced. To
do the research, I couldn't be in the gym, I couldn't be in the dormitory
watching TV, I couldn't be running around the yard shooting the breeze
with guys, I couldn't be in the visiting room and all that, or in segregation
for that matter. If I was going to follow through on these bold propositions
of mine, I had to be right in the law library, turning those pages. I didn't
have anybody there to read the pages and tell me what was meant by one
holding or another. I had to do the reasoning myself. That was good.

I guess I matured in the process of all the bickering that we went
through and having to deal with issues that I probably would never have
otherwise gotten around to considering on that scale. The adversity challenged me to develop my potentials . . . in the legal field. I certainly never
went in the penitentiary with the idea of becoming a jailhouse lawyer.

The close of 1985 marked the end of four years of personal struggles in this story of reform and change. At KSR itself, there was remarkable progress toward making the prison a decent place for human beings. New prisoners coming into KSR were the prime beneficiaries of these improvements. In a sense Shorty, Walter, and Wilgus had been working for the new inmates all along, for the young men who would make mistakes like the three plaintiffs had made when they were young and whom they did not want to see subjected to the same degrading conditions.

Shorty, Walter, and Wilgus experienced a mixture of setback and progress in their own lives. After three years of freedom, Shorty was back in prison and had lost his only child. Wilgus and Walter were also back in prison after losing their opportunities for freedom. At the same time, however, Wilgus was getting a college education, Shorty was still determined to win his freedom through the law, and Walter had achieved a much higher level of maturity and responsibility.

Substantial Compliance and Collateral Litigation

An important hearing was scheduled to begin at the federal courthouse in Louisville on July 8, 1986. The consent decree was now six years old. The state had filed a motion to terminate the federal court's supervision of the two prisons on the ground that the state had fully complied with the decree. Judge Edward Johnstone scheduled a hearing on this motion at which both sides would present testimony concerning the state's efforts to comply with the decree as reflected in the current living conditions at KSR and the penitentiary. The state had good reason to be optimistic about the hearing. By the summer of 1986, a great deal of money had been spent on building renovation, food service, medical care, education, job training, and other services.

To secure that money, George Wilson had sought and obtained massive new spending for prisons from the General Assembly. Wilson had taken the approach with the legislature that his budget requests were not draconian measures required to comply with a federal court order but rather were essential to sound corrections policy. According to Wilson,

The legislature understood the need, that the system had been neglected pretty much, and that something needed to be done. I'm sure there were varying points of departure, but I felt that when I appeared before them and talked to them about some of the problems, they listened to me, and they didn't always agree, but I think they showed a degree of sensitivity to it.

I think there was broad realization that something needed to be done. I don't know if there was any one thing. The ability to persuade them or to influence their thinking, how we presented it, how we put together our case to get their support, may have had some impact.

We tried hard not to take the approach of, "Here's this consent decree and you have to do it," because I don't think some of them understood what a consent decree was or cared. We tried to help them understand the issues involved and how the consent decree was a piece of that.

We used it as a teaching opportunity. You'll find the Kentucky legislature was aware of correctional issues about as well as anybody in the country, because of the long-standing opportunity we had. I had a chance to talk to them over and over again, kept reemphasizing and repeating certain themes and certain issues, and I think they were pretty much up on it.

Many of them even took it upon themselves to go other places and look to see if there were other ways to do it and whether or not we were correct. Because, see, obviously there was some skepticism that I was using the consent decree and that the consent decree was a whipping boy to get things we didn't need. And so they went out to find out independently if we were in the coop.

They found out that we were fairly up to date on what was going on across the country and were making a reasonable approach to it—not bent, unduly. It was a balancing act. How much? How fast? Credibility was important throughout the whole thing—personal credibility as well as credibility of the system.

Spending the money wisely represented another problem. Wilson knew that if he spent all the new money without changing how the prison system operated, he would wind up with clean, uncrowded buildings, and a larger corrections bureaucracy, but minimally better living conditions and services for the prisoners. Without systemic change, inmates would still have little to do, guards would still have inadequate control over inmates, and the prisons were likely to revert over time to squalid conditions resembling the predecree era. Wilson used an accreditation process to change the system. The consent decree required the state to formulate written plans to guide the operation of the prisons in areas such as fire safety, food service, medical care, and maintenance, but the initial plans were ineffectual because of staff inexperience. Wilson decided to counter this problem by launching an effort to have the two prisons accredited by the American Correctional Association (ACA) as a means of complying with the consent decree. The accreditation process required the state to adopt written policies and procedures for administering the prisons according to association standards. He gave that job to his lawyers, one of whom, Barbara Jones, reflected on the experience:

> *The biggest thing that stands out in my mind is the decision of George Wilson after six months of trying to come up with the plans back in 1980. There was plan after plan after plan we agreed to file. First, we were not realistic on timetables. And the second thing was, Corrections had never written a plan for anything, so we were like first-graders trying to write plans.*
>
> *Once George Wilson decided the best way to comply with the consent decree is the ACA accreditation process, that was what got us into gear. He said as soon as we sign the consent decree we're going to get accredited by the ACA. He made that decision right off the bat, but we hadn't meshed the two things together. If we get accredited by the ACA, compliance with the consent decree will be right there together. That makes sense today, but nobody thought about that at first. But that was a brilliant decision for compliance. You get accredited by the ACA, you've exceeded what we were required to do even in the consent decree.*
>
> *The plans became professional. . . . We drafted policies and procedures that addressed every phase of the institution, which in turn addressed every provision in the consent decree. The plans became the policies and procedures, and the policies and procedures became the plans. Our institutions were drafting maintenance plans, fire-safety plans, and all that, but ACA guidelines give you better ways of doing it. It gives you better suggestions on how to do it.*
>
> *So about six or eight months into this compliance process, we met with*

the inmates' lawyers to negotiate how bad they thought our plans were
and how good we thought they were. And then we started showing them
our proposed procedures and it seemed that the procedures were becoming
the plans. So they agreed to sit back, let us get these procedures drafted in
accordance with ACA standards, and submit them as our plans. Once we
got that developed, then we were on track, and then we were moving to-
ward compliance. It would cover every part of the operation of the facility,
from walking in the front door to the inmates and staff. If you look at our
consent decree, most of it said, "using ACA standards as the guidelines."
Not required to meet ACA standards, except for square footage, but using
the standards as a guideline when we drafted our plans. Well if it's written
in accordance with ACA standards, you've not only used them as guide-
lines but you've complied with them and you've exceeded them.

It changed the whole operation. . . . It made it very clear what is ex-
pected of everybody, inmates and staff. An issue comes up, you look to the
policies and procedures. There's no "That's the way we've always done
it," or "Nobody told us not to," or "Somebody sent us a letter but we can't
find it."

It changed the whole system. It made the system unified. We had a cabi-
netwide policy and then institution policies clarified those. Everybody's
disciplined according to those policies. If you don't follow them, you're dis-
ciplined. That's the guideline by which you operate and function. Inmates
are disciplined. Staff is disciplined. They're trained in it. We have all this
training. The training uses all the policies and procedures, explains the
importance of the policies and procedures: "This is the way we operate.
This is what you've got to do. If you don't do it, you're in trouble."

Judge Johnstone presided over the compliance process during these six
years. He believed from the day he signed the consent decree that the
document alone was merely thirty-five pages of promises on paper, and
that if the state decided it did not wish to reform the prisons, there would
be powerful obstacles to implementing the decree, from staff resistance to
executive and legislative recalcitrance, such as had occurred in Alabama
and Texas.[1] The judge felt that the best chance of achieving the reforms
envisioned in the consent decree was to nurture a positive attitude among
state officials toward prison reform, so he focused his efforts on keeping the
spirit of consent alive. Education was an important component of John-

stone's strategy, just as it was one of Wilson's approaches with the legislature in budget hearings. The judge continued to make unannounced visits to the prisons to get the attention of the wardens and staff, and he insisted on being escorted by prisoners and their lawyers, not by prison guards. He asked prisoners to show him where the problems were, so he could bring problems he himself had witnessed to the attention of top state corrections officials. Judge Johnstone also continued to send messages to legislative and executive leaders through the back channel and to meet with the lawyers in an effort to settle differences over implementation of the decree without having to enter coercive orders.

The Compliance Hearing

By July 1986, a great deal of money had been spent at the reformatory and penitentiary, and the prisons had been operating under the new policies and procedures for several years. The stage was set for Judge Johnstone's hearing in open court to consider the state's request that he find the state in substantial compliance with the consent decree and relinquish jurisdiction in the case. Even before the hearing, however, he had ordered the lawyers to meet in an attempt to resolve compliance issues, in accordance with his strategy of achieving maximal settlement of disputes. At the hearing, Johnstone first learned that much agreement had indeed been achieved between the state and the prisoners. The parties agreed that conditions at KSR and Eddyville were in compliance with the decree in areas such as medical care, libraries, and recreation and that both prisons had been within the population limits for five years. There was still some disagreement, however, in other areas such as jobs, sanitation, and renovation of the dorms, so the judge listened to nine days of testimony from prison officials, corrections experts, and prisoners.

Experts testified that there were 1,250 jobs for prisoners at KSR, of which 250 were vacant. Three hundred prisoners had no jobs. Prisoners testified that job opportunities were little improved in that they offered only one or two hours of work in a workday and in that most of the work was menial labor, like sweeping and mopping floors. Prisoners also testified that the eating utensils were dirty, that there were flies in the food and cockroaches in the kitchen, that bugs still infested the dorms, and that leaks in the ceilings and toilets continued. Prison officials admitted that problems remained but asserted that conditions were much improved. They testified that a maintenance man was assigned to each building to perform weekly inspections, spray living areas twice a week for bugs, and install glue traps, fly curtains, and bug lights. Expenditures on maintenance and sanitation had reached nearly $1 million during the past year at KSR alone.

One of the most important topics at the hearing was the dorm renovation process at KSR. In the consent decree, the state had promised to renovate all nine dorms at the rate of one per year. At that rate, six dorms should have been renovated by the time of the compliance hearing, with all nine dorms completed by 1989, but the state was behind schedule. By the summer of 1986, only four dorms had been renovated, and the primary reason for the delay was that renovations had been taking eighteen months per dorm rather than a year. Accordingly, renovations would not be completed until 1995, six years behind schedule. The root of the problem was, as it had been with population reduction, unintended obstacles rather than official recalcitrance. Wilson had moved as quickly as he could to renovate the dorms. Unfortunately, as one of Wilson's aides put it, to do construction on a government building, officials cannot simply "go to the bank, pull the money, and start work." Wilson had to obtain approval for each dorm project to be included in each of the governor's proposed two-year budgets, after which he was required to testify at legislative committee hearings on the budget. The committee, after approving the budget, had to send it to the entire legislature for a vote on the total budget. Once the budget was finally approved, the dorm projects had to be put up for bids from architects and contractors. Once bid selections were made, the architects had to plan each project, and once the plans were complete, work could finally begin. The work itself did not take very long. The problem lay in the numerous steps before construction could begin. Wilson had to repeat the process every two years because the state budget process ran in two-year cycles. The original promise to renovate one dorm a year was simply too optimistic. However, much progress had occurred in six years. Four dorms at KSR were completed. The men lived in single, uncrowded rooms instead of open dorms; life in these single-room dorms was safer, more relaxed, and cleaner; and the inmates appeared to take pride in keeping their rooms neat. Moreover, planning for the next two dorms was under way.

Judge Johnstone also heard testimony about the cost of compliance. Wilson's budget director, Ken Dressman, took the witness stand and presented an audit that indicated that the total amount spent for reforms mandated by the consent decree had topped $232 million, including the budget for 1986–1988. Dressman broke down the total cost into direct and indirect costs, with direct costs defined as dollars needed to pay for projects expressly written into the decree. The cost of the promised building projects was more than $27 million, including, at KSR alone, $9.2 million to rebuild six dorms, $416,000 for the mess hall, $613,000 for fire safety, $935,000 to repair the electrical system, and $216,000 for a new building for outside visitors. Also part of the direct costs was money needed to improve operations at both prisons, a total of more than $45 million. The largest operational items consisted of salary increases for guards (almost $2.5 million in 1981–1982 alone) and salaries for new employees (more than $1.5 million in 1981–1982) and included smaller items such as $14,000 for fire-safety training, $67,000 to improve the prison libraries, and $84,000 for the recreation program. This portion of his testimony was undisputed.

Dressman also testified that compliance included significant indirect costs, which he defined as money spent on items that the consent decree did not expressly require but that were needed as a result of the changes in the prison system brought about by compliance. He estimated the indirect cost of compliance to be nearly $160 million since 1980, with more to be spent in the future because many of these items were built into the ongoing budget of the Department of Corrections. The largest indirect cost, according to his estimate, was $58 million for construction of two new prisons and expansion of existing prisons to house prisoners who could no longer be housed at KSR and Eddyville because of the population cap. Dressman also included $27 million for the cost of operating the new facilities and $37 million for a variety of items such as hiring guards for the new facilities. In addition, the state sold bonds to pay for the construction projects, and interest payments and other costs of paying off the debt amounted to more than $29 million. The plaintiffs, however, disputed this testimony, contending that the state was padding the indirect costs to impress the court. Back in 1980, the consent decree had been billed in the media as a $42 million settlement, but that amount was only for the first two years of compliance. In 1980, it cost $12.25 per day to house one inmate, but by 1988, that figure had nearly tripled, to $32 a day. As Wilson had said, if the state's policy was to get tough on criminals and send record numbers of people to prison for longer terms, the people were going to have to pay the bill. Kentucky's bill was gigantic by any reckoning.

The state presented these figures to Judge Johnstone because conditions remained below minimal standards in some respects at KSR and Eddyville, and compliance with the decree was flawed. The state wanted the judge to know, however, that an enormous amount of money had been spent on improving the prisons, in a good-faith attempt to comply with the consent decree.

Substantial Compliance

Once presentation of the evidence was completed and the hearing ended, Johnstone had to decide whether the state's compliance with the consent decree was sufficient to justify his relinquishing jurisdiction over the case and terminating his supervision of the implementation process. He found little case-law precedent on this issue.[2] The few cases indicated that a judge should strike a balance between a state's two legal obligations. On one side, a judge ought to determine whether the living conditions violated the prisoners' constitutional right to be free from cruel and unusual punishment. On the other side, the judge should also determine whether the state had complied with its agreement embodied in the consent decree. The balance Judge Johnstone struck was that the state had a duty of substantial compliance with the consent decree, under which the state was obligated to perform its promises to the best of its ability. He reasoned that to impose an obligation of perfect compliance with every detail of the decree would exceed judicial power by enmeshing the court in the details of prison administration. Applying the substantial-compliance standard, Johnstone reached a compromise decision, as he had so often in this litigation. He decided the state had substantially complied with the consent decree in all areas save one: dorm renovation at KSR. He declared the court had a duty to ensure that the five remaining dorms were rebuilt or replaced. Thus, Johnstone did not relinquish jurisdiction, as the state had requested, but placed the case on the inactive docket except for dorm renovation, which would remain under active court supervision. Since major backsliding was unlikely to occur in the effort to maintain and improve living conditions at KSR, the case probably would not return to the active docket. In practical terms, Shorty's lawsuit had nearly come to an end.[3]

Reaction from two of the key inmate participants to this decision was largely positive, with some reservations. Wilgus remained at KSR, pursuing his college studies, when the decision came down, and he was satisfied with it.

> *I'll tell you, it's changed the face of corrections in this state. It's changed the attitudes. This one captain is like somebody they just hired off the street. I mean, his whole attitude has changed.*
>
> *But you know what? Guys like those old-time wardens can never be warden at LaGrange any more. That's the beautiful thing about that consent decree. It made that system so damn sophisticated that you just can't walk out of the head of a holler in Hazard, out of the logging woods, an' walk right in and be the warden. . . . That's made a tremendous difference.*

Shorty saw much progress. Although he was at Northpoint and didn't experience the changes at LaGrange firsthand, he thought most of the promises had been kept, most importantly the elimination of overcrowding and improved sanitation, the central concerns of his original complaint. But Shorty thought Judge Johnstone should not have placed any part of the case on the inactive docket.

> *I believe we got most of what we wanted. The main thing was gitting the place cleaned up and gitting the population reduced. We got that, so I'm satisfied. . . .*
>
> *I noticed that the Department of Corrections overall, they're hiring better officers now—better educated, and they seem to have more sense now, [to know] how to deal with people. 'Course there'll always be one or two assholes anywhere you go, but as a rule, officers in this place are all right. They will not mess with you.*
>
> *Most of the problems the inmates have in these prisons, they bring 'em on themselves—most of the problems, not always. 'Course there's a saying, there's always a bad apple. There's always an officer that goes out of his way just because he don't like the way you got yer hair combed or something like that. But you find that anywhere—on the streets, anywheres. . . .*
>
> *I'm pretty well satisfied—can't have ever'thing. We wanted a lot more*

than we got. I think the state stalled and stalled. I don't think the changes come about soon enough. . . . The state finagled out of some things through words, but I believe everything we got was equally important, and I think we got just about everything we asked for. I'm pretty well satisfied with it overall.

First of all, I'd like to say thank you to Judge Johnstone. And then I believe I would tell 'im that I believe he turned loose of the case too quick. When he ordered or ruled that the court would no longer supervise the thing, I believe he got out of it too quick.

I think that the court oughta stayed on it until everything—I mean everything—was done. Everything they agreed to perform shoulda been performed. I think he got off of it a little quick and I think the state had slacked up on it. I don't have no faith in these state people. I can see it now coming here at Northpoint. Before it's over with this place'll be like LaGrange was in the '60s and '70s.

There's a lot of things that they said they were gonna do that they haven't done and a lot of things that they should do that they're not doing. . . . I think the case should still be under his court's jurisdiction. I don't believe the state would have been so open about this. They said, "Well, you wouldn't let us do this at LaGrange. You wouldn't let us do this at Eddyville. Maybe we ought to do it at Northpoint." . . . They don't feel that the consent decree applies here. But it applies to the Department of Corrections, and the Department of Corrections runs this place. So I believe Judge Johnstone should have kept it under the court's jurisdiction longer.

Backup Overcrowding in Jails

Shorty soon joined a lawsuit challenging the living conditions at Northpoint, a former hospital for mentally ill people near Burgin, a small town in central Kentucky. Northpoint had been closed down as a mental hospital, but the state reopened it in 1983 to hold convicts it could not house at KSR or Eddyville because of the consent decree's population limits. Northpoint was designed to hold only five hundred prisoners when it first reopened as a prison, but by the time Shorty was transferred there in 1986, the population had risen to more than seven hundred. Over the next year, Shorty watched the population top nine hundred, and double bunk beds appeared where there had initially been single beds, making Northpoint nearly as overcrowded as the reformatory had been in 1978.

Northpoint was part of a much bigger picture, not only in Kentucky but all over the United States. The population cap at the state's two major prisons was only part of the reason Northpoint was overcrowded. Kentucky's state prisons and county jails were overcrowded. When Shorty's lawsuit was settled in 1980, Kentucky's prisons and jails held a total of 3,596 men. A year later, that number declined to 3,218, presumably as a result of Wilson's efforts to reduce technical parole violations and expedite paroles. Because of that overall decline, the state was able to end overcrowding at KSR and Eddyville without overcrowding other prisons and jails. After 1981, however, Kentucky's prison and jail population grew at a tremendous rate, reaching 4,513 in 1986. Thus, between 1981 and 1986 the number of men in prison or jail in Kentucky rose by 1,295, an increase of 30 percent in just five years.[4] These men could not, as in the past, be crowded into the reformatory or penitentiary because of the consent decree's population cap, and the minimum-security prisons were already filled to capacity. The state's answer was to overpopulate Northpoint and refuse to accept hundreds of men from county jails who were awaiting transfer to prisons that had no space for them. The overcrowding crisis of 1986 could not be attributed solely to the consent decree or to Judge Johnstone's order that the state obey the population limits at the two major prisons. Kentucky's prison population increase was part of a broader American trend. In 1969 America had fewer than 100,000 people locked up. From 1981 to 1986, the number of people, male and female, in American prisons and jails jumped from 299,514 to 506,507, an increase of 41 percent in five years and 500 percent in less than twenty years.[5] Since Kentucky's experience mirrors the national experience, the reasons for the national jump in prison population would likely explain the rise in Kentucky.

Alfred Blumstein has identified three major reasons for the national growth in prison population between 1969 and 1987. First, a few studies in the early 1970s found that prisoners who participated in rehabilitation programs were as likely to commit crime again as prisoners who had not participated in such programs. Instead of prompting calls for improvement in what were obviously deficient rehabilitation programs, these findings gave rise to a "nothing works" doctrine that criminals cannot be rehabilitated, the authority of corrections professionals to enhance treatment programs should be restricted, and prisons should be used primarily to incapacitate criminals. The decline of rehabilitation policy is related to the second reason for prison population growth, which Blumstein calls the "politicization of sentencing." The rise in crime was blamed on judges, who were accused of meting out overly lenient sentences to convicted criminals, and on parole boards, which were attacked for excessively liberal grants of parole. Such outcries found receptive audiences in legislatures, which passed new laws setting mandatory prison sentences for persons convicted of crimes and creating entirely new crimes, sometimes in response to atrocities reported in the media, sometimes to send repeat felony offenders to prison for longer periods. One result of the politicization of sentencing, according to Blumstein, is that more people were sent to prison and stayed there for longer periods of time. The third reason identified by Blumstein is demographic in nature. Studies indicate that people are most likely to commit crime in their early twenties. The baby boom generation, born between 1947 and 1962, reached this age between 1968 and 1983, which coincides with the period of rapid growth in prison population. As the number of crime-prone people swelled rapidly, so did prison populations.[6]

In the case of Kentucky, the "nothing works" doctrine probably did not play a role in the growth of prison population during this period, because the consent decree and Wilson's own philosophy of corrections reflected a view that prisoners should be provided with education, vocational training, and other programs to help prepare them for life in free society. The politicization of sentencing, however, almost certainly played an enormous role in the growth in Kentucky's prison population. The Kentucky General Assembly passed a number of laws mandating sentences for various crimes. In addition, Kentucky's persistent felony offender (PFO) law provided that a person who committed a new felony after being convicted of other felonies can be charged with a PFO violation in addition to the new felony, and, if convicted, must serve a long sentence for the PFO conviction in addition to the new felony conviction.

When Kentucky corrections officials started refusing to accept newly convicted prisoners from county jails to avoid further overcrowding in prisons like Northpoint, prisoners started backing up in the county jails, which in turn became overcrowded. Shorty watched the process and re-alized the state had a dilemma that could be traced to his lawsuit.

At the time I filed the lawsuit down at LaGrange I believe there was two thousand people in there. And I knew Eddyville was overcrowded, too. . . . So I figured if we won they'd have to do something.

They drug their feet in making space. What they should have done when the consent decree was signed, they should have right then started making a place to put 'em, and they didn't. When Judge Johnstone issued that order, they had to get rid of prisoners. . . . The result is they're over-crowded everyplace except LaGrange and Eddyville. . . . They're right in the situation in these places that they was when we filed the suit in 1978.

They're in a bind, all because they didn't go ahead, when Judge John-stone issued these orders to get the population out of Eddyville and La-Grange, they didn't go ahead and build a new prison. They just operated from day to day, like "We'll cross that bridge when we come to it." So now they're in a bind. The corrections cabinet has its ass in a bind. And of course, the corrections cabinet is partly to blame for the situation they are in. Everybody seems to have figured that once the overcrowding at LaGrange and Eddyville was corrected, that was the end of it. It was only the beginning.

$4 Million in Contempt Fines

Litigation erupted in 1984 over the jail overcrowding, and Shorty fol-lowed it closely. It eventually reached the Kentucky Supreme Court.

Some inmates . . . filed suits in the local courts asking that the prisoners be transferred out of county jail. They said they were serving more time in jail than they [were] supposed to and they had overcrowded conditions and all that.

Three different courts ruled in favor of the inmates. They threatened to fine the state so much a day for ever' day over forty-five days that they held the prisoners in these jails. And the state didn't appeal it.

Well, the state didn't have space. So a lotta time passed. The inmates, in their local courts, filed contempt motions. The local courts issued con-tempt citations and fined the state. Of course, the state appealed that to the state Court of Appeals. All three cases finally wound up in the Court of Appeals, and I believe they were transferred from the Court of Appeals to the Kentucky Supreme Court.

The Kentucky Supreme Court upheld the local courts, and now the Department of Corrections owes different plaintiffs close to $4 million. They've asked for reconsideration, but the order is so strong I don't think the Kentucky Supreme Court will even reconsider.

Robert Stephens had been appointed as a justice of the Kentucky Supreme Court to fill a vacancy in 1979, elected as a justice in 1980, and selected by fellow justices in 1982 to be chief justice. Stephens had served on the blue-ribbon commission with Johnstone in the early 1970s and was the state attorney general in 1978 when Shorty filed his lawsuit. As attorney general, Stephens had played an important role in helping to settle Shorty's lawsuit and improving conditions in the prisons. Chief Justice Stephens undoubtedly provided his fellow justices with a context in which to understand what had led to overcrowding in the county jails. The Kentucky Supreme Court handed down its decision on September 8, 1988, ruling that the state had violated the Constitution and laws of Kentucky by refusing to accept new prisoners from the county jails.

These cases present a bizarre picture of convicted felons and parole violators fighting for the right to get into state prison, joining with county officials trying to put them there. We have decided they have that right.

The Kentucky Constitution imposes responsibility on the state prison system to take custody of convicted felons and to supervise their care. We agree that the Constitution, the statutes, and Rules of Criminal Procedure impose a duty on the courts to order convicted felons be transferred to the custody of the state, meaning the state penal system operated by the Corrections Cabinet, and a duty on the Sheriff to carry out these orders. By fixing these responsibilities the Constitution and statutes necessarily create corresponding rights for prisoners being held for an unreasonable length of time in the county jail to insist upon transfer, and for county governments who are being forced to bear the expense for such prisoners when such expense is by law the state's obligation.

One of the state's defenses was that it was not violating the Kentucky Constitution at all: when the state refused to take new prisoners, those prisoners should still be seen as county prisoners because they remained in local jails because of the state policy of refusing transfer. The court poked fun at this bit of sophistry with a folksy aphorism:

> We cannot sell the people of Kentucky a mule and call it a horse, even if we believe the public needs a mule.

Shorty chuckled at this response, and in a way, it was his favorite part of the decision, for as a boy on his father's tenant farm in the foothills of eastern Kentucky, Shorty had fed, watered, saddled, hitched, and worked many mules and horses. He knew the difference between a mule and a horse, and so did the Supreme Court of Kentucky.

The state's more serious defense was that it was impossible to carry out its duty to accept all new prisoners because the Kentucky legislature had passed new criminal-sentencing laws resulting in huge new numbers of longer-term prisoners but had not funded enough new prisons to hold the influx of inmates. The court took the occasion to lecture the General Assembly:

> This then is the fundamental flaw in the Corrections Cabinet's defense based on inability to comply. The Constitution assigns the responsibility for care and custody of convicted felons to state government as a whole. The Corrections Cabinet is the correct point to impose responsibility only because it is the agency created by the General Assembly to carry out this function. It is not enough to create the agency. It must then be provided with sufficient funds for buildings, facilities and services necessary to provide for all such persons who become state prisoners by operation of state penal statutes. The basic equation is the state cannot pass penal statutes and create penalties that generate more prisoners than it is willing and prepared to provide for.[7]

The Supreme Court's fundamental message, directed at the legislature, was that there is a price for politicizing the sentencing process by legislating longer mandatory sentences and that the bill was now overdue. The legislature could not avoid its responsibility to pay for the flood of new prisoners. The court upheld the fines for contempt of court, which totaled more than $4 million, most of which was to be paid to the county governments for the expense of keeping the prisoners in jail. The fines were paid, and new jails and prisons were built to address the overcrowding problem.

Shorty's Lawsuit Reaches the U.S. Supreme Court

On June 18, 1988, the U.S. Supreme Court agreed to review one component of Shorty's lawsuit. The legal issue arose in 1985, when Judge Johnstone was still supervising implementation of the consent decree. Kenneth Bobbitt, a prisoner at KSR, had a visit from his mother and a friend. This friend had been barred from visiting at KSR for smuggling in contraband, so the officer on duty turned away the friend and Bobbitt's mother. She was then barred from visiting her son for six months because she had brought the friend with her. About the same time, another KSR inmate, Kevin Black, had a visit with his mother, who also brought along a friend. Shortly after the visit, guards found contraband on Black, so Black's mother and friend were then barred from visiting. Neither Bobbitt nor Black was given an opportunity to present reasons why their mothers should be permitted to visit them—specifically, that their mothers were innocent of any wrongdoing.

Inmates brought these incidents to the attention of the Plaintiffs' Committee, which discussed them with the lawyers. The lawyers consulted the visitation portion of the consent decree and found a relevant provision: "The Bureau of Corrections encourages and agrees to maintain visitation at least at the current level, with minimal restrictions" and to "continue [its] open visiting policy." The lawyers then read the prison's written policies and procedures, which stated that people could be barred from visiting a prisoner if they were a danger to the prison but contained no provision for giving a prisoner reasons why these people were considered a danger or for providing an opportunity for prisoners to rebut such an accusation. The lawyers thereupon filed a motion asking Judge Johnstone to order the state to give prisoners the reason for denial of visitation and an opportunity for a hearing on the matter. The lawyers contended that turning away Bobbitt's and Black's mothers without some kind of hearing violated both the consent decree and the constitutional right to due process of law.

Johnstone agreed with part of the prisoners' argument, ruling that barring a visitor without giving reasons or opportunity for a hearing did not violate the consent decree but did violate the constitutional right to due process. Relying on an earlier Supreme Court case, *Hewitt v. Helms*,[8] he found that visits were part of the "liberty" created for Kentucky prisoners by the "mandatory language" of the visiting policy agreed to by the state in the consent decree. Johnstone ordered the state to establish a procedure whereby a prisoner must be given a reason for turning away a visitor and an opportunity for a hearing.

The state appealed to the U.S. Court of Appeals for the Sixth Circuit, which affirmed Johnstone's decision.[9] The state then petitioned the U.S. Supreme Court for a writ of certiorari to review the lower courts' decisions. The Court granted certiorari to review only the issue of prison visitation, for that was the sole issue decided by the lower courts. This legal issue would affect the ability of prisoners all over the United States to have visitors.

On January 18, 1989, the U.S. Supreme Court heard oral argument in the case of *Kentucky Department of Corrections v. James Thompson.* The issue before the Court, arising from the denial of visitation by the mothers of Bobbitt and Black, was whether prison visits in Kentucky were part of the liberty guaranteed by the Fourteenth Amendment so that some sort of due process must be afforded to prisoners before guards can turn away visitors. In *Hewitt v. Helms,* the Supreme Court had ruled that if a state uses sufficiently specific and mandatory language in establishing rules for people to visit prisoners, such visits are part of the liberty protected by the Fourteenth Amendment. In this case, the state was asking the Court to overrule *Hewitt* and find that under no circumstances would prison visits be considered a constitutionally protected liberty interest. The prisoners, conversely, urged the Court to follow *Hewitt* and rule that the 1980 consent decree as well as subsequent prison regulations contained specific and mandatory language that placed such visits within the liberty protected by the Constitution.

The state's lawyer, Barbara Jones, went first in the oral argument, stating her position that visits should never be protected by the Constitution. She contended that visits for prisoners are not part of the liberty protected by the Constitution because visits are merely part of the day-to-day details of managing a prison rather than part of the length or nature of confinement. Justice Sandra Day O'Connor broke in:

> Well, I suppose the argument of the other side is that having family visitors is so vitally important in terms of a prisoner's existence, that it alters the nature of confinement. . . . What if the denial were totally arbitrary? The

guard doesn't like prisoner X and says, "I'm just not going to let you have any visitors."? [10]

After more questions from Justices Anthony M. Kennedy, William H. Rehnquist, and Antonin Scalia, Jones argued that prisoners could sue in state court rather than federal court if they were denied visits for no reason at all. Justice John Paul Stevens interrupted:

> Oh, but is that true of the particular rights at stake in this case? . . . Isn't that your position that the, if the prison officials want to do so, they can just deny, say, the inmate's mother or his wife or some friend visiting privileges and never even tell the inmate. . . . And you, and you don't even have to give the inmate notice that, telling him whether or not his wife has tried to see him or not. You just, it's just one of those minor details of prison management the prisoner has no rights in. . . . You're saying there are no constitutional rights at all. . . . And you're saying you have a right to promulgate no regulations at all. Therefore the rights you're seeking to vindicate, is one to simply say I'm sorry, I know you're curious, but we're not going to tell you.

Justices Rehnquist, Byron R. White, and Scalia fired more questions. In response, Jones repeated her theme that federal courts should not be involved in administrative details like prison visits and that constitutional protection should be reserved for matters, such as good-time credits and administrative segregation, that affect the nature or duration of confinement. She said the difference was like the prison door, that constitutional protection should be given only for matters that affect whether a prisoner gets outside the door of the prison. Justice William J. Brennan Jr. asked his only question in the case:

> How about the door between the visitors' room and the general population? . . . That's a different kind of door?

The back-and-forth continued through questioning by Justices Kennedy, O'Connor, Rehnquist, White, and others, with all nine leaning forward, expressing intense interest in this issue. Finally, Justice Kennedy asked the only question based on applying the standard set in *Hewitt* rather than on whether that case should be overruled:

> Assume for the moment that we hold that a constitutionally protected right in visitation can be created. Did this regulation have sufficiently specific and mandatory language to do that?

Jones answered, "No, Your Honor." After a few more questions, she sat down.

Now it was time for the prisoners' lawyer, Joe Elder. He got one sentence out of his mouth before Justice O'Connor again jumped in with the first questions.

> Is this a class action? . . . And are any of the named plaintiffs still incarcerated? . . . Is it possible that this is moot?

Justices Kennedy, White, Rehnquist, Thurgood Marshall, and Scalia all chimed in, wondering how long the consent decree would continue to command the attention of the federal courts. Once Elder informed them that Judge Johnstone had already found substantial compliance with the decree and put the case on inactive status, except for dorm renovation, the justices abandoned this topic. Elder then articulated the heart of his argument, that the specific and mandatory language in the consent decree and in the state's own prison policies had made visits part of the liberty of a Kentucky prisoner, so that the Constitution guaranteed due process of law in the form of some kind of hearing if visitors were turned away. Justices Rehnquist, O'Connor, and Kennedy queried how the state had created this right to have visitors, and Elder answered that the state had created the right to visits by agreeing to mandatory language in the decree and using mandatory language in its own visiting regulations. Sensing that some justices were reluctant to impose a cumbersome hearing process on prison authorities, Elder said that the inmates were not asking for a formal hearing in court every time a visit was denied but merely an informal review by prison staff. That led to the most heated exchange of the day, between Elder and Justice Scalia:

> *Elder:* The State of Kentucky drops the inmate a note saying, "Your mother brought contraband to the prison last week. We're going to suspend her visitation." The inmate writes back and says, "I'm sorry, that was inmate Jones' mother and not mine. If you'll check your records, you've made a mistake." That's all the Sixth Circuit requires. I cannot see how that—
>
> *Scalia:* Does that satisfy you?
>
> *Elder:* That would satisfy me. That's all the Sixth Circuit requires. It's all that Judge Johnstone requires.
>
> *Scalia:* And if you found out the warden was just taking that note and not even reading it, chucking it in the wastebasket, you wouldn't be back here

saying, "Now wait a minute." You have to, you have to consider the note, don't you? And don't you have to investigate whether it's correct that it was so and so instead of—right? . . . He'd have to look into the matter. Wouldn't the warden have to look into the matter?

Elder: I think he has some good faith duty to do something with—

Scalia: Legal duty.

Elder: Some legal duty to do something with the note rather than just put it in his round file next to his desk.

Scalia: So, it's not nothing.

Elder: It's not nothing. And neither is visitation. One of the things that's important to remember is the potential that could affect the inmate. If an inmate's visits are suspended for, say, six months with his mother, this potentially is as many as 72 visits. The regulations which the state has promulgated say that in case of contraband, it could be indefinitely. Now, if a man's serving 30 years and his wife brings contraband to the institution and the warden says indefinitely, that's where we're at. That could be for the rest of that inmate's time. And that is an extremely serious matter indeed.

By this time a red flush was flooding up Elder's neck. If the Supreme Court did not think that visits were important to a prisoner, he would surely lose this argument. Justice Scalia, however, did not pursue the point. After a few more questions from Justices Rehnquist, Scalia, Stevens, and Kennedy, Elder's time was up. Jones spoke for a few more minutes in rebuttal, and the oral argument was over. These two lawyers had spent ten years on Kentucky's prison litigation, and it had led to oral argument before the U.S. Supreme Court. The Justices asked 121 questions in one hour, an average of one question every thirty seconds. The state's lawyer was asked sixty-two questions, the prisoners' lawyer fifty-nine. It was apparent that the justices were keenly interested in the issue, but there was one very disturbing element in the oral argument. Some of the justices—notably Scalia, Rehnquist, White, and Kennedy—seemed to indicate by the tone of their questions that they did not feel that visits were important to a prisoner.

The Supreme Court handed down its decision four months later, on May 15, 1989. By a six to three vote, the Court ruled that Bobbitt, Black, and the other prisoners at KSR were not entitled to a hearing if guards turned away their mothers, friends, or other visitors. The Court rejected the state's main argument and adhered to its precedent in *Hewitt v. Helms,* but the six-justice majority found that the state's visiting regulations did not have the kind of mandatory language required to make visits a constitutionally protected liberty interest. This finding, however, was clearly inconsistent with the plain language of the prison rules, which used the mandatory word *will* repeatedly. The Court's bewildering decision could only have been based on an unspoken moral premise that visits are not important to prisoners and that the human need for contact with family and friends is merely a detail of prison administration.

Justice Marshall wrote a dissenting opinion for three justices and addressed this premise directly. He argued that visits are so important to a prisoner that they should be considered part of the liberty kept by prisoners after they have entered prison. He expressed dismay about the practical effect of the majority ruling.

> As a result of today's decision, correctional authorities at the Kentucky State Reformatory are free to deny prisoners visits from parents, spouses, children, clergy members, and close friends for any reason whatsoever, or for no reason at all. Prisoners will not even be entitled to learn the reason, if any, why a visitor has been turned away. In my view, the exercise of such unbridled governmental power over the basic human need to see family members and friends strikes at the heart of the liberty protected by the Due Process Clause of the Fourteenth Amendment. Recognizing a liberty interest in this case would not create a right to "unfettered visitation," but would merely afford prisoners rudimentary procedural safeguards against retaliatory or arbitrary denials of visits.[11]

This decision marked the end of major legal proceedings in Shorty's lawsuit. The Supreme Court's decision neither affected the consent decree nor reversed any of the improvements in living conditions at KSR and Eddyville. The population at KSR remained within the limits set by the decree, most of the dorms had been rebuilt, more were on the way, and the job of cleaning up continued.

Back at the federal courthouse in Paducah, Kentucky, Judge Johnstone received the news that his decision on prison visits had been reversed. He put it all in perspective, for he realized that the Supreme Court's decision would not affect the massive reforms in Kentucky's prison system.

I don't worry about being reversed. I have enough trouble worrying about my own mistakes without worrying about mistakes appeals courts think I made. Oftentimes, appeals courts see it differently. We get along. If I'm wrong, I certainly want to know it. I don't keep score.

You can't tell what the Supreme Court is going to do. I thought that case was solid. Things balance out. The Constitution works. I'm not afraid of a conservative judge. I'm not afraid of a liberal judge. If they get too far out of line, the legislature will fix it. I don't worry too much anymore.

We've got a good system. The system works.

If we did nothing else with those prison cases, we created a more professional staff running that system. The people running the Kentucky prisons today are better and more professional. I think they welcomed the lawsuits. I think the Kentucky prisons are out in front today because of that.

Aftermath

The litigation was completed by 1989, ten years after it had begun. Much of the literature on prison-reform litigation has analyzed its impact on the operation of prison systems, but there has been little examination of the major participants' lives in the aftermath of such litigation. The Kentucky litigation had a significant impact on the lives of several of the people featured in this study, particularly Walter Harris.

George Wilson: Ohio Commissioner of Corrections and Rehabilitation

Kentucky elected a new governor in 1987, and he appointed a new secretary of corrections to replace George Wilson. For eight years, Wilson had presided over the greatest expansion of resources for prison programs and facilities in Kentucky history. The two-year corrections budget nearly quadrupled, from $58 million in 1980 to $203 million in 1988. The workforce grew more than 50 percent, from 1,400 to 2,200 employees. The system added 2,800 new beds for prisoners and 3,100 new beds for those released into community programs. Under Wilson, these resources were used to improve the prisons and create opportunities for prisoners to reform their own lives. He gained a national reputation not only for transforming a neglected, backward corrections department into a progressive, professional system but also for achieving termination of extensive federal court intervention in a relatively short six years. Ohio's reform-minded governor, Dick Celeste, recruited Wilson to run that state's prison system, one of the largest in the country, and Wilson became a national spokesman for criminal-justice reform. After his stint in Ohio, he returned to Kentucky and continued a career in corrections and politics.

Judge Johnstone: Senior Status

Judge Johnstone achieved even greater prominence throughout Kentucky as a result of the prison litigation, and he presided over many other federal cases. One of these cases was especially noteworthy, involving a prosecution of ten members of the notorious Hell's Angels motorcycle gang, including its leader, Ralph Hubert "Sonny" Barger. The Hell's Angels had been charged with conspiracy to violate federal explosives laws by blowing up a clubhouse of a rival gang, the Outlaws, as well as lesser offenses. During the trial, Johnstone was an island of serenity in an ocean of tension engendered by the Hell's Angels' reputation for violence. The tension was exacerbated by reports that U.S. Marshals, without the judge's knowledge, had stationed snipers on the courthouse roof. The veteran of the Battle of the Bulge ordered the snipers off the roof.

> *That's the kind of foolishness that can blow a trial, cause a mistrial. It's a bunch of foolishness. Just like with prisoners, if you taunt someone enough, you're going to stir them up! The marshals put those snipers on the roof, and it just stirs the defendants up. If you tell a guy he's bad, he's a criminal, he'll act that way! I couldn't ask for any more polite, respectful behavior than these Hell's Angels gave. There's no reason for those guns — just foolishness. It's up to the judge to command respect, not because he's high or big or mighty, but because he treats people with respect.*

The trial ended without incident, with some of the Angels acquitted and others, including Barger, convicted of conspiracy.[1]

Judge Johnstone's high esteem within the legal profession was reflected in the Kentucky Bar Association's decision, soon after the U.S. Supreme Court decision on prison visits, to name him the outstanding judge for 1989. Lawyers who had cases before him found him to be courteous to everyone, not influenced by personalities, knowledgeable about the law, and decisive in his rulings. The award surprised Judge Johnstone.

When you handle controversial matters—like the prison cases—you don't expect awards like this. I don't think the majority of the organized bar understands the problems of prisoners. They don't understand the problems of the poor. They don't understand the whole problem of access to the courts. I guess people may not agree with what you decide, but they can appreciate that you handled the case fairly.

Back at the barbershop in Princeton, Kentucky, Herby heard all this news about the Supreme Court case, the judge of the year award, and the prison lawsuit, and he reflected on Judge Johnstone.

Ed enjoys the fact he was an enlisted man in World War II. He likes to say, "I wasn't one of the officers. I was one of the soldiers." He really believes all people are equal and he does not put himself above anybody else. . . .

He was sitting in my barbershop one day. It was about the time of the $42 million prison lawsuit. A guy from Hopkinsville was here, and he didn't know Ed Johnstone. Well, he gave that federal judge the devil about the prison case! Ed just got up and started sweeping hair off the floor! . . . Most people in his position would live in Louisville. Ed stays here. He doesn't try to be a big shot. He's easygoing. He does not try to impress anyone. Most people here are working-class people. They don't think about how important his job is. Ed likes it that way.

He was a leader here in Democratic politics. But he's done more favors for small people. You can't imagine how many people he's helped. One time my health wasn't very good. I had some firewood that needed to be split. Ed come over and helped me bust it with a wedge. He worked on a tobacco farm when he was young. He was one of the best tobacco cutters around. He's big, and he could cut tobacco with the best. He likes busting wood. There was this high school boy from a poor family. One day he asked the judge for some money. Ed asked him to come out to his house and help out with some work. Ed worked that kid hard and then he paid him! Instead of just giving it to him, he taught that kid to work for his money. . . .

Ed paid me the nicest compliment I've ever had. We were down by the creek one day, busting up wood or planting a tree or something like that. And he up and looked at me and said, "Herby, I just want to thank you for being my friend." That was the nicest thing. I'm just a two-bit barber. He has lunch with the governor, has dinner with Supreme Court justices, has this big, important job. I grew up on the wrong side of the tracks, I guess you'd say. . . . We were honest and worked hard, but we were poor. Ed and I came from different backgrounds. Just a two-bit barber, and he says to me, "Herby, I just want to thank you for being my friend."

Johnstone was later elected to the University of Kentucky Hall of Fame. He chose senior status as a federal judge, which in theory meant he would have a reduced workload, but according to his longtime secretary, Barbara DeAngelo, he has continued to work as hard as ever. He does not agree with the proposition that prisoners file so many frivolous lawsuits that they are disrupting the federal courts. He reads all petitions filed by prisoners and finds that it does not take long to separate the serious grievances from the silly ones. Reading prisoners' petitions is his method of continuing to monitor the prisons and, if several petitions repeat the same problem or one petition recounts an apparently serious incident, he takes steps to ensure that the prisoner is afforded a hearing. The prisoners who receive hearings usually lose, but they are treated with dignity in Johnstone's courtroom. In some cases, the judge encourages a settlement, and in others juries have awarded money damages to prisoners. An inmate at KSR named Bernie Harris, for example, filed a lawsuit alleging that prison officials had ignored him one morning when he complained of illness. His condition deteriorated, and he eventually was taken to a hospital emergency room, where he was diagnosed as having pneumonia. He was returned to prison, but his condition continued to deteriorate, and he was finally admitted to the hospital. The state agreed, in an order signed by Judge Johnstone, to pay Harris five hundred dollars in damages.

Shorty Goes Home

After Shorty was transferred to Northpoint Training Center in 1986, he continued to pursue his habeas corpus petition to vacate his persistent felony offender (PFO) conviction and gain his release. In the interim, he found useful work at Northpoint and refused transfer to a minimum-security prison near the state capitol.

They don't have any work down at the capitol for me. I'm a welder and a painter and a body man and mechanic. They don't do any of that stuff. All they have is janitors for the state office buildings and maintenance people for the state office buildings—plumbers and buffers and waxers, stuff like that.

I've got minimum-custody status. I've had minimum custody since March of '88. They tried to transfer me up to the capitol in March of '88, but my supervisor up at Northpoint, I asked him to get it stopped. He knows somebody in Frankfort in prison industries, and they must have had a little pull. Anyhow, they got it postponed for over two years.

So at Northpoint I kept working in upholstery, making furniture. I just stayed on.

I kept working on guys' cases. I got one in the United States Supreme Court and one in the federal district court in Louisville and one in federal district court in Lexington—habeas corpus. The public defender at Northpoint's working with me on one. I got some records from him yesterday on a guy's case. Their caseload's so heavy, they're glad to get any help they can, even if it's a nonskilled person like me.

Well, my success rate is higher than the public defender at Northpoint, I'll say that. I've won twenty-seven cases. I've lost, I'd say, seventy-five or a hundred. Like I say, I'm working on three of 'em. I got two that I'm pretty sure 'll win. I don't know about the other one, the one in the Supreme Court.

Shorty's own habeas corpus petition became enmeshed in a procedural problem. His argument for overturning his PFO conviction was that the state did not have sufficient evidence of his prior felony convictions to convict him as a PFO. The federal district court initially ruled, however, that Shorty was procedurally barred from even raising the claim of insufficient evidence because he had failed to make that claim at trial or in earlier appeals.

Shorty appealed the district court decision to the U.S. Court of Appeals for the Sixth Circuit, which ruled on October 13, 1989, that he was not barred from raising the insufficient-evidence claim and ordered the federal district court to determine whether there was sufficient evidence to support the PFO conviction. On May 17, 1990, the district judge ruled in Shorty's favor because the prosecutor had failed to introduce certified copies of the prior felony judgments of conviction. The state's only evidence of the earlier conviction was testimony from a court clerk, but the law required a certified copy of the earlier judgment. Thus, the federal judge vacated the PFO conviction.

The judge's order did not affect Shorty's other 1984 conviction for theft, but Shorty had long since served his time on that conviction, so Shorty was a free man after six years of appeals. Now fifty-five years old, he returned to his home area in Bath County on the periphery of the Appalachian Plateau. He had thirty years of experience in car and truck bodywork, so he opened his own business, Thompson's Body Shop, in Owingsville. The business prospered for several years, but in 1993 Shorty experienced severe headaches and dizziness that made it difficult to work. Tests revealed he had a brain tumor. Surgeons removed the tumor and it was benign, but Shorty could no longer do body shop work and had to close the business. Today he lives quietly in a mobile home on a younger brother's farm, supported by a monthly government benefit for disabled people.

Wilgus: Waiting

By the end of 1987 Wilgus had obtained all the academic credit possible in the college program at KSR. He made top grades, won academic honors, and achieved the equivalent of a junior-college education. Wilgus started making plans to earn a bachelor of arts degree.

> I made the dean's list all five semesters, and I graduated with distinction, associate of arts degree. I had a scholarship offered to me from three different places. I'm gonna choose the one at the University of Kentucky. I'll be transferred there next year. The political science department or the English department, either one'll take me.

Wilgus's older daughter, Shannon Dawn, who had encouraged him to go to college, became pregnant just before finishing high school and abandoned her plans to attend college, marrying instead and giving birth to a son. In 1988 the new grandfather, now forty-one years old, finally received permission to transfer to the Blackburn Correctional Center near Lexington, enroll in its study-release program, and attend the University of Kentucky. In the few remaining months at KSR before the transfer to Blackburn, he passed the time writing short stories and tutoring other prisoners in English courses.

I write short stories. I can write fiction, and I can lace it with the truth. I do a lot of features for the prison magazine. I make sure there's no dangling modifiers, there's good noun-verb agreement, and the mechanics are in proper order.

The guys that's in the program now is struggling with English 101. I'm the unofficial tutor. Here's the stuff I'm doing. I'm diagramming sentences. I'm busting 'em down, showing 'em the basic rules. And they're paying me. I get a pack of cigarettes here, a pack there, a tube of toothpaste here — just whatever I can get, whatever they offer.

If they're having problems, they're referred to me. I'm not doing anything wrong. I'm not writing anything for 'em. I'm just showing 'em how to build good, solid paragraphs, how to make good transition sentences from one paragraph to the next. Or they're leaving a block of paragraphs and they want a transition paragraph going into another subject. . . .

I didn't have anybody to teach me that stuff. I was so intimidated and so frightened by that English 101 experience in the beginning, that I went to the library and dug up ever'thing I could possibly dig up. I got Harbrace, Donald Hall's Writing Well, *Elizabeth McMahon's* Writing, *McCrimmon's. In my cabinet is all English books and dictionaries. . . .*

Next spring, University of Louisville is gonna come in and . . . set up a business management and economics program. Louisville's saying, "We'll do this, we'll set this up at our own expense." They're wanting to move in, 'cause boy, University of Kentucky got lots of miles out of its program — "Taking education to the people!" They've reached down into the bottom pits of mankind, boy, and got us!

The University of Kentucky admitted Wilgus as an undergraduate with sixty-three hours already to his credit from the KSR program, giving him a scholarship. He transferred to Blackburn in July 1988, with his bachelor of arts curriculum scheduled to begin a year later.

I want a Bachelor of Arts degree. Other than that, I'm not looking too far beyond that because it's too far to look. There's too many things that could happen.

While Wilgus was waiting at Blackburn for the study-release program to begin, his daughter's marriage ended in divorce.

She's a receptionist, file clerk, and that kind o' thing, and she went back to school. She's going to Hazard Community College. And as soon as she graduates at Hazard Community, she's gonna transfer to the University of Kentucky—physics, double major. Same time as me.

But without Wilson as its head, the Department of Corrections abolished the study-release program without explanation on July 21, 1989, four days before Wilgus would have matriculated. The study-release program was replaced by a program operated by Eastern Kentucky University. The new plan would offer a four-year college program inside the prison but would begin with introductory survey courses such as English 101, which Wilgus had already completed. No upper-level courses would be offered for at least two years, so Wilgus would have a lengthy wait.

At first Wilgus felt ambushed, bewildered, and frustrated. He had done everything the authorities had asked of him, but then the program had been canceled in a move that appeared directly aimed at him. Wilgus eventually recovered from his disappointment and continued to read books and write stories on his own.

We were all disappointed about the college program, the folks at UK and I were. I didn't know what to do. The people in the honors program had open arms for me, so what I did was, I wrote to the adult academic office. They told me to write some essays and they'd take 'em before the academic committee and see if I couldn't get some money to where I could take some independent study courses for credit.

So I wrote one essay and there was seventy-seven people involved in it—I assume it was a competition. And then they cut it down to twenty. And then we had to write another essay. So I wrote another essay and sent it over. Then they took fifteen out of the twenty, and they asked us to write another essay, and so I did. I was one of the ones who got awarded. They paid for my books, they paid the professor's fee, and they paid the course fee.

But now I lost out on one, too. There was another program. There was something called the Anna Johnson Scholarship Fund for exceptional students. I wrote an essay for that and I made the first cut. Then I wrote an-

other essay and I didn't make that cut. So obviously there was some pretty stiff competition!

Wilgus continued to write for a while but finally gave up when it became clear that his opportunity for education in prison was stalled. He remained at Blackburn Correctional Center and worked at the Kentucky Horse Park. Wilgus married a woman named Martha whom he met when she came to visit her brother in prison. Martha visits Wilgus regularly, and he occasionally receives a furlough to visit her. Wilgus was denied parole in 1996, but he could be released in 2004 based on good-time credits. He waits for that day, although there is no guarantee of parole.

Walter: Struggle for Success

Walter experienced a rocky start in 1986. At Northpoint Training Center, he was assigned to the legal office, doing work for other prisoners. An inmate named Ross Webster planned to sue the prison for having asbestos materials in the buildings, and he sought Walter's assistance. On Walter's advice, Webster sent a sample of the asbestos material to the national Centers for Disease Control in Atlanta, which examined the material, wrote a report, and sent it to the prisoners. Unfortunately, the center also sent a copy of the report to the warden, who transferred Walter back to KSR on January 15, 1986, after just four months at Northpoint. He remained for only thirty-five days at KSR. Another inmate from Northpoint wrote and asked Walter to do some legal work on his criminal case. Walter replied that he would not provide assistance because the work would require a law book that cost more than fifty dollars, which Walter would not buy with his own money. The inmate wrote back that his brother would send Walter the money for the law book and demanded that Walter do the work. Walter responded that he would do no work until the brother produced the money for the book, and that if the brother did so, Walter might advance some of his own money to pay for some of the inmate's other legal expenses. Guards at KSR obtained Walter's letter and charged him with violating the rule against charging other inmates for legal services. Walter contended that he was not charging for his services and was only insisting that the other inmate arrange payment for the law book, but he was found guilty by a two-to-one vote of the hearing panel. He was transferred to the maximum-security penitentiary at Eddyville, placed in isolation for thirty days, and then assigned to work in the legal office.

Through the rest of 1986 and into the winter of 1987, Walter remained at Eddyville, working to overturn his own criminal conviction. It was a tangled case. He originally had a life sentence for murder and armed robbery, for which he had served eight years. He also had a new ten-year sentence for the crime he had committed while on parole, which the judge had ruled would run "concurrently" with the old sentence. It was unclear what *concurrently* meant when applied to Walter's case—specifically whether Walter's new ten-year sentence began to run when the judge imposed it, when Walter first returned to KSR after the parole violation, or when the first sentence had started to run.

Walter researched the meaning of the word *concurrently* in the context of criminal sentencing. It was difficult, often boring work, but he found some cases that said a concurrent sentence begins to run on the day the original sentence began to run, and a prisoner was entitled to credit on his concurrent sentence for all time he had served on his original sentence. By the time Walter was returned to KSR in 1986, he had already served more than ten years on his original life sentence, so he developed an argument that, under the case-law definition of *concurrently*, his new sentence began to run the day his original sentence commenced, and he was entitled to ten years' credit on his new ten-year sentence, so that his new sentence had expired.

He presented his argument to the Department of Corrections without great confidence, but the department surprised him by agreeing with his argument and declaring that the ten-year concurrent sentence had expired. Walter still had time left on his original life sentence, but he became eligible for parole on the life sentence, since the now-expired new sentence had blocked his eligibility.

The Kentucky Supreme Court soon handed Walter another surprise by vacating his original 1973 murder conviction. Through all these years, through Shorty's lawsuit, through the first failure at parole, through bouncing around from prison to prison, Walter had fought his 1973 murder conviction in the appeals courts. Walter did not deny that he had killed a liquor-store employee in the course of a robbery, but he had contended that the act was not intentional murder because the employee provoked

Walter to shoot by attacking him with a glass bottle. Walter was convicted of intentional murder, but after the trial new evidence had come to light, showing that the police had tampered with the evidence in order to make it appear the shooting was unprovoked.

The parole board provided a third surprise, granting parole on the remaining armed-robbery sentence. Walter was released from Eddyville on February 20, 1987. He first applied to reside in a halfway house in Lexington and enroll at the University of Kentucky, but his application was denied. Walter then decided to return home to the ghetto and attempt to find a job as a paralegal in a law firm, but his initial forays were unsuccessful.

For about six months I beat my head up against the wall trying to find a job. The parole officers were trying to find me a job as a paralegal instead of being practical about it. . . . They were trying to oversell. They were just harping on the fact that I had been involved in litigation and legal programs over the thirteen years that I was locked up in Kentucky. . . . People that they were introducing me to, they were all impressed, but it was a question of what they could do with the limited resources that they had.

Here there's a requirement that you have a college degree, generally, a four-year degree. And most lawyers don't want to hear what you have to say if you don't have a degree or you can't come up with the equivalent degree of experience in this city. It doesn't matter where you acquire experience prior to that. If you don't have any in this city, they can't really use you.

So I kinda gave up on obtaining a position as a paralegal for a while. I was looking for basically just about anything I could lay my hands on — factory work, dish washing, you name it. Nothing was happening. As soon as they found out about my past record, which the people said I was obliged to mention, they lost interest. . . .

It finally dawned on me that there wasn't going to be any real progress until I got back in school and got some private recognition of whatever capabilities I had. So I stayed in the house with my mother, paid tuition at a career-training program, and was there for six months. [I] completed a paralegal course, a word-processing course. It was combined. And went job hunting again.

Initially, it didn't do me too much good. I went to a law firm downtown. They had a paralegal position open. They wanted someone who was capable of just sitting in front of a terminal or just analyzing papers the better part of a day. They had a pretty nice benefits package. But as soon as I told the personnel director about my personal history, he kinda shook his head, and it didn't go any further than that.

So, I went around to a number of places. One was a permanent employment office. The president of the company kinda laid out what the economic situation of the city was at that time, what the political situation was. He was of the opinion that my background per se wouldn't prevent me from getting a job. It was just the fact that I didn't have any experience in this city as a paralegal or legal secretary to fall back on. Nobody was gonna take a chance.

So I just kept on trying. I was getting kinda discouraged. And I got to the point where I figured that the best thing to do was to work for the temporary employment agencies until they were successful in getting me a temporary position with a law firm or a legal department in a corporation. And they were trying, but things just weren't developing as they had anticipated. I don't know if they were mentioning my background to people or not, but they were aware of it. . . .

[Through a temporary agency, I finally found] a position as a legal secretary. I thought it was a nice idea. It was a position I was interested in as a stepping stone to a position as a paralegal, but I didn't really see myself getting the position. I saw them finding out about my background and, "Oh, wow. You have to go." But fortunately, to my amazement, that isn't what happened. I got the temporary position.

I think they were satisfied with my work and the extra effort I put in, going out of my way to do some things which someone else might consider to be running errands—things like that. That's the way you get your foot in the door. You gotta do that little bit extra. I didn't too much like it, but realistically I didn't have too much of a choice. It was the difference in hiring me and hiring someone else. If I was just going to do what everyone else was willing to do, if I just wanted to sit back and wait until that someone came along that they felt was just a little bit better than me, then I'd be out the door.

About two weeks went by after that without me taking any action on the permanent position as a legal secretary. They began to doubt whether I was really interested in the permanent position. During that second week, the director of pilot development for the aging and the associate counsel set up an interview with me. I thought it was going to be kinda informal chit-chat. Turned out that it wasn't so informal. It was a prelude to a formal interview for a position.

And I just straight-out told them, before the formal interview, I wanted them to know that even though everybody who interviewed me prior to that had indicated they didn't want to hear that I was an ex-con, they didn't even bother to ask what I had been in prison for. I didn't volunteer. I knew they'd get around to it sooner or later, but I thought I'll wait until they do.

The formal interview came around, and no mention was made of it. They were, the two of them, prepared at that point to extend the offer of employment. But they went and discussed the situation with the senior vice president and general counsel of the corporation that was head of the legal department. And she gave them the OK with the provision that they contact the parole office to find out what was really going on as opposed to what I might have been leading them to believe.

They wanted me to meet with a fellow in employee relations. We talked, and basically it was straightforward conversation. He wanted to know where I had been and how I had been and where I was. And in my own rambling way I finally got around to spelling it out for him. He seemed satisfied that I was on the level, that I wasn't just looking for a nest to roost for a while or wreak havoc. And he recommended that I be retained.

The director of pilot development and the associate counsel in the meantime, had gotten chewed out. I don't think the vice president was very pleased to hear about it for the first time so late in the day. Well, they are pretty shrewd women. They know the corporation. They know when to reveal things and when to keep to themselves. And they were determined to hire me. The associates and directors usually made the hiring decisions subject to the approval of the head of the department, but it was generally a foregone conclusion that once the director or associate agreed to hire you, the head of the department would go along with their decision unless there was something really exceptional.

So, they kinda played around until they felt that they had the best *hand. At which point they presented the issue to the vice president, and she looked at it. She knew what the situation was, how they felt about me coming to work for them. It wasn't as though she had been deceived or misled or anything like that. It was just a delay in presenting it to her. I guess she mentioned it to the president of the corporation to find out how he felt about it. And he said OK.*

It was essentially a paralegal position, but they just had a different name for it, legal secretary. Their paralegal positions went by other titles like the contract analyst position. They wanted someone with a four-year degree and about three years' experience in contract analyst work. There aren't too many people around training for that.

I did substantially less on that job than what I did when I was working as a legal aide at Eddyville and LaGrange. Basically it was secretarial work, quite a bit of word processing, answering the telephone. . . .

I told them I would stay in the position for at least eighteen months before I moved on if a position became available elsewhere as a paralegal. I pretty much stuck by that. It was just an informal agreement between myself and my immediate supervisors, because they wanted somebody that would stay around at least that long.

Walter had been out of prison for a year and was nearly thirty-eight years old when he landed the job as legal secretary. The job fell short of his goal of being a paralegal, but it was a beginning, and it was steady work. Walter became a very useful employee. His supervisors came to realize that he was dependable and wanted to attain professional status. Less than a year after starting work, Walter enrolled in college, and the corporation helped pay his way.

The corporation had a tuition loan program, and through the tuition loan program it paid for associates' educational programs, with the exception of books. So I applied for that. The senior vice president sent me to a woman in the human resources department. I got my career guidance from her. We sat down and talked over my ambitions and the corporation's objectives and how I could best satisfy their criteria with respect to an entry-level paralegal position. That's why they paid for my education at that point.

Walter's full-time job necessitated that he take courses at night. He enrolled in two schools, a university for liberal arts courses to obtain a bachelor's degree, and a paralegal school for the purpose of becoming certified as a paralegal.

Much had changed in free society in the fifteen years since Walter first entered prison in 1974. In particular, everything was much more expensive, but he could cope with that problem because he lived with his mother and had little time for social life between work and school. After his disillusionment in Vietnam and his years in prison, Walter simply wanted to be a free man and make a decent living. He soon learned, however, that achieving these goals would require more patience.

At times it's great to be free. At times, it's not so great in terms of additional responsibilities that I have to cope with now. You have to eat. That's the first thing you gotta think about when you get some money, is ensuring that you have some food. And I'm not talking about just from one day to the next, but for the whole month. Even when that paycheck is gone, first thing you have got to get out of the habit of doing is living from one paycheck to the next. That necessitates a bank account, so you don't get into a situation where you get paid today and next week you're broke.

It's not just for food. It's for all the little necessities. Things that at one time you could kind of take for granted because things were far less expensive then. I almost choked at the price of beers! That was one of the hardest things. Shoot, I got my hands on fifty dollars when I first got out, I thought I had some money. So I went into the store and found out there wasn't very much that I could buy with fifty dollars. Can't lay anything away. A meal—one meal, two people—would take about that. I said, "God, I couldn't go out to any clubs. Shoot, it's a crazy world!" I didn't have enough money.

I mean, a guy my age would like to have his own place and would like to have a car, the kind of things that I was used to before I was initially incarcerated in Kentucky. But doing it legitimately takes a lot longer than when you're out there on the other side of the fence. It hasn't been that bad. For all the turmoil, it's been worth it.

There's something to be learned, something that may prove beneficial in the long run in terms of my merging back into the mainstream of society. So I'm kinda taking it one step at a time. Guarding against that pitfall that guys like me usually run into, when you get uptight because the pressure is building up. Slipping back, get yourself into a situation where you feel that you don't have any other choice but to go back to what you were doing before, because that's what you know best—stealing, robbery, selling drugs, whatever. Drugs're out there. No problem about that. . . .

I have a pretty fair idea of what direction I want to go in. My ultimate goal is to become a paralegal. At that point I will have accomplished one goal that I set for myself when I got out and that was that I was going to be a paralegal, and I'd go through hell or high water to do it.

A jailhouse lawyer would never be anything else but a jailhouse lawyer. . . . The reality is, there's no way anyone is going to hire you, unless someone makes an exception. I read this book, Guardians of Satan, *where a Jewish jailhouse lawyer had a life sentence, and at the time he started out at this jailhouse lawyering they didn't have parole in New York. It was through his involvement that he created a certain amount of momentum to change the law with respect to parole. With the help of some judges and some Catholic preachers, it was changed. He ultimately got out of prison and became a lawyer. In fact, he's working in New York. I was doing some research one day, and I came across his name in a case I was reading.*

And that's where I got my idea. Maybe some of us can do it. It's just a matter of setting certain things in place, building the foundation for the next step, and formalizing a program. If we had succeeded in getting a paralegal program at LaGrange, then when we walked out the door, we would have had a certificate that said we had received formal training, professional training. Then we'd've been that much better off when we left the institution than when we came in.

I was looking from the point of view, we had all these jailhouse lawyers that were making these contributions, wanting something but not getting anything, and being discouraged from participating on that basis. In addition to reaching out to all the other guys in the institution that we thought of as less fortunate, we had to deal with our own needs. I was reading Ebony *one day. There was an article about a prison, I think it was the Missouri state prison. They had a computer-programming curriculum, and they have a plant outside the prison that the inmates ran. There was a guy in there who had earned a Ph.D. He was getting offers from all over the country to come to work as a systems analyst, but his chances for parole were nil. And I said, "Well, despite all these great things you're saying about this guy, and despite his education and the fact that he won't*

have to go back to robbing, he's just not gonna make parole. If this guy,
in the six years he's in the penitentiary, he did all that, why can't we do
something like that?"

Correctional officials, when they institute programs of that sort, they
take a gamble. But something had to be done in terms of at least getting
them to think about it. I think through what we did, we succeeded in that
they thought about it for a time. They're not thinking about it now, but if
it comes up later on, they may not be so opposed to it.

I guess it's through repetition that ideas become reality. You have a
dream, you want something, go after it. You have to be persistent about it.

Walter experienced a downturn after a few years at the corporation. His
job was eliminated, and he had to withdraw from school since the corporation no longer paid the tuition. Discouraged, he resorted to his old, post-
Vietnam drug habit. With help from family members, however, he entered
a drug-rehabilitation program, refocused on his goal of becoming a paralegal, and took a series of temporary jobs through employment agencies. A
law firm eventually hired him as a legal secretary, a position he has now
held for four years, working primarily in computer programming and office
systems development. Walter has earned paralegal certification, but firms
in his city generally also require paralegals to have a four-year college degree, so he must also finish his undergraduate education. His mother has
retired and moved to Florida, leaving Walter in possession of her house,
and Walter has been renovating it. Once the renovations are complete, he
plans to return to college to earn a bachelor's degree, the final step on the
path to becoming a viable candidate for a paralegal position.

In the aftermath of the Kentucky prison litigation, these three main inmate participants continued to struggle through their lives in a pattern of
progress and setback. Having engaged in a daily struggle for dignity in the
squalor of an overcrowded, filthy, lawless institution and in litigation that
resulted in sweeping reform of those conditions, each in turn obtained
release from prison and encountered the problems ex-convicts often encounter in returning to free society. All three men sought to lead lawful,
productive lives but experienced difficulty in achieving that goal. Now approaching old age, Shorty has overcome personal troubles and remained a

free man for more than a decade. Wilgus awaits 2004, when he hopes to join his wife. Of the three, Walter has achieved the greatest progress. Perhaps anchored in the realization that his many disadvantages in life are primarily the result of forces beyond his control but that he has the responsibility to achieve a measure of control over his destiny, Walter got off drugs, found new steady employment, earned a paralegal certificate, and now awaits the opportunity to resume his academic education.

Epilogue

The *Thompson* and *Kendrick* cases ended with vastly improved living conditions for the inmates, but the state's prison population continued to skyrocket. When Judge Edward Johnstone placed Shorty's case on the inactive docket in 1986, 4,513 men were incarcerated in Kentucky.[1] That number had more than tripled to 15,107 by mid-1998.[2] Kentucky followed the pattern of the nation as a whole. In 1986, 544,972 people—male and female—were incarcerated in American prisons and jails, and by mid-1998 that number had reached 1,802,496.[3] At this rate, well over 2 million people will be imprisoned in the United States come the millennium.

A considerable portion of the increase in prison population is a function of tougher sentencing laws and new crimes created by legislatures, particularly in the war on drugs. Burgeoning narcotics laws and sentencing guidelines have resulted in drastic increases in the number of prisoners, especially in the federal system. While violent offenders are the largest source of the increase, drug offenders accounted for 25 percent of the increase between 1990 and 1996.[4] Crime rates have declined slightly since the mid-1990s, but the controversy continues to rage over whether aggressive incarceration policies have contributed significantly to the decrease in crime rates.[5] However, these policies clearly have resulted in a massive increase in prison and jail populations.[6] It is even more important today than it was at the dawn of Shorty's prison-reform litigation to strive for decent and humane living conditions for prisoners, because the increase in prison population will result in the return of even greater numbers of ex-convicts to free society after they have been released. Will their time in prison have done anything to help them become productive, law-abiding citizens, or will they simply be, as Larry W. Yackle warns, "kept in cages . . . long enough to ensure that they could never again function as ordinary citizens?"[7]

Federal judicial intervention may have fallen short of achieving complete compliance with court decrees, but as this and other studies have demonstrated, such intervention has resulted in prisons that are cleaner, safer, and less crowded.[8] Moreover, many new prisons have been built to accommodate the vast upsurge in prison population, and their newness suggests that, at least for the time being, most of them will have at least minimally habitable living conditions. Nevertheless, as these prisons age, massive public expenditures will be needed to maintain and repair the facilities. If future executive and legislative officials refuse, as many did in the past, to provide sufficient resources to maintain constitutional prisons, the judiciary will have the responsibility to intervene on an even broader scale than in the final third of the twentieth century.

There is more immediate cause for concern in the areas of race, drugs, human rights, and prisoner access to court. Widespread racial disparities prevail throughout the nation's prison system. Whereas the number of white male prisoners increased by 46 percent from 1990 to 1996, the numbers of blacks increased by 55 percent and of Hispanics by 53 percent. In 1993 black male inmates outnumbered whites for the first time and did so by 6,200; that gap grew to 17,300 in 1996.[9] The rate of incarceration among blacks and Hispanics is sharply higher than among whites. In 1996, more than 3 percent of the black male population and nearly 1.3 percent of the Hispanic male population was in prison but less than .04 percent of white males were incarcerated: blacks and Hispanics are far more likely than whites to go to prison.[10] This racial disparity suggests that racial tensions in prison are likely to rise in coming years, creating a greater potential for violent disorder unless preventive measures are undertaken. There are correlations among race, poverty, and incarceration, as Walter Harris's life illustrates.

If one way to reduce racial tensions exacerbated by disparities in incarceration rates is to remedy the disadvantages that burden racial minorities, then it is incumbent on correctional authorities to provide meaningful opportunities for education and training for all inmates. If authorities fail to do so and judicial intervention is required, it would be difficult to prove that officials violated equal protection by intentionally treating racial minorities less favorably because of their race, but it might be feasible to prove that officials were deliberately indifferent to harm caused by racial disparity in incarceration, in violation of the Eighth Amendment. Litigation based on such a legal theory would differ markedly from the sort of litigation described in this book, for it would require massive amounts of sociological and economic data to prove the correlations among race, poverty, and incarceration. The model for this type of approach to legal issues is provided by *Muller v. Oregon*.[11] In that case, Louis Brandeis filed a brief with the U.S. Supreme Court that supported his legal arguments with hundreds of pages of statistics and "social facts" showing that women's health is harmed far more than men's health by long working hours. This data persuaded a Court unsympathetic to laborers' claims to rule that a law limiting women's work hours was constitutional.[12] Thurgood Marshall and others provided another example of supporting legal argument with social facts in *Brown v. Board of Education*, in which the Court's decision invalidating racial segregation in schools relied heavily on extensive documentation of the harmful effects of racially segregated schools on the education of black children.[13]

The drastic increase in the number of drug offenders in prison has created a second area of concern, a rise in the number of inmates with drug problems ranging from addiction to mental illness. Corresponding increases in drug-treatment programs are a necessary means not only of maintaining prison order but also of preparing such inmates for release and reducing the risk of reincarceration for new drug offenses. Deliberate indifference in failing to provide adequate drug treatment could be another source of future prison litigation, if corrections officials fail to act.

Since the greatest increase in prison population has come from violent offenders, a plausible, though not inevitable, inference is that prisons are now more dangerous and violent than they were a decade ago. If such is the case, sound correctional policy requires more stringent security. Prison litigation of the past three decades, however, revealed that security measures are subject to abuse, and history may well repeat itself in the effort to control what is perceived to be a more dangerous inmate population. The opinion of federal district judge Thelton Henderson in *Madrid v. Gomez* offers a stark reminder that, behind the facades of new, clean supermaximum security prisons equipped with the latest in technological security devices lies the potential for abuse of power wrought by chilling disregard for basic and elemental rights. California's Pelican Bay State Prison opened in 1989 and was hailed as the prison of the future. Trial in a prisoners' lawsuit protesting conditions of confinement, however, revealed numerous, wide-ranging violations of the Constitution. In particular, Judge Henderson found a conspicuous pattern of excessive force in three areas: firing tear gas and taser guns at inmates in their cells for no legitimate security reason; locking inmates in a "fetal restraint," with handcuffs in the front and leg irons and a chain connecting the handcuffs and leg irons until only a few inches separated the wrists and ankles, creating painful contortions merely for punishment rather than security; and confining naked or partly naked prisoners in outdoor cages in cold, wet weather in full public view. After concluding that such conditions were unconstitutional cruel and unusual punishment, Henderson explained the moral basis of the legal conclusions:

> [D]ry words on paper can not adequately capture the senseless suffering and sometimes wretched misery that defendants' unconstitutional practices leave in their wake. The anguish of descending into serious mental illness, the pain of physical abuse, or the torment of having serious medical needs that go unmet is profoundly difficult, if not impossible, to fully fathom.[14]

Such treatment may become an international legal issue as well as a source of profound embarrassment for this nation. Amnesty International conducted research on American prisons and found widespread torture and ill treatment of inmates, in violation of the Universal Declaration of Human Rights. Human-rights abuses included brutality and excessive force, sexual abuse, inadequate medical care, inordinate isolation and sensory deprivation in "supermax" units, use of remote control electroshock belts, and unnecessary use of pepper spray and four-point restraints.[15]

Amnesty International also addressed prisoner access to court, the fourth area of concern, saying that human-rights abuse occurs when undue restrictions are placed on inmates' ability to use the courts to end ill treatment. Amnesty International specifically mentioned the Prison Litigation Reform Act of 1995 (PLRA), in which Congress severely restricted prison-reform litigation. The PLRA was a response to perceptions that federal courts had overstepped their authority in ordering extensive changes in state prisons and that prisoners were overburdening the federal courts with frivolous complaints. Since prisoners generally lack the money needed to pay the costs of litigation, they historically have been permitted under federal law to proceed in forma pauperis, without payment of costs. The PLRA, however, provides that prisoners can sue in forma pauperis only if prison officials provide certified copies of the prisoners' trust fund accounts (containing money, if any, earned through job assignments or other means). Even if the prisoners are allowed to proceed in forma pauperis, 20 percent of all court fees will be collected from their trust accounts. Prisoners are not allowed to proceed in forma pauperis if they have had three previous actions dismissed as frivolous, malicious, or groundless unless they are in immediate danger of serious physical harm.[16] Thus, if prison officials refuse to provide copies of trust accounts or if prisoners have had three prior actions dismissed as frivolous, suits cannot go forward even if they have merit unless the prisoners pay the litigation costs. Since prisoners almost without exception cannot do so, the practical effect of these provisions is that suits cannot be filed. Even prisoners allowed to proceed in forma pauperis will have a significant portion of their meager financial resources collected to pay court fees, bringing these people closer to the edge of destitution and thus discouraging suits. Even those who can surmount all these obstacles will surely pause to consider whether doing so is worth the effort, because the PLRA also severely limits the authority of federal courts to provide remedies to prisoners.[17] Although Congress's stated purposes were to deter frivolous prisoner suits and prohibit courts from overstepping their authority, these provisions appear to have overshot the mark because they will prevent the filing of meritorious lawsuits. Thus, Amnesty International's concern that the PLRA will unduly hinder prisoners' access to court for redress of ill treatment is well founded.

The voice of James M. "Shorty" Thompson, embodied in a one-page handwritten petition, initiated the KSR litigation and brought the attention of Judge Edward H. Johnstone to the squalid living conditions at that prison. The end result, though imperfect, was a vastly improved prison system. If the PLRA had been in effect at that time, Shorty might have been unable to file the lawsuit. Would prison officials have provided a copy of the trust account (if any) to an inmate who they knew intended to sue them? Knowing that he intended to file a complaint, would they have opened all his mail, refused to mail the petition, and transferred him elsewhere? Would Shorty have been willing to have 20 percent of what little money he had in his account collected for court fees? What if he had three prior suits dismissed as groundless, so that he would have had to pay litigation costs he could not afford, no matter how unconscionable the conditions at KSR? Restrictions on prisoner access to the courts are of grave concern to the extent that they silence prisoners' voices. Such voices made a difference—for the better—in the KSR litigation. With more than 2 million people incarcerated in the United States today, it is even more important that the courts heed the voices of prisoners with legitimate grievances.

Appendix A: Methodology

This book uses three primary sources of evidence for case-study research: (1) interviews, (2) direct observations, and (3) court records and other legal documents. Sources consisted of both qualitative and quantitative evidence.

The interviews were conducted with the key inmate-plaintiffs and the key decision makers and participants in the *Thompson* litigation. The author's participation as attorney for the inmate class permitted identification of those inmates who played key roles in the *Thompson* litigation and of the other key participants, such as the judge, attorneys for the state, prison officials, and the newspaper reporter who provided primary news coverage. Subject areas for the interviews were established prior to conducting the interviews, including the interviewee's personal history prior to the litigation, observations of the prison conditions, participation in the litigation, negotiation and implementation of the consent decree, and life history subsequent to the lawsuit. The interviews were conducted in an open-ended conversational manner to achieve a free, spontaneous flow of information.

Three inmates and ten other key participants in the *Thompson* lawsuit were selected and interviewed by this method. The interviews with all three inmates and five of the other participants were recorded on tape, with their permission. The untaped interviews were also conducted with the subjects' permission, and the author kept detailed notes of each such interview. The interviewees gave permission for their names and the interviews to be used in this book.

The direct observations encompassed this author's many visits to KSR as lead attorney for the inmate class. Most important among these visits were tours of the entire prison provided by prison officials, investigations of particular areas of the prison while accompanying expert witnesses, tours of the prison on inspection visits by the judge, and discussions with many inmates in their dormitories to gather evidence in the case and, after the negotiations, to explain the settlement to the inmates. Direct observations also included meetings with the Plaintiffs' Committee at KSR, personal participation in conferences in the judge's chambers, negotiations with state and Justice Department attorneys, and hearings in the judge's courtroom as well as attendance at oral argument in the U.S. Supreme Court. These direct observations are listed in appendix B, including dates, where possible.

The legal records consisted of court records in the *Thompson* case, transcripts of hearings, and the author's records of participation. All of these documents were available because of the author's role as attorney for the plaintiff class. Appendix C contains these records.

Appendix B: Direct Observations

Tours of KSR

With prison officials: March 14, 1979; January 20, February 21, June 4, 1981; June 7, 1989.

With Judge Johnstone: February 6, 1980.

With expert witnesses: June 23, 24, July 9, 11, 12, November 16, 17, 1979; January 22, 23, 24, 1980.

With newspaper reporter: March 5, 1980.

Tours of the Kentucky State Penitentiary, Eddyville

With expert witnesses: December 20, 21, 1979.

Meetings with Plaintiffs' Committee at KSR

1979: March 30; April 17, 18; May 3; June 8; August 29; September 7, 25, 27; October 4, 25, 31; November 1, 7, 8, 28; December 4, 13, 19.

1980: February 14, 15, 18; March 3, 6, 11, 14, 31; April 8, 14, 21, 22; May 7, 9, 21; June 6, 26; July 16; December 9, 18, 24.

1981: January 7, 9, 20; March 18, 31; May 8, 19; July 24, 29; August 5, 12.

Conferences and Hearings with Judge Johnstone

Meeting to discuss court appointment of counsel to represent inmate plaintiffs in *Thompson* case, March 8, 1979, judge's chambers, U.S. Courthouse, Louisville, Kentucky.

Pretrial conferences to discuss renovation of cell block at Kentucky State Penitentiary, April 26, June 15, 1979, judge's chambers, U.S. Courthouse, Louisville, Kentucky.

Pretrial conferences, June 4, 16, 1979, January 25, 1980, judge's chambers, U.S. Courthouse, Louisville, Kentucky.

Hearing on harassment of inmate class members, November 27, 1979, judge's chambers, U.S. Courthouse, Louisville, Kentucky.

Pretrial conferences to discuss settlement of case, February 8, March 7, 1980, judge's chambers, U.S. Courthouse, Louisville, Kentucky.

Hearing to announce settlement of case, April 3, 1980, judge's courtroom, U.S. Courthouse, Louisville, Kentucky.

Hearing on objections to and approval of consent decree, May 28, 1980, judge's courtroom, U.S. Courthouse, Louisville, Kentucky.

Hearing on motion to hold defendants in contempt for noncompliance with consent decree, October 22, 1980, judge's courtroom, U.S. Courthouse, Louisville, Kentucky.

Conference to discuss defendants' compliance with consent decree, November 7, 1980, judge's chambers, U.S. Courthouse, Louisville, Kentucky.

Hearings on defendants' compliance with consent decree, December 22, 1980, July 22, 1981, judge's courtroom, U.S. Courthouse, Louisville, Kentucky.

Depositions of Defendants and Other Prison Officials

(All depositions taken in Frankfort, Kentucky, unless otherwise noted.)

1979: July 25, 26; August 20 (Louisville, Kentucky), 21, 22; October 8, 9, 10, 11.

1980: January 8 (Louisville, Kentucky), 9, 11, 16, 25, 30, 31; February 5, 6, 7, 21; December 16.

1981: April 22, 23, 27, 28, 29; May 4 (Louisville, Kentucky), 7, 13, 18.

Oral Argument in the Supreme Court of the United States

January 18, 1989, Washington, D.C.

Appendix C: Court Records and Other Legal Documents

This appendix consists of court records in the *Thompson* case, transcripts of hearings, legal documents, and the author's records of participation as attorney for the inmates.

Court Records (adapted from the Civil Docket Sheet, *Thompson v. Commonwealth of Kentucky,* Case No. C79-0092P(J), U.S. District Court, Western District of Kentucky)

1979

January 2: ORDER by Magistrate Long that plaintiffs' tendered complaint be filed, and motion to proceed in forma pauperis granted. Complaint filed.

February 7: ANSWER by defendants.

March 17: Professor Leslie W. Abramson of the University of Louisville School of Law and Mr. Lloyd C. Anderson, Legal Aid Society of Louisville, are appointed as counsel to represent plaintiffs from KSR.

May 1: Order by Judges Allen, Johnstone, and Ballantine (1) that the following cases be consolidated with 76-0079P(J): *Kendrick v. Bland,* concerning living conditions at the Kentucky State Penitentiary in Eddyville; *Thompson v. Commonwealth of Kentucky,* C 79-0001 L; *Thompson v. Bland,* C 79-0154 L; *Gardner v. Sowders,* C 79-0036 L; *Jones v. Bland,* C 79-0124 L; *Curry v. Bland,* C 78-0029 L; *Stohler v. Sowders,* C 78-0111 L; (2) that *Thompson v. Commonwealth of Kentucky,* C 79-0001-L is designated as the controlling action in all consolidated actions identified herein from inmates at KSR; (3) all claims for injunctive relief sought in consolidated actions are severed from claims for monetary damages; (4) all matters pertaining to monetary damages are STAYED pending further orders of the court; . . . (9) these consolidated cases are hereby assigned for trial to Judge Johnstone.

June 4: Findings of Fact and ORDER regarding KSR by Judge Johnstone that: (1) action may be maintained as a class action; (2) named plaintiffs James M. Thompson, Harry B. Gardner, Johnny Sutton, James R. Bone, Joel Tinch, Kevin Jones a/k/a/ Farid Muhammad, Terry Thornton, James E. Robinson, Richard Stewart, Arnold Alexander, Arthur C. Sewell, and Gary T. Hayes are certified as representatives of a class defined as all persons who currently and/or will be confined in KSR at LaGrange; (3) defendants are responsible for immediate notification of this class at KSR; (4) members of the class who are or will be confined at KSP are designated as EDDYVILLE CLASS; members of the class who are or will be confined at KSR are designed as LAGRANGE CLASS; (5) order is entered pursuant to Rule 23(c)(1) of the Federal Rules of Civil Procedure.

June 7: Memorandum of Pretrial Conference and ORDER by Judge Johnstone of June 4, 1979, that (1) evidentiary hearing on pending motions is set for June 15, 1979, at 9:00 A.M. in Louisville, (2) on or before June 15, 1979, parties shall confer and prepare a schedule for discovery proceedings. If parties are unable to agree, each shall submit a proposed schedule on or before June 20, 1979, and (3) this consolidated case, including the Eddyville class action and the LaGrange class action, is set for trial on April 7, 1980, with expected length of twenty-five days.

June 12: Motion for appointment of additional counsel for KSR class filed by plaintiff.

June 16: Order by Judge Johnstone that plaintiffs are granted leave to file their amended complaint. Amended complaint filed.

June 27: ORDER by Judge Johnstone that plaintiffs' motion for additional counsel is GRANTED, and Joseph Elder and Alan Schmitt (Legal Aid Society of Louisville) are appointed as additional counsel to represent LaGrange class.

June 28: Answer to complaint, filed by defendants.

June 29: AGREED ORDER signed by Judge Johnstone that (1) parties shall exchange preliminary lists of potential expert witnesses by November 1, 1979, (2) parties shall complete discovery by February 15, 1980, unless for good cause shown a party requires further discovery. Leave shall be freely given to allow further depositions after such date, and (3) potential expert witnesses, who have previously inspected KSP and/or KSR, will be allowed to reinspect institutions after such date without leave of court.

First set of requests for production of documents, filed by plaintiffs. First set of interrogatories, filed by plaintiffs: Definitions, Demographics, Identification of Personnel, Physical Facilities and Environment, Inmate Security and Property, New Institution and Forensic Unit, Activities and Programs, Classification and Orientation, Religion, Discipline and Segregation, Legal Research and Grievances, Medical and Psychiatric.

July 6: Notice of taking of depositions of corrections officials Max Weaver, Irving Bell, William Gardner, Joan Wooten, Ellen Dean, and Michael Samberg, filed by U.S. Department of Justice. Cross-notice of depositions filed by plaintiffs on July 13 and July 23.

July 25: Order by Judge Johnstone that motion of Kentucky Department of Human Resources for a protective order against taking depositions of its employees DENIED.

August 13: Notice of depositions of corrections officials William Cowley, Art Brockman, Michael Samberg, Tom Peterson, Kenneth Hutcherson, and James Dent filed by U.S. Department of Justice. Cross-notice of depositions of same witnesses, filed by plaintiffs on August 15.

September 10: Answers to first set of interrogatories filed by defendant Bland.

September 11: Depositions of corrections officials Ellen Dean, Max Weaver, Irving Bell, and Thomas Peterson filed by court reporter.

September 12: Response to plaintiffs' first set of requests for production of documents filed by defendants.

September 18: Notice to take deposition of James Stephens, deputy warden, KSR, filed by U.S. Attorney.

September 21: Notice to take depositions of corrections officials Wayne Dunn, Walter Powell, Tom Campbell (deputy warden, KSR), Ed Akers, Robert Schneider, David Vislisel, and Steven Barry, filed by U.S. Department of Justice.

September 24: AGREED ORDER by Judge Johnstone that defendants and their agents are permanently enjoined from the following: (1) No Bureau of Corrections personnel shall take any action, including, but not limited to, disciplinary charges, lock up, job transfer or loss, or call transfer against an inmate because he is a named plaintiff in a lawsuit, is representing himself in a lawsuit, or has given testimony or will be a witness in a lawsuit; provided, however, that such prohibitions do not apply to individuals who violate institution rules nor to transfers of inmates to other institutions through the normal classification process; (2) No Bureau of Corrections personnel shall take any action against an inmate who causes to be filed or delivered to the administrator a complaint about corrections officers or other bureau personnel. If such complaint is without merit, the inmate shall be notified in writing of the reasons why the complaint was without merit. All complaints and responses thereto shall be kept in a separate file at the institution. Provided, however, that such prohibitions do not apply to individuals who initiate complaints which constitute a threat to institution discipline or security; (3) No Bureau of Corrections personnel shall take any action against an inmate who initiates or places his signature upon a petition to any bureau official, public official, or court (state or federal) regarding either sentence or conditions of confinement. Provided, however, that such prohibitions do not apply to individuals who initiate petitions that constitute a threat to institution discipline or security.

October 3: Cross-notice to take depositions of corrections officials Steve Barry, Wayne Dunn, Walter Powell, Tony Campbell, Ed Akers, Robert Schneider, and Dave Vislisel, filed by plaintiffs.

October 10: Deposition of corrections official Arthur Brockman filed by court reporter.

October 17: Second set of requests for inspection and production of documents filed by plaintiffs.

October 23: Depositions of corrections officials James Dent, Kenneth Hutcherson, and William Gardner filed by court reporter.

October 29: Third set of requests for production of documents filed by plaintiffs.

October 30: Request to permit entry upon property for inspection filed by plaintiffs.

November 5: Preliminary list of potential expert witnesses filed by LaGrange plaintiffs.

November 20: Response to plaintiffs' second set of requests for inspection and production of documents filed by defendants.

November 30: Response to plaintiffs' third set of requests for inspection and production of documents filed by defendants.

December 5: Depositions of corrections officials Ed Akers, Wayne Dunn, Robert Schneider, Walter Powell, and Steve Barry filed by court reporter.

December 6: Motion to compel production of documents specified in Paragraphs 2A, B, C, D, E, and G of plaintiffs' second set of requests for inspection and production of documents filed by plaintiffs.

December 10: ORDER by Judge Johnstone that plaintiffs' motion to compel is granted.

December 13: First set of requests for admission filed by plaintiffs.

December 19: Deposition of corrections official Dave Vislisel filed by court reporter.

December 26: Notice to take depositions of corrections officials James Stephens (deputy warden of KSR), Michael Samberg, Luther Luckett, and David Bland (commissioner of the Bureau of Corrections) filed by U.S. Department of Justice. (Cross-notice of depositions of same witnesses filed by plaintiffs, January 7, 1980.)

1980

January 16: Response to plaintiffs' first set of requests for admissions filed by defendants.

January 18: ORDER by Judge Johnstone that pretrial conference shall be held on January 24, 1980, at 3:30 P.M. in Louisville.

January 21: AGREED continuance of deposition of Commissioner David Bland.

January 28: Notice to take depositions of corrections officials George Wilson (new commissioner of the Bureau of Corrections), Mike Young, Jack Simpson, William Turner, James Stephens, Steve Smith (warden of KSR), and Barry Bannister, filed by U.S. Department of Justice.

MEMORANDUM OF COURT CONFERENCE AND ORDER by Judge Johnstone that (1) motion of defendants for continuance of trial is DENIED, and (2) pretrial conference will be held at 9:30 A.M. in chambers in Louisville on February 8, 1980.

February 1: Motion to add additional plaintiffs to LaGrange class action filed by plaintiffs.

February 6: MEMORANDUM of court visit to KSR by Judge Johnstone.

February 12: First set of interrogatories filed by defendants.

February 14: Interrogatories and request for production of documents filed by AMICUS CURIAE (United States).

Response to plaintiffs' second set of requests for inspection and production of documents filed by defendants.

February 21: ORDER by Judge Johnstone that plaintiffs' motion to add Wilgus Haddix, Walter Harris, Clifford Elliott, and George Sholar as named plaintiffs is GRANTED.

February 22: ORDER by Judge Johnston and Memorandum of pretrial conference of February 8, 1980, that Trial of Actions to commence April 7, 1980; FURTHER, (1) parties shall complete discovery by March 28; (2) parties shall submit to court pretrial briefs by March 31; (3) parties shall exchange witness and exhibit lists and submit copy to court by March 21; (4) parties shall exchange summaries of witness testimony and submit copies to the court by March 28; (5) parties shall submit to the court by April 3 stipulation of facts agreed on by all parties; (6) settlement conference shall be held on March 7 in Louisville; (7) final pretrial conference shall be held on April 3 in Louisville.

February 28: Second set of requests for admissions, filed by plaintiffs.

March 11: Depositions of corrections officials David Bland, Michael Samberg, and William Turner filed by plaintiffs.

March 24: Witness lists, exhibit lists, and stipulations filed by plaintiffs and by United States.

March 26: Answers to defendants' first set of interrogatories, list of experts, and list of witnesses filed by plaintiffs.

April 4: NOTICE OF PROPOSED CONSENT DECREE to inmates of KSR and KSP of hearing on May 28, 1980, at 3:00 P.M. in Louisville to determine final approval of the proposed CONSENT DECREE for equitable relief pursuant to Rule 23(e); terms of settlement are contained in consent decree tentatively approved by court on April 4, 1980—copies are to be distributed to inmates not later than April 13; OBJECTIONS to proposed consent decree must be filed by May 15 in writing and mailed to clerk, U.S. Courthouse, Paducah. Papers received after May 15 will not be filed.

ORDER by Judge Johnstone that: (1) Notice is in compliance with Rule 23(e); (2) defendants' attorneys shall immediately provide notices to members of plaintiff class by posting notice on all bulletin boards and other appropriate locations at KSP and KSR and by distributing notices for all members of plaintiff class.

CONSENT DECREE by Judge Johnstone with provision that court has reserved power to modify the decree after any objections to the decree have been filed and reviewed by the court.

April 24: Depositions of corrections officials George Wilson, Mike Young, and Luther Luckett filed by court reporter.

April 17–May 21: Objections to proposed consent decree filed by various inmates.

May 23: Response to objections made by prisoners to proposed consent decree filed by United States.

May 27: Depositions of corrections officials Barry Bannister and Steve Smith filed by court reporter.

Response to objections by members of class filed by defendants.

May 30: AGREED ORDER by Judge Johnstone that consent decree tentatively approved on April 4 be amended (1) such that Section 2, paragraph C read as follows: "C. For purposes of determining the rated capacity of the Kentucky State Reformatory, the open wing dormitories are adequate to house 144 inmates using the American Correctional Association standard of sixty (60) square feet per inmate"; (2) to include the following additional paragraph: "K. Except where a specific implementation time is called for by the Decree, a provision for implementation of the plan as soon as possible after the plan is approved by the court."

June 2: Report on inmate-grievance procedure filed by defendants.

July 21: Motion to cite defendants for contempt and/or for supplemental relief filed by plaintiffs. Notice to take deposition of Wayne Dunn, deputy warden, KSR, filed by United States.

July 22: Supplemental partial consent decree by Judge Johnstone.

July 24: Cross-notice to take deposition of Wayne Dunn, deputy warden, KSR, filed by plaintiffs.

July 31: Response to motion to cite defendants for contempt and/or for supplemental relief filed by defendants.

August 21: Motion for order acknowledging compliance with consent decree filed by defendants.

August 29: Motion for agreed order for additional thirty days beyond period stipulated in consent decree in which to complete evaluation of defendants' classification program through National Institute of Corrections filed by plaintiffs. ORDER by Judge Johnstone that defendants shall have such additional thirty days.

September 8: Response to defendants' motion to be deemed in compliance with consent decree filed by plaintiffs.

September 12: ORDER by Judge Johnstone that provision of consent decree dealing with grievances, having been completed by defendants and no objections having been filed within sixty days, submitted grievance procedure has been reviewed by court and is APPROVED.

September 17: Objection to supplemental partial consent decree by Leslie Brannum, James Thompson, and Dennis McDonald.

September 23: Motion to cite defendants for contempt and/or for supplemental relief filed by plaintiffs.

October 6: Notice of compliance with consent decree filed by defendants.

October 8: MEMORANDUM OF COURT CONFERENCE of October 7 AND ORDER by Judge Johnstone that attorneys appear in chambers at Bowling Green on October 15 for court conference to consider simplification of issues and other matters to aid in disposition of hearing scheduled for October 22 and 23 in Louisville. ORDER by Judge Johnstone that hearing will be held on October 22 in Louisville at 9:00 A.M. on plaintiffs' motion to hold defendants in contempt. Pursuant to telephone conference held on October 7, Eddyville class is granted permission to file contempt motion on issues common to ones currently pending before court, and hearing on that motion will be consolidated with hearing this day ordered.

October 14: Motion to cite defendants for contempt and/or for supplemental relief filed by Eddyville plaintiffs.

October 20: Response to plaintiffs' supplemental motion to cite defendants for contempt filed by defendants.

October 24: ORDER by Judge Johnstone that (1) Defendants shall implement due-process provisions encompassed in section 6 of consent decree; (2) Inmates placed in confinement in punitive segregation, administrative segregation, or administrative control unit, without benefit of procedures set forth in Section 6 of consent decree, shall be returned to their prior status until due-process provisions encompassed in that section are complied with; (3) Initial charges and classifications entered against inmates in violation of Section 6 of consent decree shall be expunged.

October 30: ORDER by Judge Johnstone that objections to supplemental partial consent decree be overruled in all respects.

November 12: MEMO OF PRETRIAL CONFERENCE of November 7 AND ORDER by Judge Johnstone that (1) Defendants have until November 21 to reexplain terms of consent decree to staff at KSR; (2) Defendants shall review length and duration of lunch lines at KSR and take steps to eliminate lines or submit evidence to court that lines have been eliminated; (3) Defendants shall repair plumbing at KSR by December 1 with leave for extension of time upon showing appropriate steps toward accomplishing this goal have been taken by December 1; (4) Defendants shall provide copy of consent decree to each inmate in assessment and orientation unit by November 18; (5) Defendants shall within thirty days of entry of this order submit to court a report on provision of flame-retardant waste containers and lids at KSR; (6) Plaintiffs shall submit suggested errata and addendum to handbooks being distributed to population at KSR by November 15; plaintiffs' motion for an order recalling these handbooks OVERRULED; (7) Defendants shall hire sufficient personnel to provide minimum of one guard per floor in each open dormitory and one moving supervisor per unit per shift by January 28, 1981.

November 25: Notice of compliance (20 percent salary increase for correctional officers) filed by defendants.

December 1: Motion for extension of time, including opening of Luther Luckett Correctional Complex, to comply with consent decree re reduction of population, filed by defendants.

Motion to cite defendants for contempt filed by plaintiffs.

December 4: ORDER of the court that hearing shall be held on defendants' motion for extension of time to comply with consent decree re reduction of population, on December 22 at 1:00 P.M., at Federal Courthouse, Louisville.

December 8: Cross-notice to take deposition of George Wilson, commissioner of corrections, on December 16 at 9:00 A.M. filed by plaintiffs.

December 10: Response to plaintiffs' motion to cite defendants for contempt filed by defendants.

December 12: Notice of compliance filed by defendants.

December 17: HABEAS CORPUS AD TESTIFICANDUM by Judge Johnstone that James Thompson, Steve Brannum, William Kimbrew, and Dennis McDonald be transported by Bureau of Corrections from KSR to Federal Building, Louisville, to be transferred to the custody of U.S. Marshal for hearing on December 22 and shall be returned to custody of Bureau of Corrections at conclusion of hearing to be returned to KSR.

December 23: Deposition of George Wilson, commissioner of corrections, filed by court reporter.

1981

January 7: Plan of reduction of population at KSP and KSR, filed by defendant, in compliance with order of December 22.

January 12: Response to defendants' plan of reduction of population at KSP and KSR filed by plaintiffs.

January 14: FINDINGS OF FACT AND ORDER by Judge Johnstone that (1) defendants' motion for extension of time to decrease inmate population at KSP and KSR is GRANTED, subject to terms and conditions of this order; (2) defendants shall have until February 28, 1981, to reduce the population at these facilities by a total of six hundred inmates, as required by consent decree; (3) defendants are enjoined as of March 1, 1981, from accepting into these facilities any inmates, except escapees and technical parole violations, until they have reduced the population at these facilities by agreed-upon six hundred inmates; (4) defendants shall maintain population at these facilities at, or below, the agreed-upon population levels unless defendants show good cause to this court why such numbers should be increased or otherwise modified; and (5) this order does not prohibit internal transfers from one institution to another or within an institution but forbids any admission into either institution from outside until agreed-upon population levels have been reached.

June 1: Order by Judge Johnstone that one attorney for each party shall appear in chambers to discuss progress on negotiation on differences on compliance.

September 15: Order by Judge Johnstone that motion of plaintiffs for appointment of special master is denied.

September 25: Order by Judge Johnstone that any party alleging noncompliance shall confer with opposing counsel in effort to resolve all issues of alleged noncompliance.

1982

February 22: Action on KSR contempt motion stayed until counsel for LaGrange class files report to court detailing efforts and progress made toward informal resolution of issues.

March 29: With regard to pending LaGrange class contempt motion, plaintiffs are directed to gather affidavits concerning custodial staff interference in food preparation. Parties shall report to court if settlement is possible. Should negotiations fail, trial is set for July 19, 1982.

1983

September 12: Order by Judge Johnstone that defendants shall take immediate steps to fill all correctional officer positions and shall continue to do so in the future as vacancies occur, as defendants' policy of not filling authorized correctional officer posts violates consent decree.

1984

April 4: Order by Judge Johnstone that plaintiffs' motion for enforcement of Section 4 of consent decree to require defendants to establish full-blown bachelor of arts degree program at KSR is denied.

June 28: Temporary restraining order by Judge Johnstone that defendants are enjoined from taking any action that would cause reduction of beds at any community-release center or halfway house.

December 18: Order by Judge Johnstone that defendants' motion to temporarily modify the consent decree by lifting the population cap is denied.

1986

January 31: Ruling by Judge Johnstone that consent decree is modified to permit construction of new dormitories instead of renovating old dormitories.

February 19: Inspection of KSR by Judge Johnstone.

June 27: Order by Judge Johnstone that defendants shall implement minimal due-process procedures for revocation or suspension of plaintiffs' visitation privileges, including notice to inmate of reasons for revocation or suspension and opportunity for inmate to be heard.

1987

March 3: Order by Judge Johnstone that defendants are in compliance with consent decree in all areas except construction and renovation; case transferred to inactive docket for receipt of semiannual reports on progress of construction and renovation; in event of major violations of consent decree, any party may apply to court for reinstatement of case on active docket.

July 15: Judgment of District Court concerning due-process procedures for prisoners denied visitation affirmed by Court of Appeals for the Sixth Circuit.

Transcripts of Hearings

Hearing on Nomination of Edward H. Johnstone for U.S. District Court Judge, in U.S. Senate Committee on the Judiciary, *Hearing on Nominations for District and Circuit Court Judges,* 95th Cong., 1st sess., September 27, 1977.

Official Transcript, Proceedings before the U.S. Supreme Court, *Kentucky Department of Corrections, Petitioner, v. James M. Thompson,* Case No. 87-1815, Washington, D.C., January 18, 1989.

Legal Documents in *Thompson v. Commonwealth of Kentucky*

Complaint, pro se, *James M. Thompson, et al., v. Commonwealth of Kentucky,* No. C79-0001(2), U.S. District Court, Western District of Kentucky.

Amended complaint.

Reports of expert witnesses David Fogel, Richard Korn, Frank Rundle, Paul Keve, Theodore Gordon, Herbert Wood, Shirley Snarr, and Brad Fisher.

Offer of judgment, filed by defendants.

Response to offer of judgment, filed by plaintiffs.

Amended offer of judgment, filed by defendants.

Consent decree.

Author's Records

Appointment books for 1979, 1980, and 1981.

Notes

Introduction

1. See, e.g., Blumstein, "American Prisons."

2. See, e.g., DiIulio, "Help Wanted." For a general overview of this debate, see Beale, "Rethinking Federal Criminal Law."

3. Gilliard and Beck, "Prisoners in 1993"; Gilliard, "Prison and Jail Inmates at Midyear 1998."

4. The KSR lawsuit was consolidated with *Kendrick v. Bland,* a similar case concerning conditions of confinement at the Kentucky State Penitentiary in Eddyville. Although the two cases were interwoven throughout the litigation and this book makes various references to the Eddyville case, this work focuses primarily on the KSR litigation and the lives of major participants in that case.

5. Yackle, *Reform and Regret,* 8–12; see also Chilton, *Prisons under the Gavel,* 2–3.

6. Crouch and Marquart, *Appeal to Justice,* 4–6.

7. 378 U.S. 546 (1964). The decision in *Cooper* was a brief, per curiam opinion, which means that it is the opinion of the Court as an institution rather than

an opinion written by an individual justice for the Court. Such an opinion usually indicates that the legal proposition and its application to the case is, in the justices' view, beyond serious question.

8. Chilton, *Prisons under the Gavel,* 4–6; Crouch and Marquart, *Appeal to Justice,* 6–7; Yackle, *Reform and Regret,* 3–8.

9. Chilton, *Prisons under the Gavel,* ix, 107.

10. Yackle, *Reform and Regret,* viii.

11. Crouch and Marquart, *Appeal to Justice,* 2, 11–12, 226–233; Martin and Ekland-Olson, *Texas Prisons,* 238–239.

12. DiIulio, *Governing Prisons,* 6–7, 246–250.

13. Yarbrough, *Judge Frank Johnson,* 212–214, 227–228.

14. Feeley and Rubin, *Judicial Policy Making,* 3–7.

15. Ibid., 12–15, 18, 338–339, 341–344.

16. Chilton, *Prisons under the Gavel,* 75.

17. Crouch and Marquart, *Appeal to Justice,* 238.

18. DiIulio, *Governing Prisons,* 235; Crouch and Marquart, *Appeal to Justice,* 229, 237.

19. DiIulio, *Governing Prisons,* 256.

20. Crouch and Marquart, *Appeal to Justice,* 238.

Judge Johnstone

1. See, e.g., Grossman, "Social Backgrounds." See also Dorsen, "A Change in Judicial Philosophy?"; Ulmer, "Are Social Background Models Time-Bound?"; Tate and Handberg, "Time Binding."

2. See, e.g., Carrington, "Of Law and the River." See also Segal and Spaeth, *Supreme Court and the Attitudinal Model;* Ashenfelter, Eisenberg, and Schwab, "Politics and the Judiciary."

3. Sisk, Heise, and Morriss, "Charting the Influences on the Judicial Mind."

4. Ibid., 1477–1478.

5. "W. C. Johnstone: A New Kind of Pioneer."

6. U.S. Senate Committee on the Judiciary, *Hearing,* 6.

7. Yarbrough, *Judge Frank Johnson,* 33–152.

8. 347 U.S. 483 (1954) (holding that segregation of children in public schools solely on the basis of race deprives minority children of equal-education opportunities in violation of the Equal Protection Clause of the Fourteenth Amendment to the U.S. Constitution).

9. 356 U.S. 86 (1958).

10. *Holt v. Sarver,* 300 F. Supp. 825 (E.D. Ark. 1969).

11. *Hutto v. Finney,* 437 U.S. 678 (1978).

12. *Pugh v. Locke,* 406 F. Supp. 318 (M.D. Ala. 1976).

13. Yackle, *Reform and Regret,* 108–167.

Wilgus

1. Caudill, *Night Comes to the Cumberlands.* Caudill's version of Appalachian history is controversial, and it should not be considered fully accurate or universally accepted. For contrasting views of this history, see Eller, "Harry Caudill and the Burden of Mountain Liberalism"; Salstrom, *Appalachia's Path to Dependency;* Rasmussen, *Absentee Landowning;* Dunaway, *First American Frontier.* The sole purpose in describing Caudill's version of Appalachian history is to provide a broad context for understanding Haddix's background, since the oral history of Haddix's maternal ancestors dovetails with at least a portion of Appalachian history as described by Caudill.

Walter

1. Richard R. Korn, "An Examination of Conditions at the Kentucky State Penitentiary and the Kentucky State Reformatory," in possession of author, 14.

2. Theodore J. Gordon, "Report on Environmental Health and Safety Standards of the Kentucky Bureau of Corrections' Facilities at Eddyville and LaGrange, Kentucky," in possession of author, 5–17.

3. Martinson, "What Works?"

4. Blumstein, "American Prisons."

5. Korn, "Examination," 14–15.

6. David Fogel, "Visit to LaGrange Reformatory, Kentucky, November 16–17, 1979," in possession of author, 19–20.

Politics and Litigation

1. Chilton, for example, estimates that the total cost of the Georgia prison-reform litigation exceeded $250 million, even allowing for the impact of other factors, such as inflation, on the state's budget (*Prisons under the Gavel,* 86–93).

2. *Missouri v. Jenkins,* 495 U.S. 33, 50–52 (1990).

3. Chilton, *Prisons under the Gavel,* 43–72.

4. Yackle, *Reform and Regret,* 108–185.

5. Stastny and Tyrnauer, *Who Rules the Joint?* 19–25. See also Chilton, *Prisons under the Gavel,* 2–4; Yackle, *Reform and Regret,* 8–9.

6. Stastny and Tyrnauer, *Who Rules the Joint?* 25–28.

7. Ibid., 28–30.

8. Ibid., 30–32.

9. Ibid., 32–33.

10. Ibid.

11. Yackle, *Reform and Regret,* 168–185.

12. Powell, "$50 Million."

13. This debate is described in Taggart, "Redefining the Power," 266–268. See also Feeley, "Significance of Prison Conditions Cases."

Judge Johnstone Visits LaGrange

1. *Holt v. Sarver; Gates v. Collier,* 349 F. Supp. 881 (N.D. Miss. 1972); *Battle v. Anderson,* 376 F. Supp. 402 (E.D. Okla. 1974); *Pugh v. Locke.*

2. *Hutto v. Finney,* 685–688.

3. For an example of the view critical of judicial activism, see Horowitz, *Courts and Social Policy.* Opinion supportive of proactive efforts is expressed in Chayes, "Supreme Court, 1981 Term."

4. DiIulio, *Governing Prisons,* 248.

Negotiation and Settlement

1. Ramsey, "Overcrowding a Big Problem"; Gatz and Howington, "Inmates' Suit Could Hinge on State Budget Requests."

2. Shafer, "Negotiations Start in Prisoners' Lawsuit."

3. Shafer, "Crowded Reformatory Tense."

4. Isaacs interview.

5. "Courts Right in Demanding That Prisons Meet Standards."

6. For a more detailed discussion of the hybrid nature of a consent decree in that it is both a contract between the parties and a court order, see Anderson, "Approval and Interpretation," 584–586.

7. The plaintiffs' attorneys in the Eddyville litigation negotiated separately with the state's attorneys, after which the two agreements were consolidated in the proposed consent decree.

8. Federal Rule of Civil Procedure 23(e) requires that judicial approval must be obtained for class-action settlements. For a detailed discussion of the standards governing whether a court should approve such a settlement, see Anderson, "Approval and Interpretation," 598–615.

9. The entire text of the consent decree appears in *Kendrick v. Bland,* 541 F. Supp. 21 (W.D. Ky. 1981) (Appendix).

10. Shafer, "Settlement of Inmates' Suit."

Compliance: Obstacles and Impact

1. Crouch and Marquart, *Appeal to Justice,* 2, 226–227. See also Martin and Ekland-Olson, *Texas Prisons,* 238–239.

2. Yackle, *Reform and Regret,* 107–186. See also Yarbrough, *Judge Frank Johnson,* 182–212.

3. Chilton, *Prisons under the Gavel,* 56–71.

4. Jones interview.

5. DiIulio, *Governing Prisons,* 246.

6. Shafer, "Corrections Chief."

7. "Prisoners Should Bend a Little, Too."

8. Shafer, "State to Get More Time."

9. Shafer, "State Expects to Meet Deadline."

10. Shafer, "Prison Upgrading Could Be Delayed."

11. "Conflict in Kentucky's Justice Department."

12. *Canterino v. Wilson,* 546 F. Supp. 174, 180–206 (W.D. Ky. 1982) (findings of fact).

13. *Glover v. Johnson,* 478 F. Supp. 1075 (E.D. Mich. 1979).

14. *Canterino v. Wilson,* 206–217 (conclusions of law).

15. See, e.g., *Pinkston v. Orr,* 1986 U.S. Dist. LEXIS 28266 (S.D. Ind. 1986) (Indiana); *Jeldness v. Pearce,* 30 F. 3d 1220 (9th Cir. 1994) (Oregon); *Women Prisoners of the District of Columbia Department of Corrections v. District of Columbia,* 877 F. Supp. 634 (D.D.C. 1994) (District of Columbia). The *Canterino* decision has been cited in at least thirty-three published opinions, including all but three of the U.S. Circuit Courts of Appeals. While the great majority of these opinions adhere to Johnstone's reasoning in *Canterino,* a few disagree, in part, with his conclusions. See, e.g., *Klinger v. Department of Corrections,* 31 F. 3d 727 (8th Cir. 1994) (male and female inmates are not similarly situated with respect to prison programs and services, so that inferior programs and services for women do not violate equal protection).

One supplemental order by Judge Johnstone concerning early-release programs was reversed on appeal (*Canterino v. Wilson,* 869 F.2d 948 [6th Cir. 1989]), but the original, sweeping decision was left undisturbed.

Substantial Compliance and Collateral Litigation

1. Yackle, *Reform and Regret,* vi–viii, 17–18, 108–255; Crouch and Marquart, *Appeal to Justice,* 2–3, 127–150.

2. For a discussion of the case-law precedent and a proposal for standards that

should govern the decision whether to relinquish jurisdiction, see Anderson, "Release and Resumption of Jurisdiction."

3. Judge Johnstone's decision is reported at *Kendrick v. Bland,* 659 F. Supp. 1188 (W.D. Ky. 1987).

4. "Statistical Summary, Adult Institutional Populations," in *Directory* (1981), xii; "Statistical Summary, Adult Inmate Populations," in *Directory* (1987), xvii.

5. "Statistical Summary, Adult Inmate Populations," in *Directory* (1988), xxii.

6. Blumstein, "American Prisons."

7. *Campbell County v. Commonwealth of Kentucky,* Ky., 762 S.W. 2d 6 (1988).

8. 459 U.S. 460 (1983).

9. *Kentucky Department of Corrections v. Thompson,* 833 F. 2d 614 (6th Cir. 1987).

10. U.S. Supreme Court Official Transcript, *Kentucky Department of Corrections v. Thompson* (Washington, D.C., January 18, 1989). All excerpts from the oral argument are from this transcript. Identification of individual justices is derived from the author's personal record of the oral argument.

11. *Kentucky Department of Corrections v. Thompson,* 490 U.S. 454 (1989). The Supreme Court eventually abandoned the reasoning of *Hewitt v. Helms* in *Sandin v. Conner* (515 U.S. 472 [1995]) (holding that mandatory language in prison regulations cannot create a constitutionally protected liberty interest).

Aftermath

1. For a full history of this case, see *United States v. Barger,* 931 F. 2d 359 (6th Cir. 1991), in which the Court of Appeals affirmed Barger's conviction and upheld various rulings Judge Johnstone made during the trial.

Epilogue

1. "Statistical Summary, Adult Institutional Populations" in *Directory* (1987), xvi.

2. Gilliard, "Prison and Jail Inmates," 3.

3. "Statistical Summary, Adult Institutional Populations," in *Directory* (1987); Gilliard, "Prison and Jail Inmates," 1.

4. Gilliard and Beck, "Prisoners in 1997," 11.

5. See, e.g., Beale, "Rethinking Federal Criminal Law."

6. One of the most prominent advocates of tougher sentencing laws and more aggressive use of incarceration has recently called for less harsh sentencing policies, particularly in the war on drugs, and for zero population growth in prison. He contends that the "value of imprisonment is a portrait in the law of diminish-

ing returns" and "two million prisoners are enough" (DiIulio, "Drug War Follies). DiIulio first expressed these views in "Two Million Prisoners."

7. Yackle, *Reform and Regret,* 260.

8. See, e.g., Chilton, *Prisons under the Gavel,* 107–108; Crouch and Marquart, *Appeal to Justice,* 226–233.

9. Gilliard and Beck, "Prisoners in 1997," 9.

10. Ibid., 1.

11. 208 U.S. 412 (1908).

12. Just three years before the *Muller* case, the Court had invalidated a state law limiting men's work hours as an unwarranted interference with liberty of contract and thus violative of due process of law (*Lochner v. New York,* 198 U.S. 45 [1905]). Brandeis's immediate task in *Muller* was to distinguish *Lochner,* although the jurisprudence of the *Lochner* decision eventually came into disrepute and was abandoned (*Ferguson v. Skrupa,* 372 U.S. 726, 728–733 [1963]) (Strum, *Louis D. Brandeis,* 114–131).

13. *Brown v. Board of Education of Topeka,* 347 U.S. 483, 493–495 (1954).

14. *Madrid v. Gomez,* 889 F. Supp. 1146, 1280 (N.D. Cal. 1995).

15. *Amnesty International's Recommendations,* 3–5.

16. 28 U.S.C. Sec. 1915(a)(2), (b)(1), and (g).

17. 18 U.S.C. Sec. 3626. Serious questions have been raised about whether these remedial restrictions unduly intrude on the independence of the judicial branch in violation of separation of powers. See, e.g., *Hadix v. Johnson,* 144 F.3d 935, 937 (6th Cir. 1998) (interpreting the "automatic stay" provision narrowly to avoid ruling it unconstitutional); *French v. Duckworth,* 178F.3d 437 (7th Cir. 1999) (finding that the "automatic stay" provision cannot be given a narrow interpretation and holding it violative of separation of powers). The Supreme Court granted certiorari in *French* and a descision is expected by the time this book is in print.

Bibliography

Interviews

Collins, Carl, director of support services, Kentucky Bureau of Corrections and Department of Corrections, 1978–1988: June 7, 1989, Ohio Department of Rehabilitation and Corrections, Columbus, in person, taped.

Dressman, Ken, director of resource allocation, Kentucky Bureau of Corrections, 1979–1981; fiscal branch manager, Kentucky Department of Corrections, 1981–1988: May 3, 1990, Frankfort, Kentucky, telephone, not taped.

Haddix, Wilgus Gray, named inmate plaintiff, key member of Plaintiffs' Committee, 1979–1981: May 10, 1988, Kentucky State Reformatory, LaGrange, in person, taped; October 28, 1988, May 15, 1990, Blackburn Correctional Center, Lexington, Kentucky, in person, taped; various letters and telephone conversations, 1991–present.

Harris, Walter McKinley, named inmate plaintiff, key member of Plaintiffs' Committee, 1980–1981, chairman of Plaintiffs' Committee, 1983–1987: July 19, 1988, law school in major urban center, in person, taped; January 19, 1989, motel room, major urban center, in person, taped; various letters and telephone conversations, 1991–present.

Isaacs, Paul, deputy general counsel, Kentucky Department of Justice, 1977–1982; general counsel, Kentucky Department of Justice, 1982–1983: May 7, 1991, Frankfort, Kentucky, telephone, not taped.

Johnstone, Edward Huggins, judge, U.S. District Court for the Western District of Kentucky, 1977–present: May 3, 1984, October 24, 25, 26, 1988, June 6, 1989, U.S. Courthouse, Louisville, Kentucky, in person, not taped; October 31, 1988, U.S. Courthouse, Paducah, Kentucky, in person, not taped; various conversations, 1991–present.

Jones, Barbara, assistant attorney general for the commonwealth of Kentucky, general counsel, Kentucky Department of Corrections, 1978–1996: June 8, 1989, Kentucky Department of Corrections, Frankfort, in person, taped.

Merrick, Herby, owner, Herby's Barber Shop, Princeton, Kentucky: October 31, November 1, 1988, in person, not taped.

Shafer, Sheldon, reporter, *Louisville (Kentucky) Courier-Journal*, 1973–present: November 2, 1988, private home, Louisville, Kentucky, in person, taped.

Shepard, Phil, law clerk, Judge Edward Johnstone, 1980–1982: June 6, 1989, Frankfort, Kentucky, telephone, not taped.

Thompson, James McClellan "Shorty," original named inmate plaintiff, chairman of Plaintiffs' Committee, 1979–1981: May 9, October 17, 24, 1988, Northpoint Training Center, Burgin, Kentucky, in person, taped; May 15, 1990, Frankfort Career Center, Frankfort, Kentucky, telephone, taped; also various letters and telephone conversations, 1991–present.

Wilson, George, commissioner, Kentucky Bureau of Corrections, 1979–1981; secretary, Kentucky Department of Corrections, 1981–1988: June 7, 1989, Ohio Department of Rehabilitation and Corrections, Columbus, in person, taped.

Published Works

"About 380 Inmates File Formal Objections to Terms of Settlement on Prison Conditions." *Louisville (Kentucky) Times*, May 17, 1980.

Amnesty International's Recommendations to the United States Government to Address Human Rights Violations in the USA. London: Amnesty International, 1998.

" . . . And Timely Call to Upgrade Prisons." *Louisville (Kentucky) Times*, February 7, 1980, A10.

Anderson, Lloyd C. "The Approval and Interpretation of Consent Decrees in Civil Rights Class Action Litigation." *University of Illinois Law Review* 1983 (1983): 579–632.

————. "Release and Resumption of Jurisdiction over Consent Decrees in Structural Reform Litigation." *University of Miami Law Review* 42 (1987): 401–417.

Ashenfelter, Orley, Theodore Eisenberg, and Stewart J. Schwab. "Politics and the Judiciary: The Influence of Judicial Background on Case Outcomes." *Journal of Legal Studies* 24 (1995): 257–281.

Beale, Sara Sun. "Rethinking Federal Criminal Law: What's Law Got to Do with It? The Political, Social, Psychological, and Other Non-Legal Factors Influencing the Development of Federal Criminal Law." *Buffalo Criminal Law Review* 1 (1997): 23–66.

Blumstein, Alfred. "American Prisons in a Time of Crisis." In *The American Prison: Issues in Research and Policy, Law, Society, and Policy,* ed. Lynn Goodstein and Doris Layton MacKenzie, 4:13–22. New York: Plenum Press, 1988.

Brooks, Verne. "Judge of the Year." *Paducah (Kentucky) Sun-Democrat,* February 1, 1987.

Carrington, Paul D. "Of Law and the River." *Journal of Legal Education* 34 (1984): 222–228.

Caudill, Harry M. *Night Comes to the Cumberlands: A Biography of a Depressed Area.* Boston: Little, Brown, 1963.

Chayes, Abram. "The Supreme Court, 1981 Term—Foreword: Public Law Litigation and the Burger Court." *Harvard Law Review* 96 (1982): 4–60.

Chilton, Bradley Stewart. *Prisons under the Gavel: The Federal Court Takeover of Georgia Prisons.* Columbus: Ohio State University Press, 1991.

"Conflict in Kentucky's Justice Department Dims a Great Potential." *Louisville (Kentucky) Courier-Journal,* March 20, 1981, A10.

"Courts Right in Demanding That Prisons Meet Standards." *Louisville (Kentucky) Courier-Journal,* March 15, 1980, A4.

Crouch, Ben M., and James W. Marquart. *An Appeal to Justice: Litigated Reform of Texas Prisons.* Austin: University of Texas Press, 1989.

DiIulio, John J., Jr. "Drug War Follies: 2 Million Prisoners Are Enough." *Sacramento Bee,* April 14, 1999, H1.

————. *Governing Prisons: A Comparative Study of Correctional Management.* New York: Free Press, 1987.

————. "Help Wanted: Economists, Crime, and Public Policy." *Journal of Economic Perspectives* 10 (1996): 3–24.

————. "Two Million Prisoners Are Enough." *Wall Street Journal,* March 12, 1999, A14.

Directory of Juvenile and Adult Correctional Departments, Institutions, Agencies, and Paroling Authorities. Laurel, Md.: American Correctional Association, 1981, 1987, 1988.

Dorsen, Norman. "A Change in Judicial Philosophy?" *National Law Journal,* February 18, 1985, 13.

Dunaway, Wilma A. *The First American Frontier: Transition to Capitalism in Southern Appalachia, 1700–1860.* Chapel Hill: University of North Carolina Press, 1996.

Eldridge, Ann. "Prisons Called 'Beneath Human Decency.'" *Oldham (Kentucky) Era,* July 12, 1979, A1.

Eller, Ron. "Harry Caudill and the Burden of Mountain Liberalism." In *Critical Essays on Appalachian Life and Culture,* ed. Rick Simon, Grace Edwards, Ron Eller, Joan Moser, and Barry Buxton, 21–29. Boone, N.C.: Appalachian Consortium Press, 1982.

Feeley, Malcolm M. "The Significance of Prison Conditions Cases: Budgets and Regions." *Law and Society Review* 23 (1989): 273–282.

Feeley, Malcolm M., and Edward L. Rubin. *Judicial Policy Making and the Modern State: How the Courts Reformed America's Prisons.* Cambridge: Cambridge University Press, 1998.

Garrett, Robert T. "All Sides Find a Good Word for This Judge." *Louisville (Kentucky) Courier-Journal,* June 8, 1980, E7.

Gatz, Carolyn, and Patrick Howington. "Inmates' Suit Could Hinge on State Budget Requests." *Louisville (Kentucky) Times,* February 21, 1980.

Gilliard, Darrell K. "Prison and Jail Inmates at Midyear 1998." In *Bureau of Justice Statistics Bulletin,* 1–11. Washington, D.C.: U.S. Department of Justice, Bureau of Justice Statistics Clearinghouse, 1999.

Gilliard, Darrell K., and Allen J. Beck. "Prisoners in 1993." In *Bureau of Justice Statistics Bulletin,* 1–12. Washington, D.C.: U.S. Department of Justice, Bureau of Justice Statistics Clearinghouse, 1994.

———. "Prisoners in 1997." In *Bureau of Justice Statistics Bulletin,* 1–16. Washington, D.C.: U.S. Department of Justice, Bureau of Justice Statistics Clearinghouse, 1998.

Grossman, Joel B. "Social Backgrounds and Judicial Decision-Making." *Harvard Law Review* 79 (1966): 1551–1594.

Horowitz, Donald. *Courts and Social Policy.* Washington, D.C.: Brookings Institution, 1977.

Howington, Patrick. "$42 Million Settlement of Corrections Suit Is Termed 'Historic.'" *Louisville (Kentucky) Times,* April 3, 1980, A1.

"Kentucky to Aid Prisons in Settlement of Lawsuit." *New York Times,* April 4, 1980.

Long, John C. "Ball and Change." *Louisville (Kentucky) Courier-Journal,* June 1, 1980, A1.

Martin, Steve J., and Sheldon Ekland-Olson. *Texas Prisons: The Walls Came Tumbling Down.* Austin: Texas Monthly Press, 1987.

Martinson, Robert. "What Works? Questions and Answers about Prison Reform." *Public Interest* 35 (1974): 22–54.

Miller, Howard L. "Delay in Corrections Complex Worrying State." *Louisville (Kentucky) Times,* June 21, 1980, A1.

Powell, Bill. "$50 Million to Be Sought to Improve State's Prisons." *Louisville (Kentucky) Courier-Journal,* November 21, 1979.

———. "Prisons out of Dark Ages, Warden Says." *Louisville (Kentucky) Courier-Journal,* September 30, 1979, B10.

———. "State Inmates Can Thank Former Jailhouse Lawyer for Bettering Their Lot." *Louisville (Kentucky) Courier-Journal,* April 14, 1980, A1.

"Prisoners Should Bend a Little, Too, in Seeking Their Greater Goals." *Louisville (Kentucky) Courier-Journal,* November 12, 1980, A10.

Ramsey, Sy. "Overcrowding a Big Problem in Kentucky Prisons, New Corrections Commissioner Says." *Louisville (Kentucky) Times,* February 7, 1980, B8.

Rasmussen, Barbara. *Absentee Landowning and Exploitation in West Virginia, 1760–1920.* Lexington: University Press of Kentucky, 1994.

Salstrom, Paul. *Appalachia's Path to Dependency: Rethinking a Region's Economic History, 1730–1940.* Lexington: University Press of Kentucky, 1994.

Segal, Jeffrey A., and Harold J. Spaeth. *The Supreme Court and the Attitudinal Model.* New York: Cambridge University Press, 1993.

Shafer, Sheldon. "Corrections Chief Works to Give Prison System, Personnel 'A New Face.'" *Louisville (Kentucky) Courier-Journal,* November 10, 1980, A1.

———. "Crowded Reformatory Tense, Inmates Say." *Louisville (Kentucky) Courier-Journal,* March 11, 1980, A1.

———. "Federal Judge Finds Pattern of Harassment at Eddyville." *Louisville (Kentucky) Courier-Journal,* October 23, 1980.

———. "Inmates Say Problems Linger at LaGrange." *Louisville (Kentucky) Courier-Journal,* April 20, 1981, A1.

———. "Most Caseworkers at State Reformatory Object to Agreement." *Louisville (Kentucky) Courier-Journal,* May 28, 1980.

———. "Negotiations Start in Prisoners' Lawsuit." *Louisville (Kentucky) Courier-Journal,* March 8, 1980, A1.

———. "New Prison in Oldham Will Provide Full Psychiatric Services for Inmates." *Louisville (Kentucky) Courier-Journal,* September 30, 1979, B1.

———. "Prison Upgrading Could Be Delayed by Budget Problems." *Louisville (Kentucky) Courier-Journal,* March 20, 1981, B1.

———. "Settlement of Inmates' Suit Means Changes at Prisons." *Louisville (Kentucky) Courier-Journal,* April 4, 1980, A1.

———. "State Expects to Meet Deadline for Prison Cuts." *Louisville (Kentucky) Courier-Journal,* February 19, 1981, B1.

———. "State to Get More Time to Cut Prison Populations." *Louisville (Kentucky) Courier-Journal,* December 23, 1980, B1.

———. "State's Going Back into the Business of Making Auto Tags at Reformatory." *Louisville (Kentucky) Courier-Journal,* October 9, 1979, B1.

———. "Superintendent Named for State's New Prison." *Louisville (Kentucky) Courier-Journal,* June 25, 1980.

———. "U.S. Judge Dismisses Inmates' Objections, Approves Agreement." *Louisville (Kentucky) Courier-Journal,* May 29, 1980, B1.

Shafer, Sheldon, and Bill Powell. "Brown Announces Reformatory Warden Is Being Replaced." *Louisville (Kentucky) Courier-Journal,* November 7, 1980, B1.

Sisk, Gregory C., Michael Heise, and Andrew P. Morriss. "Charting the Influences on the Judicial Mind: An Empirical Study of Judicial Reasoning." *New York University Law Review* 73 (1998): 1377–1500.

Stastny, Charles, and Gabrielle Tyrnauer. *Who Rules the Joint? The Changing Political Culture of Maximum-Security Prisons in America.* Lexington, Mass.: Lexington Books, 1982.

Strum, Philippa. *Louis D. Brandeis: Justice for the People.* Cambridge: Harvard University Press, 1984.

Taggart, William A. "Redefining the Power of the Federal Judiciary: The Impact of Court-Ordered Prison Reform on State Expenditures for Corrections." *Law and Society Review* 23 (1989): 241–271.

Tate, C. Neal, and Roger Handberg. "Time Binding and Theory Building in Personal Attribute Models of Supreme Court Voting Behavior, 1916–1988." *American Journal of Political Science* 35 (1991): 460–480.

Taylor, Diana. "Brown Tours Prison at Eddyville, Sees Merit in Court Order." *Louisville (Kentucky) Times,* November 7, 1980, C11.

U.S. Senate Committee on the Judiciary. *Hearing on Nominations for District and Circuit Court Judges,* 95th Cong., 1st sess., September 27, 1977.

Ulmer, S. Sidney. "Are Social Background Models Time-Bound?" *American Political Science Review* 80 (1986): 957–967.

Voskuhl, John. "Prison Panel Backs Plan to Shift and Reclassify Convicts to Get More Space." *Louisville (Kentucky) Courier-Journal,* November 2, 1988, B5.

"W. C. Johnstone: A New Kind of Pioneer." *Paducah (Kentucky) Sun-Democrat,* April 9, 1978, 2C.

Yackle, Larry W. *Reform and Regret: The Story of Federal Judicial Involvement in the Alabama Prison System.* New York: Oxford University Press, 1989.

Yarbrough, Tinsley E. *Judge Frank Johnson and Human Rights in Alabama.* University, Ala.: University of Alabama Press, 1981.

Yopp, Kevin. "State Prisoners Make 'Sweeping Changes.'" *Oldham (Kentucky) Era,* April 7, 1980, 1.

Index

Alaimo, Judge Anthony, xiv, 92, 146

Alexander, Larry, 64–66, 78

American Correctional Association (ACA), 84, 89, 125, 135, 138, 155, 170, 201–202

Ballantine, Judge Tom, 23–24, 37

Bland, David, 92–93, 97, 100, 116, 128; conflict with George Wilson, 101–102, 104

Breathitt, Governor Edward T. ("Ned"), 25, 30–31

Brown, Governor John Young, Jr.: appointments, 101, 107; budgets, 100, 133–134, 138; cabinet controversy, 158, 160, 163, 165–167; compliance with consent decree, 143, 147, 154; election, 98–99, 104, 135; negotiations to settle prison litigation, 128, 131, 141–142; spending freeze, 116, 159

Bureau of Corrections, 3, 96; budgets, 105; compliance with consent decree, 155–157, 214; hiring freeze, 160; old guard v. reformers, 93, 97, 101–102, 104, 107, 116, 122, 163; separation from Justice Department, 165. *See also* Department of Corrections

Carroll, Governor Julian, 31, 93, 96, 100

Casselberry, Brad, 117, 119–120

class action, xvii, 38, 40, 140, 169

consent decree: approval by court, 141–142; college degree controversy, 183; compliance, 180, 199–206, 217; funding, 181, 195; gender disparities resulting from, 169–170; inmate participation in enforcement, 172–173, 175–177, 193–194, 197; mediation by judge, 3, 115; obstacles to compliance, 146–147, 149–151, 155, 159–160, 162, 164, 167–168, 171; population cap, 209; rehabilitation of prisoners, 210; signing by prisoners, 138–140; visitation controversy, 214

Constitution of Kentucky, 212–213

Constitution of the United States: as a living document, xv, 33, 39, 144–145, 220; and policy making, xvi; and prison conditions, 133, 138, 242. *See also* Eighth Amendment; Fourteenth Amendment

cruel and unusual punishment, 23, 34–36, 83, 91, 109, 169, 206. *See also* Eighth Amendment

Department of Corrections, 166, 205, 208, 212, 228, 230. *See also* Bureau of Corrections

Eddyville: administration, 104, 138, 159, 163; and consent decree, 139, 141, 148–149, 174, 203, 208; improvements, 100, 135, 152, 155, 160, 209, 219; inmates, 40, 42–43, 61, 64, 76–77, 179, 230–231, 234; and Judge Johnstone, 33, 37, 60, 108; and litigation, 38, 63, 92, 101, 116–117, 125–127, 132, 168; living

conditions, 25, 85, 93–94, 98, 119, 124, 206; newspaper articles about, 121, 133; population cap, 156, 205, 211. *See also* Kentucky State Penitentiary

Eighth Amendment, xii, xiv, xvi, 34–36, 109, 169, 241. *See also* cruel and unusual punishment

Elder, Joe, 217–218

equal protection, 169–170, 241

Fourteenth Amendment, 35, 169, 215, 219

Haddix, Wilgus: criminal history, 51–58, 75; education in prison, 181–187, 226–228; life in prison, 104, 112, 130, 177–181, 207; participation in litigation, xvii–xviii, 40–44, 58–64, 67, 78, 80, 109, 116, 123–126, 139–141, 171, 198; personal history, 44–51, 73, 128; postlitigation life, 228–229, 238

Harris, Walter: criminal history, 69, 74–76, 241; life in prison, 76–78; participation in litigation, xvii–xviii, 64–67, 78–90, 116, 123–126, 134, 139, 171–177, 184, 193–198; personal history, 67–74, 118, 179; postlitigation life, 221, 229–238

Johnson, Judge Frank, xiv–xvi, 33, 36–38, 92, 100, 109, 115, 146

Johnstone, Judge Edward H.: compliance with consent decree, 146, 151–152, 154–156, 161–165, 168, 180, 195, 199, 202–203, 205–206, 209, 211, 214, 217; judicial decisions, 183, 215; KCIW litigation, 169–170; KSR litigation, xvii–xviii,

22–25, 37–40, 42–43, 58, 60–61,
78, 81, 84, 99, 105, 176, 207–208,
219, 239; personal history, 26–29,
72, 144; postlitigation life, 222–224;
and prisoner rights, 63; professional
career, 29–37, 98; visits to KSR,
107–114, 120
Jones, Barbara, 201, 215–217

Kendrick, Jerald, 33, 37–38, 40–43,
58
Kentucky Constitution, 212–213
Kentucky Correctional Institution for
Women (KCIW), 118, 168–170
Kentucky Department of Justice, 97,
133, 158–159, 165
Kentucky General Assembly, 96–97,
99–100, 105, 108, 116–117, 131,
134, 142–143, 180, 195, 199, 210,
213
Kentucky State Penitentiary, 24, 31,
41, 57, 94, 130, 155, 157. *See also*
Eddyville
Kentucky State Reformatory (KSR):
administration, 67, 77, 86, 95–96,
121, 148; consent decree, 123, 139,
141–142, 193; history, xiii, 95–96;
improvements, 100, 117, 138, 149,
152–153, 155–157, 194–195, 198,
203–209, 229–230; inmates, xvii,
40, 43, 55, 58, 64, 76, 82, 171–172,
177, 179–181, 185, 188–189, 226–
227, 229–230; litigation, xii, xviii,
38, 62, 92, 99, 101, 125, 135–136,
150, 168, 214, 218–219, 224, 243;
living conditions, 20–21, 59, 63, 83–
89, 93, 114, 118–121, 124, 127,
130–132, 199, 244; population cap,
156, 205; visits by Judge Johnstone,
108–113, 151. *See also* LaGrange

Kentucky Supreme Court, 4, 31, 211–
213, 230

LaGrange: administration, 3, 207;
improvements, 134, 193; inmates,
11–13, 20, 42, 179–180, 195, 234,
236; litigation, 97, 101, 110, 116,
133, 211; living conditions, xii,
1–2, 43, 65, 86, 129, 208. *See also*
Kentucky State Reformatory
Luther Luckett Correctional Complex,
149, 152–158, 160

Moore, Shawn, 139

Northpoint Training Center, 179, 188–
189, 194, 207–208, 224–225, 229;
overcrowding, 209–210

Plaintiffs' Committee: consent decree,
139, 149, 172–173; inmates, 43–44,
58–60, 63–64, 66–67, 78–80, 82,
89, 92, 120, 129, 175, 194, 196;
litigation, 108–109, 116, 123, 134–
136, 138; and living conditions,
150–151, 214
prison-reform litigation, xii, xiv–xvii,
xix, 62, 64, 67, 91–92, 97, 128, 146,
221, 240
Pritchard, Edward, 127–128, 131,
162–163, 165

Roederer Farm Center, 177

Shafer, Sheldon, xviii, 117–120;
investigation of KSR, 120–122, 125,
141, 152, 164–165; newspaper
articles, 129–134, 143–144, 152–
158, 160–161, 164
Stephens, Robert, 31, 98–99, 212

Thompson, James M. ("Shorty"):
complaint, 23–25, 37–38, 83, 89;
consent decree, 136, 139–142, 155,
170; criminal history, 10–20, 55, 75;
and Kentucky politics, 92–93, 97–
101, 131; and Kentucky Supreme
Court, 211–213; negotiations, 135,
183–184; newspaper articles about,
120, 129, 132, 157; participation in
litigation, xvii–xviii, 207–208, 240;
personal history, 4–10, 45, 54, 73;
petition, 1–4, 20–22, 40, 96, 243–
244; Plaintiffs' Committee, 43, 58–
60, 64, 67, 78–80, 82, 175, 230;
plaintiffs' counsel, 115; postlitigation
life, 171, 187–193, 198, 208, 211,
224–226; and settlement, 116, 123,
125–126, 128, 172, 209; and U.S.
Constitution, 144–145; and U.S.
Supreme Court, 214, 219; and visits
by Judge Johnstone, 109, 111–113,
151

United States Department of Justice,
37–38, 81–82, 84, 105, 139, 145,
156, 169

United States Supreme Court: and
civil rights, 34; justices, 127–128,
224, 241; KSR litigation, 4, 214–
220, 223; prison-reform litigation,
xiii, 35–36, 109, 225; and United
States Constitution, 145
University of Kentucky, 26–29, 75,
171, 177, 184, 224, 226–228, 231
U.S. Constitution. *See* Constitution of
the United States

Wallace, Governor George, 33, 37,
92
Welch, Neil, 158–166, 172
Wilson, George, xviii, 101, 107, 171;
cabinet controversy, 158–168, 172;
compliance with consent decree,
145–154, 156–158, 180–181, 194–
195, 199–201, 203–206, 209–210;
negotiations, 115, 137–138, 141;
newspaper articles about, 121–122,
130, 153–154, 158, 160–161, 163;
and old guard v. reformers, 102–
104, 128; postlitigation life, 221–
222, 228